ROGUE
SPOOKS

ALSO BY DICK MORRIS AND EILEEN McGANN

Armageddon

Power Grab

Here Come the Black Helicopters!

Screwed!

Revolt!

2010: Take Back America

Catastrophe

Fleeced

Outrage

Condi vs. Hillary

Because He Could

Rewriting History

ALSO BY DICK MORRIS

Off with Their Heads

Power Plays

Vote.com

The New Prince

Behind the Oval Office

Bum Rap on America's Cities

ROGUE
SPOOKS

THE INTELLIGENCE WAR
ON DONALD TRUMP

DICK MORRIS
AND
EILEEN McGANN

ALL
POINTS
BOOKS

All Points Books is an imprint of St. Martin's Press.

www.allpointsbooks.com

The Library of Congress Cataloging-in-Publication Data is available upon request.

ISBN 978-1-250-16786-6 (hardcover)
ISBN 978-1-250-18280-7 (signed edition)
ISBN 978-1-250-16787-3 (e-book)

Our books may be purchased in bulk for promotional, educational, or business use. Please contact your local bookseller or the Macmillan Corporate and Premium Sales Department at 1-800-221-7945, extension 5442, or by email at MacmillanSpecialMarkets@macmillan.com.

First Edition: August 2017

10   9   8   7   6   5   4   3   2   1

This book is only for sale in the United States.

CONTENTS

"You're missing it right now. It's happening in front of your faces. We have a disinformation campaign designed to discredit the president-elect and as of today we have boots on the ground like the protesters I had to wade through to get here. Does that seem familiar to any of you? Because it does to me. It's what we did in Nicaragua, Chile, Congo, a dozen other places. All the way back to Iran in the '50s. And it does not end well for the elected regime. You're fighting for your lives here, do you get that? Can't afford to stay silent."

—CIA director Saul Berenson to
President-elect Elizabeth Keane,
Homeland

PROLOGUE

THE SCHEME HAS ALL THE ELEMENTS OF A RIVETING SPY NOVEL: A POLARIZING
billionaire presidential candidate, considered crude and unworthy of the
Oval Office by the political establishment he threatens, along with ris-
qué sex, blackmail, bribes, betrayal, special interests, back channels to
Russia, spies, political intrigue, envy, and hatred.

And the plot is in the tradition of the best-selling spy novels written
by former British MI6 officers: Nameless moneymen supporting the
first female candidate for U.S. president are secretly bankrolling a former British spy to find lethal dirt on the opposing candidate's activities
in Russia.

Behind the scenes, the ex-spook, an expert on Russia, compiles the
dossier of sensational reports, allegedly based on intelligence gleaned
from high-level sources in Russia. The result is a narrative alleging that
the candidate and his associates were involved in illicit activities in Russia that make him extremely vulnerable to blackmail.

The goal: Destroy him. Humiliate him. Get him out of the race.

During the campaign, the British rogue spook—at the behest of
his American paymasters—orchestrates an audacious plan to create and
publicize a shocking dossier to besmirch the billionaire candidate and
assure that he will never become president.

The explicit accusations center on extensive collusion with the Russian government to influence the U.S. election—including the hacking

of the Democratic National Committee and campaign officials' personal emails. To add a little color, claims of Trump's involvement in vulgar sexual acts in a Moscow hotel room are thrown in, too.[1]

Beyond that, the dossier makes the far-fetched claim that the now president-elect is, in effect, a Manchurian candidate who has been under the influence and control of Russia for more than five years.[2]

But from the start, a doubt nags. Too many things in the dossier don't add up. Could there be someone else—or some other country—involved in preparing this explosive document?

Because the rogue spook is not acting alone.

Later, we learn that he didn't actually write much of the dossier. Someone else did and gave it to him. Who was that person?

And how did anyone know to give it to him? What was the arrangement?

More questions arise: Did the stunning allegations in the dossier really come from the Russian sources it quotes? Or were there other players? Could other intelligence agencies—like those of the British or of other European allies—have been involved? What about the CIA? The FBI? Or could it have been someone else entirely?

There's more to this story.

The "sources" for the material are vaguely described as "Kremlin insiders," "current and former FSB officers," and others with a "direct line" to the Russian president as well as colorful characters who claim to be close to the candidate.[3] (The FSB, or Federal Security Service, is the successor to the KGB, Russia's secret police organ.)

Later, a look back at them would raise serious questions about their reliability, and even whether most of them ever existed at all.

The ex-spook describes his findings as "hair-raising" and decides (without alerting his American client) to secretly relay the material to U.S. law enforcement officials.[4] Since he is already known and respected by the FBI, he contacts the Bureau in early July and shares his alarming findings.[5] Eventually, based in part on the unsubstantiated dossier, the

FBI begins a secret federal counterterrorism investigation of the presidential candidate and his associates.[6]

Several months later, the FBI gets more aggressive in the Russian meddling probe and is suddenly interested in talking to the ex-spook. They meet him in Rome and that's when the FBI makes a baffling decision: It agrees to pay him $50,000 if he can "get solid corroboration of the material in his reports."[7] In the meantime, the FBI pays for some of his expenses.[8]

"The material," of course, refers to the accusations against the candidate in the dossier. So, now, weeks before the presidential election, the FBI agrees to pay an opposition researcher who is simultaneously being paid by the political supporters of the opposing candidate. While one employer pays him to find embarrassing—or even incriminating—information about the nominee of a major political party, the other hires him to prove those very same allegations about the same candidate it is investigating.[9]

The ex-spook never collects the $50,000. Media reports suggest that the arrangement lasts only a few weeks, ending "abruptly" before the U.S. election, "in part, because of frustration that the FBI wasn't doing enough to investigate [the candidate's Russian] ties."[10]

The spook and his patrons seem desperate. What if their client's opponent wins the election before the salacious claims ever see the light of day?

Time is running out. As election day approaches, the sordid details of the dossier still remain secret. Although the dossier was available to major news outlets for months, not a single media outlet dares to take a chance on publishing the unproven, scandalous dossier.[11]

Then the worst happens. Time does run out and the Manchurian candidate wins the election and is about to enter the Oval Office.

But the female candidate's loss doesn't end the project—not by a long shot. Now the American spooks in the outgoing administration and their British allies are even more desperate to legitimize the dossier and make it public, because now their target is not just a candidate, but the president-elect.

To get the dossier out there, to make sure that all its sordid and possibly treasonous claims go public, the FBI director—himself something of a rogue spook—as well as current and former intelligence agents in the United States, Britain, and maybe other countries, a prominent U.S. senator, a former assistant secretary of state, and a highly esteemed UK diplomat—all play a role.[12]

That's when the rogue spooks see triumph around the corner. And they are right.

Because two weeks before the inauguration, the director of the FBI huddles with the three leaders of the other top intelligence agencies in the United States—the heads of the CIA and the NSA and the director of national intelligence—to discuss the dossier and what to do with it. They unanimously agree to brief the outgoing president, the president-elect, congressional leaders, and the chairmen of the House and Senate Intelligence Committees on the existence of the dossier and summarize its still-unsubstantiated stunning charges. But they also unanimously agree that there is no evidence to prove the shocking allegations. A few days later, the director of national intelligence confirms that he can "not corroborate or validate the information."[13]

Part One of the Intelligence Coup is set in motion.

Not surprisingly, within hours, the specifics of the still-unproven allegations in a classified document are illegally leaked to the press by rogue spooks inside the U.S. intelligence and/or the White House, who want to be sure the documents are in the system and can't be buried by a new administration.

Soon, the entire unverified dossier is published by BuzzFeed, an online organ, causing great embarrassment and humiliation to the president-elect.

Not a single media outlet can verify most of the sensational claims. In fact, many of the specifics are easily proven to be false. Soon, a number of the allegations are challenged in defamation lawsuits.

But the game plan works: By the time the new president is sworn in, serious questions surround him about his relationships with the Russians.

The FBI, the CIA, congressional leaders, intelligence committees, and the media all clamor for answers to questions raised by the phony information in the dossier.

Unfortunately none of this is simply the outline of an enthralling but fictional spy thriller. It is the true story of how Hillary Clinton supporters paid for a secret investigation that resulted in a dossier that was filled with lies that rogue British ex-spooks—and possibly others—and the U.S. intelligence community are using in a brazen attempt to undermine and shatter Donald Trump's presidency.

Why is the dossier important? Because it was no less of an attempt by foreigners to influence the presidential election than the hacking incidents were. Unknown, unnamed persons conspired to produce and disseminate a document filled with lies in order to damage a presidential candidate and, later, the president-elect of the United States. It should be taken as seriously as the hackings. The rogue spooks, wherever they are from—and any other persons or entities behind them—should be exposed and treated with the same seriousness as the hackers. This was an unacceptable intrusion into our sovereign political process. And we still don't know who was behind it. That it could have been one or more of our allies is truly shocking.

But it didn't end with the dossier. From the minute Donald Trump was elected, "deep state" bureaucrats still serving in the highest levels of government were leaking and plotting to destroy Donald Trump and his aides at any cost. Daily leaks of transcripts of his phone calls, diplomatic meetings, internal memos, private conversations, and intelligence reports on his associates—including his son-in-law—were eagerly fed to a hungry press.

Even the former director of the FBI, James Comey, admitted that he deliberately arranged to leak sensitive material to the press in the hopes of stirring up a demand for the appointment of a special prosecutor to go after the president. A few weeks later, he got his wish: Robert Mueller was named as a special prosecutor to investigate possible collusion between Russia and Trump and his associates.

What else did James Comey leak?

The unauthorized leaks continue. And, yet, only one low-level clerk has been arrested. Not a single person has been held accountable.

The intelligence war on Donald Trump is now in full swing.

INTRODUCTION

ON MAY 17, 2017, THE U.S. DEPARTMENT OF JUSTICE ANNOUNCED THE APPOINT-
ment of former FBI director Robert Mueller as special counsel to investigate possible Russian interference in the 2016 U.S. presidential
election, including whether there was any collusion between the Kremlin and Donald Trump and his campaign associates to defeat Hillary
Clinton.

The extraordinary decision to appoint a prosecutor followed several
tumultuous days in Washington that reached a crescendo with President
Trump's abrupt firing of FBI director James Comey. For days before
that, a series of leaks by anonymous intelligence officials had followed
in rapid succession—about Trump's comments to Russian diplomats in
confidential White House meetings; about alleged inappropriate over-
tures to the FBI director and other intelligence leaders concerning the
Russian collusion allegations; and about Comey's memos memorializing
his concerns about Trump.

The leaks demonstrated a new menace to our democracy: the "Intel/
Media complex." Almost sixty years ago, President Dwight Eisenhower
warned us about the dangers of the emerging coalition of defense contractors and Pentagon generals he referred to as the "military-industrial
complex." Now, spooks from both sides of the Atlantic coalesce with
the liberal mainstream media to form this new phenomenon, the Intel/
Media complex, as potent as its predecessor but far more dangerous because it operates anonymously behind the cloak of the First Amendment.

The intelligence war on Trump was now out in the open.

It was suddenly all-Russia, all-the-time in Washington.

The allegations about Russian interference in the election were certainly not new. In September 2015, more than a year before the election, British intelligence agents had explicitly warned the FBI about Russian hacking into Democratic National Committee computers.[1] A year later, in August 2016, well after the hack of the DNC computers had been exposed, the Brits were back with another heads-up, this time to warn the CIA director of suspicious contacts between Trump associates and Russians.[2]

But none of this information was made public at the time.

Later, it was revealed that, beginning in July 2016, Comey had overseen the FBI's secret investigation of the unsubstantiated claims of collusion—without producing any evidence to prove it.[3] A parallel probe by the CIA likewise failed to substantiate even any coordination between Trump and the Kremlin.[4]

And from the very beginning, President Trump vehemently denied the charges.

All these investigations had one thing in common: They each failed to find any evidence, any substantiation, any documentation, or any proof that Trump or his campaign or his associates had anything to do with Russian interference in the U.S. election.

No one knows for sure whether there is some yet-uncovered evidence of a Trump-Kremlin collusion that escaped all the previous investigators. But what we do know is that the full force of the top American intelligence agencies—along with some help from the Brits—could not uncover any such evidence during a year-long investigation. And the former FBI director James Comey, the former CIA director John Brennan, and the former chairman of the Senate Intelligence Committee Senator Dianne Feinstein have all confirmed that they have seen no evidence of collusion.[5]

There is a lot of evidence that the Russians were behind the hacking of the DNC computers.

Yet the lack of any evidence of collusion didn't get in the way of the media-hyped charges suggesting otherwise with blaring headlines and sensational accusations.

And with no evidence to support their claims, Hillary Clinton and her top aides invented and promoted a Trump-Kremlin connection throughout the campaign—and indeed for months following election day.

How did the situation become so extreme that a special prosecutor had to be appointed six months after the election? Just as important: How did the idea of Russian interference become such a central issue in the 2016 presidential campaign to begin with? Why did questions about ties between President Trump and his associates and Russia continue to dominate the headlines for months and months after the election?

The first public mention of possible Russian involvement in the presidential election appeared on June 14, 2016, when the DNC announced that its computers had been hacked. Private security analysts determined that the DNC systems had been compromised by "Russian government hackers" who gained access to the "entire database of opposition research on GOP presidential candidate Donald Trump."[6]

Whoever they were, the cyberstalkers had actually accessed the DNC database almost a year earlier—when Donald Trump had just entered the presidential race and was lagging in the polls. When the DNC disclosed the hacking, the media originally treated it as "business as usual" for the Russians and for the spy business in general. There was no suggestion at all of any Trump connection.

Here's what the *Washington Post* reported:

The intrusions are an example of Russia's interest in the U.S. political system and its desire to understand the policies, strengths and weaknesses of a potential future president—much as American spies gather similar information on foreign candidates and leaders.[7]

Nothing shocking there.

According to the *New York Times*, American intelligence officials did not view the hacking as "extraordinary" since "foreign spies had hacked previous campaigns, and the United States does the same in elections around the world, officials said. The view on the inside was that collecting information, even through hacking, is what spies do."[8]

The hacking was no surprise to the U.S. intelligence agencies since they had been alerted to the possibility of Russian hacking by the British intelligence counterpart to our NSA (National Security Agency), known as GCHQ (Government Communications Headquarters).[9] Despite the warning, however, neither the FBI nor the DNC took the necessary steps to shut the hacking down.[10] Why didn't the FBI begin an immediate investigation of this serious intrusion into our political system—in the middle of an election year? Why didn't they insist on reviewing the DNC's computers—and take legal steps to take them into FBI custody and have them examined by the FBI's own experts? Because that's the only way to actually see what was going on. But the FBI caved in to the Democrats and the Russian hackers nestled in.

Where was Comey when this was going on right underneath his own nose?

The reaction of the FBI was somewhat lackadaisical.

The reaction of the DNC was worse—it wasn't just careless, it was idiotic. When the FBI initially called the DNC, the agent was referred to the committee's technical help desk. After receiving the information about the Russian hacking, Yared Tamene, the IT officer on duty, did a perfunctory search and found no sign of hacking. Even though the FBI agent called him back numerous times to follow up, Tamene ignored him, claiming that he had no way of knowing if "the caller was a real FBI agent and not an imposter."[11]

Seriously, how many FBI imposters are out there warning of Russian hacking into a political party's website in the middle of a presidential election? Apparently, no thought was given to simply calling up the FBI and verifying that the agent was for real. And the FBI didn't physically sit down with the DNC to discuss it for another nine months. Obviously, there was no sense of urgency there. Even after the DNC learned of the hacking, it refused to let the FBI physically examine the hacked computers, insisting that any analysis be done by a third party.[12]

So the system remained vulnerable and the hackers remained embedded in the DNC computers for almost a year. But at this point, although the hackers had stolen the opposition research on Trump, there was no public disclosure of anything inside the DNC computers.

After the DNC announcement of the Russian hack, David Sanger and Nick Corasaniti of the *New York Times* raised for the first time the possibility of Russian involvement. Still, they said it might have an innocent explanation:

> The connection to Russia may be explained simply by the global fascination with the presidential campaign and the mystery surrounding Mr. Trump, who has not been a major subject of foreign intelligence collection.[13]

Now a new name—political consultant Paul Manafort—surfaced. As far as Americans knew, Manafort was simply Trump's new campaign manager, after the firing of Corey Lewandowski on June 20. But few realized that Manafort had also been the chief advisor to Russian president Vladimir Putin's protégé Viktor Yanukovych, the ousted pro-Russian president of Ukraine. Until late July, very little was written about Manafort's connection to Putin's favorite Ukrainian politician. Most press about him focused instead on delegate selection and his attempts to impose discipline on Trump.

But now, in the Sanger-Corasaniti story in the *New York Times*, the fact that Trump had hired Manafort became suddenly relevant. They wrote that the development "also recalls a subplot to the race: Paul Manafort, Mr. Trump's campaign chairman, previously advised pro-Russian politicians in Ukraine and other parts of Eastern Europe, including former President Viktor F. Yanukovych of Ukraine."[14]

The linkage of Trump with Putin and Yanukovych through Manafort was the beginning of a narrative that continues to this day and has become the central theme of what can only be described as an on-going intelligence coup against Donald Trump: The fact that Trump's associates had economic interests in Russian-related projects has been deemed sufficient proof of their motivation to bond with the Kremlin in an effort to elect Donald Trump.

Now, anyone who was in any way involved with Trump and had any former or current financial interest in anything vaguely related to Russia suddenly became suspect and was portrayed as a conspirator working with Moscow to try to influence the U.S. presidential election. As a result, a never-ending series of articles about Trump associates began to dominate the media.

Meanwhile, far from putting this conspiracy theory to rest, Trump's own remarks stoked the burgeoning Trump-Kremlin narrative. He called Putin a "strong leader" and said he "respects him."[15] On July 21, 2016, Trump told the *New York Times* that if NATO countries did not pay their fair share of military expenses, he was prepared to tell them: "Congratulations, you will be defending yourself."[16] This was a shock to U.S. policy makers and European nations who had relied on the U.S. commitment to defend NATO countries for nearly seventy years. Shortly after those comments, Trump said that he would "take a look at" recognizing Russia's claims to the Crimea and suggested that the "people of Crimea, from what I've heard, would rather be with Russia than where they were."[17]

The pro-Ukraine, pro-NATO foreign policy folks were on full alert. David Kramer, a former senior State Department official in the George W. Bush administration and a close associate of Senator John McCain, stepped up: "Trump's attitude on Russia is not in line with most Republican foreign-policy thinking. Trump has staked out views that are really on the fringe."[18] Kramer indicated that Trump's out-of-sync view "raises some questions in my mind about what's driving it."[19]

On July 22, 2016, a bomb dropped. Two days before the opening of the Democratic National Convention in Philadelphia, WikiLeaks released a trove of over 19,000 emails from the DNC. These emails chronicled the DNC's deliberately favorable treatment of Hillary Clinton over Bernie Sanders during the primaries, in violation of party rules. The Democrats were furious and demanded to know who was behind the hacking. Several days later, Nancy Pelosi publicly blamed the Russians. "I do know this: that the Russians did the D.N.C. hack." She reportedly added that she had learned this "not through intelligence briefings, but through other means."[20]

A few days later, Trump added to the banner headlines when he called on Putin to release Hillary Clinton's missing personal emails—if he could find them: "Russia, if you're listening, I hope you're able to find the 30,000 emails that are missing."[21] This struck a nerve. Now there were widespread claims that Trump was "actively encouraging another country to commit a crime against the U.S. to directly affect the presidential election."[22] One of Hillary Clinton's senior policy advisors, Jake Sullivan, jumped in: "This has to be the first time that a major presidential candidate has actively encouraged a foreign power to conduct espionage against his political opponent."[23]

Trump, for his part, repeatedly indicated that his goal was, in fact, to improve relations with Russia. "Wouldn't it be nice if we actually got along with people, wouldn't it be nice if we actually got along, as an example, with Russia?"[24]

From then on, everything Trump said was viewed through the prism of a possible Trump-Putin collusion.

The hacking had now turned from a passive foreign presence lurking on the DNC computers to an active plot to embarrass Hillary Clinton. The story of Russian intelligence intervention moved onto the front pages of the campaign coverage. As the Democrats began their convention in Philadelphia, a sense of outrage and opportunity combined to galvanize a massive assault on Donald Trump.

The conventional wisdom was that the revelations in the DNC emails would seriously hurt Hillary Clinton. But, in fact, the contents of the email dump itself did not do Hillary any lasting damage. Before the emails were released, Hillary had trailed Trump by 4 points in the polls as the Republicans wrapped up their convention. After the leak, and at the close of Hillary's convention, she was 11 points ahead. Any fleeting damage the emails may have caused seemed to have been totally offset by her highly successful convention.

The conventional wisdom, unfortunately, never noticed its mistake. Failing to read the polls, the media clung to its story that the emails had been devastating to the Clinton campaign. This misconception has done a lot to magnify the impact of the hacking and to justify Hillary's use of Russian interference as a reason she lost the election. In October, as the election approached, WikiLeaks (and Russia?) tried for an Act 2 by releasing 60,000 emails to and from Hillary's campaign chairman, John Podesta. The release certainly had embarrassing revelations, as when Doug Band, a key aide to Bill Clinton, called his daughter, Chelsea, a spoiled brat in a message he assumed would remain private. Other emails exposed concerns about Hillary's inability to articulate any reason for her candidacy, as well as DNC operative (and then CNN contributor) Donna Brazile's advance notice of questions to be asked at a televised town hall meeting on CNN. Then there was former Hillary aide Neera Tanden discussing Hillary's bad judgment.

The emails probably ruffled some Clinton feathers but did Hillary's campaign no harm. In fact, Hillary had been losing her lead throughout September as concerns about her health multiplied. But in October—despite the Podesta emails—she recovered smartly. No specific fact or allegation in the emails had much to do with her campaign one way or the other.

In fact, the release of the emails actually served Hillary's campaign, handing it a resonant theme against Trump. It was then that the Clinton campaign and the media began to spin the story that the DNC email release was a deliberate act by the Russians to help the Trump campaign.

Immediately following the DNC email dump, Clinton campaign manager Robby Mook told CNN:

"What's disturbing to us is that experts are telling us Russian state actors broke into the DNC, stole these emails, and other experts are now saying that the Russians are releasing these emails for the purpose of actually helping Donald Trump."[25]

Mook did not reveal the identity of those other "experts" who apparently knew that the Russians were doing this to help Donald Trump. Who were they?

Mook never told us who the experts were, but we can make an educated guess.

Back then, there was only one place, one source that was spinning the theory that Trump was working with the Russians to sabotage Hillary. It was a former British MI6 intelligence agent—a rogue spook—named Christopher Steele. He and his associates, it later turned out, had been secretly paid $160,000 by Hillary Clinton supporters to investigate Trump's ties to Russia.

Unbeknownst to the voters, Steele had started providing his "intelligence reports" to the Clinton paymasters in June 2016. Eventually his reports were bound together in a "dossier" that documented Trump's collaboration with Putin in vivid, but totally inaccurate, detail.

The dossier's charges were specific but outlandish, and many have since been proven largely false. Nevertheless, it was these "findings" that provided the fodder for media stories of Trump-Putin collusion and led to leaks from the U.S. intelligence agencies that fueled the narrative.

Buoyed by Steele's intel, the Clinton campaign embarked on a continuous stream of allegations of Russian support for Trump and questions about Trump's Russian involvement.

Mook's assertions signaled a pivotal moment in the campaign. David E. Sanger and Nicole Perlroth of the *New York Times* recognized that he had crossed a line and escalated the charges to a new level.

Even at the height of the Cold War, it was hard to find a presidential campaign willing to charge that its rival was essentially secretly doing the bidding of a key American adversary. But the accusation is emerging as a theme of Mrs. Clinton's campaign, as part of an attempt to portray Mr. Trump not only as an isolationist, but also as one who would go soft on confronting Russia as it threatens nations that have shown too much independence from Moscow or, in the case of Lithuania, Latvia and Estonia, joined NATO.[26]

The *New York Times* also noted the Clinton strategy: "the Russian-intervention narrative fits with Mrs. Clinton's efforts to establish the idea that President Vladimir V. Putin of Russia wants to see Mr. Trump elected to weaken America and hurt its closest NATO allies."[27]

It was during this period, in the immediate aftermath of the DNC email release, that the intelligence community and the media coalesced around the story line that they would follow throughout the election, the transition, and the early months of the Trump presidency: that he had been elected because he was Russia's handpicked candidate.

Even President Obama weighed in, coyly mirroring the Clinton campaign's suggestion that something was up between Trump and Putin. "What the motives were in terms of the [email] leaks, all that—I can't say directly. What I do know is that Donald Trump has repeatedly expressed admiration for Vladimir Putin."[28] The president's implication was obvious.

The story line was in place.

The Clinton campaign stayed on message. On August 5, 2016, it released a new campaign ad entitled "What Is Donald Trump's Connection to Vladimir Putin?" that "insinuates that Trump has some kind of business or political alliance with Russia's president."[29]

The *Washington Post* correctly reported: "At this point, however, there is no evidence that anyone in the Trump campaign has a direct connection with the Kremlin, as Clinton's spot insinuated."[30]

The ad featured ominous music and clips of Trump talking about Putin, while comments and questions appeared on screen:

- We don't know why Trump praises Putin.
- We don't know why Trump and Putin share foreign policies.
- We don't know why Trump's top campaign aides have ties to Russia.
- We don't know why Putin is trying to influence this election.
- We don't know how much Trump has invested in Russia.
- We don't know what's going on here and Donald won't tell us.

"We'll let you guess."[31] This ad voiced what became a central theme for the Clinton campaign. As the campaign progressed, Hillary hit the issue harder and harder. Previous attacks on Trump had been ineffective, but in the Putin collusion story, the Clinton campaign felt they had struck gold.

With no evidence against Trump, the Clinton campaign focused its fire on his associates, particularly Paul Manafort.

Starting on July 31, 2016, details about Manafort's consulting business in the Ukraine suddenly became page-one news. Manafort was under siege, with stories in every media outlet filled with information leaked by pro-Ukraine partisans:

- How Paul Manafort Wielded Power in Ukraine Before Advising Trump (*New York Times*, July 31, 2016)
- Secret Ledger in Ukraine Lists Cash for Trump Campaign Chief (*New York Times*, August 14, 2016)
- Ukraine Documents Detail Cash Payments to Paul Manafort (*U.S. News & World Report*, August 15, 2016)
- Manafort Tied to Undisclosed Foreign Lobbying (AP, August 17, 2016)
- Bombshell Reports Allege Paul Manafort Was Involved in Potential Felony, Staged Pro-Russian Protests (*Slate*, August, 17, 2016)

- How Trump Adviser Manafort Revived His Career— and Business Fortunes—in Ukraine (*Washington Post*, August 18, 2016)
- Donald Trump Aide Paul Manafort Scrutinized for Russian Business Ties (NBC News, August 18, 2016)
- Trump Advisers Manafort and Gates Waged Covert Influence Campaign for Previous Ukraine Ruling Party (CNBC, August 18, 2016)

You get the picture.

On August 19, 2016, Manafort resigned from the Trump campaign. But his resignation did nothing to stop the stories about his work in the Ukraine, his real estate deals, his lobbying, his financial situation, the hacking of his daughter's cell phone. There are still reports that he is under investigation for various alleged crimes, but none of them have anything at all to do with Donald Trump.

With Manafort effectively destroyed, the media moved on to Carter Page, a foreign affairs volunteer to the Trump campaign who had never met Trump and had a long history of business endeavors in Moscow, including heading Merrill Lynch's office there at one time. Page was by no means a close associate of Trump, but his circumstances made him an attractive target, especially for the intelligence agencies. Using the soon-to-be-discredited Christopher Steele dossier, the FBI applied for a FISA warrant to surveil Page and his contacts and communications.[32]

Meanwhile, behind the scenes, the rogue spooks were desperately trying to get the phony dossier published. But no media outlet in the United States or the UK would publish it. Even left-wing websites turned up their noses at its wild and totally unsubstantiated accusations.

The rogue spooks did manage to get one U.S. publication, *Mother Jones*, to run a short story on October 31,[33] a week before election day, recounting the importance of the tales in the dossier and an overview, without actually publishing the unproven details. Nobody else dared to pick it up and the *Mother Jones* story had no impact.

In October, the FBI hired Steele for a very short time to verify the charges in the dossier.[34]

This raises a serious question: Why would the highest law enforcement bureau in the United States choose to collaborate with Steele—a for-hire private spook, who was being paid by one candidate's supporters to try to destroy the other candidate—right in the middle of the presidential election? So much for the political independence of the FBI, so loudly touted by its director, James Comey. And why would the FBI rely on someone who admittedly relied on uncorroborated "intelligence" that was simply passed on to him and not verified?

Meanwhile, the dossier's fanciful charges and unsubstantiated accounts of secret meetings between Trump and Putin operatives—which never actually happened—came to form the basis of very damaging leaks that came pouring out of the U.S. intelligence community.

It didn't work. Trump won.

But his victory was not the end of the story. Rather, it sent the Obama administration and parts of the intelligence community into shock. They had expected Hillary to win and hadn't given serious thought to the idea that Trump might prevail.

But as the truth sank in—that their work was about to be undone and Obama's presidential legacy all but destroyed—they went into overdrive to taint Trump's win and strengthen the story line of Russian interference in the hopes that it would seriously hamper him as president and ultimately lead to his impeachment.

Here, the disgruntled spooks' years of training at the CIA in the art of destabilizing and toppling regimes in foreign countries began to kick in. That the CIA playbook—applied in successful coups in Guatemala, Chile, and Iran—was originally written by right-wing agents anxious to destroy leftist governments made no difference. The radical liberals who had taken over the Agency—and the entire U.S. intelligence community—in the years after the end of the Cold War eagerly picked up its lessons and applied them to the task at hand: an intelligence coup against Donald Trump. As in those foreign coups, the chosen weapon was the leak.

The media, equally shocked and aghast at Hillary's defeat, willingly accepted and promoted these (often illegal) classified leaks. Covering up the real source behind innocuous words like "officials familiar with the situation" or "former or current government employees," they concealed often treasonous leaks by officials with the highest security clearance. The people we have appointed to guard our secrets, in whom we have reposed the ultimate trust, are spilling them to the media, which willingly publishes them. They suffer no repercussions, criticism, or even public exposure.

The Obama administration's efforts to tie Trump to Putin bled over into foreign relations three weeks before the Republican's inauguration when the president imposed sanctions on Russia to punish Moscow for its alleged hacking of the DNC.

A week later, the unsubstantiated dossier that Steele and his rogue spooks had developed was finally disseminated. FBI director James Comey and director of national intelligence James Clapper, despite their reservations about the lack of verification of the charges in the document, appended a summary of it to an intel briefing for President Obama. They sent the summary to congressional leaders and even briefed Trump on its contents. Their efforts had the desired effect of lending an air of authenticity to the flawed document. Its very existence was news, and therefore its contents—verified or otherwise—were now of public interest. Encouraged, the website BuzzFeed published it in full.

Apparently it was FBI director James Comey who insisted on including information about the dossier in the intel briefing.[35] That was surprising because he knew very well that the material in the dossier was unverified. And had he been investigating it for months, as he claimed, he would have learned how easy it was to prove the lies in the document. All the King's horses and all the King's men could not verify the dossier.

(The dossier became—and still is—the source of endless stories speculating on the Trump-Putin relationship. There is much more about the origin and contents of this spurious document later in the book.)

Even after Trump took office, anti-Trump partisans have been scheming to overturn the will of the American electorate by attempting to paralyze the Trump presidency. Make no mistake about it, paralysis is only their immediate goal. Their endgame is impeachment.

And they have help from within our government from the permanent bureaucrats who are leaking classified and embarrassing material.

It's a plan for an intelligence coup d'etat.

These leaks are designed to show a president incapable of governing, in over his head, and undermined by his own unreliable temperament.

The rogue spooks within the government were silently embedded and ready for anonymous targeted action as soon as Donald Trump became president. Suddenly private phone calls with foreign heads of state found their way into print. Oval Office meetings became the fodder of the evening news. Where did these stories come from? The "deep state," the permanent bureaucracy that exercises its will over democratically elected leaders.

As soon as Obama and his people realized that Trump was definitely coming to the White House, they scurried to convert the positions that they had staffed with liberals up and down the line into exempt civil service jobs from which they could not be fired by the new president. These hidden moles infested the CIA, the FBI, the NSA, the State and Defense departments, and the White House. Like spooks of old, they sat figuratively hunched over their wireless sets tapping out purloined information to a waiting press corps outside. The leaks framed the narrative. It was through leaks that:

- A phone call by incoming national security advisor Mike Flynn to the Russian ambassador to forestall Moscow from retaliating against U.S. sanctions and expressing his hope for better relations came to be seen as grounds for his removal.

- President Trump was accused of telling FBI director Comey to go easy in investigating Flynn.

- Attorney General Jeff Sessions was accused of lying to Congress when he did not disclose his own meetings with the Russian ambassador when asked about any contacts by Trump campaign people with Moscow. As a senator on the Foreign Relations Committee with no formal role in the campaign, he saw his own contacts with Russia as having nothing to do with the election, but he was forced, anyway, to recuse himself from the investigation into the Trump-Putin relationship.

- The president's decision to share classified material with Russia in order to increase their ability to collaborate in the fight against ISIS was seen as a breach of security and part of the Putin-Trump conspiracy.

And now, after the appointment of the special prosecutor, we have learned through a leak to the *Washington Post* that "according to people familiar with the investigation who were not authorized to speak publicly," Jared Kushner, the president's son-in-law and top aide, is under scrutiny for contacts, meetings, and interactions with the Russian ambassador and the head of a Russian bank.

The leakers are still at it.

Pounded by leak after leak about Moscow, the mirage of Trump-Putin collusion has grown into what one senator called "a huge shadow over the incoming Administration. The more we know the darker the cloud becomes."[36]

But this cloud has no corpus, no substance, no proof, no facts at all. It is just that, a cloud, a fog obscuring our vision of Trump's very real accomplishments as president and of the lack of evidence against him.

Today we face a growing movement to effect the removal of a popularly elected president based on leaks from the intelligence community, eagerly picked up by a compliant and leftist media. This Intel/Media complex has replaced the once feared military-industrial complex as the core of the "deep state" and the most potent threat to our democracy.

How did the American intelligence community move, decade by decade, from being a group of agencies that protected Americans to one that uses its power, budget, and independence to threaten our most sacred national institutions—even to the extent of mounting a virtual coup d'etat against the elected government of Donald Trump?

That's what this book is about. We want you to know all about the details that are deliberately kept in the shadows.

ONE

WHO IS BEHIND THE INTELLIGENCE COUP?

IT BEGAN WITH AN UNVERIFIED DOSSIER COMPILED BY CHRISTOPHER STEELE, the former MI6 spy who was hired by a U.S. opposition research firm and paid by Hillary Clinton supporters to find dirt connecting Donald Trump with the Kremlin during the campaign.

In retrospect, this highly flawed dossier was the catalyst that triggered everything else. A loss leader. False though it may have been, its allegations were sufficiently outrageous and sensational to attract the kind of nonstop media attention necessary to put the phony issue of a Trump-Putin arrangement on the front pages.

We still don't know who was behind the dossier. We don't know the identities of the Hillary supporters who paid for it. More important, we don't know who actually made up the allegations that have been proven false and were passed to Steele. Who went to all that trouble?

It seems unlikely that the Russians would implicate themselves, but they certainly might have. Was it rogue British—and/or U.S.—spooks? Spies from other countries?

The Democratic/Hillary Clinton supporters? Political operatives?

If Steele played the main role in assembling the dossier, who brought it to the public's attention? There were a number of people who definitely helped out. But more than anyone else, it was former FBI director James Comey who insisted on bringing the unsubstantiated document to the attention of President Obama and congressional leaders, which ultimately led to its widespread publication. And he, more than anyone else, knew how unreliable the document was, but he passed it on anyway. The FBI had actually offered to pay Steele $50,000 to help them verify the allegations in the dossier. They ended up paying him expenses (while he was still working for the Hillary supporters right in the middle of the campaign).

When the *New York Times* reported that anonymous government officials alleged that Trump campaign associates had "repeated contacts with Russian intelligence," Comey stayed on the sidelines and didn't correct or clarify the story. Did the FBI know that the story wasn't true? According to the White House, it was Comey's deputy, Andew McCabe, who had assured Trump's chief of staff that the *Times* story was "BS" but who later reportedly said, "We'd love to help but we can't get into the position of making statements on every story."[1]

So, with no comment from the FBI, the claims that Trump aides were frequently in touch with Russian intelligence entered into the bloodstream of the Trump-Russia story line.

And, knowing that Trump was not under investigation, Comey deliberately leaked his own memos about his private meetings with President Trump, no doubt expecting they would trigger the appointment of a special prosecutor.

He succeeded.

Why was Comey so invested in the anti-Trump dossier? And how did his relationships with others help kickstart this massive investigation that got so out of hand and so off track?

There is little doubt that Comey has an exalted self-image. Does he think he is the last good man on earth? Sometimes it looks like that. Others in Washington may wallow in half-truths, evasions, and corruption, but sometimes it seems that Comey believes he stands like a beacon above them all, a model of honesty and integrity.

Is he really that, or is he a headline hunter?

Comey seems addicted to the limelight. His career has been a parade of revolving headlines, always with Comey center stage, accompanied by an adrenaline rush from the publicity and controversy. To the outside observer, he looks like he's suffering from an inside-the-Beltway strain of attention deficit disorder (ADD)—when he doesn't get enough attention, he becomes disordered.

Don't get between Comey and a camera.

HOW THE COUP IS UNFOLDING

The coup progressed when the unverified allegations in Steele's dossier went public. But when Steele had first tried to pitch it to media outlets, he came up cold. They wouldn't touch it without verification and proof.

So Steele and his colleagues asked Senator John McCain for help. With the senator's intervention, Steele got the dossier to Comey. It was Comey who considered the dossier "so important that he insisted the document be included in January's final intelligence community report on Russian meddling in the U.S. election." That got it distributed to the president and leaders of Congress.[2]

Comey had to know that the very act of giving a summary of the dossier to the president and Congress would lead to its leaking and publication all over the Internet. He once testified that he knew how Congress works—you give them something confidential and they leak it. So he was not blind to the likely consequences of his actions.

Once the dossier leaked, the other half of the new Intel/Media complex kicked in, as every major news organ breathlessly featured each new leak by the rogue spooks to give the impression that the president was nothing more than a desperate criminal trying to cover up his fraud during the election.

Trump knew he had done nothing wrong and had been assured several times by Comey in private that he was not under investigation personally.[3]

But all this noise was getting in the way of the real progress he wanted to make. He couldn't be an effective president with this nonsense—which he knew had no basis in fact—obscuring his presidency. Confronted with this kind of false narrative overshadowing his administration, it was predictable that Donald Trump, activist that he is, would ask for a public affirmation of exactly what he had been told in private—that he was not under investigation. After all, he knew they wouldn't find anything. That there was nothing to find.

But Comey did not comply with that request. Instead, Trump's intervention created a new narrative: The president was obstructing justice. After Comey met with the president, he wrote a memo to himself about their discussion. In his telling, it sounded as if Trump had leaned on him to discontinue his investigations of former national security advisor Mike Flynn.

But that wasn't the end of it. Comey, no stranger to the ways of Washington, leaked the memo through a friend to the *New York Times*.

We don't have to speculate what his goal was. He explained it himself: "I thought that might prompt the appointment of a special counsel."[4] He got fired in the process, but no matter, that goal was achieved: A special prosecutor was now inevitable.

But who?

Attorney General Jeff Sessions—a loyal Trump friend—had already removed himself from the process surrounding the Russian investigation, and thus could not appoint a special prosecutor. Instead, it was done by Deputy Attorney General Rod Rosenstein, a step down in the food chain. He named Robert S. Mueller, former head of the FBI.

But Mueller has a problem—there is no evidence that the president actually conspired with Putin. Comey had already told Trump that he was not under investigation several times. Now, instead, the investigation shifted to whether Trump obstructed justice by asking his appointees to bring the Russia investigation to an end (the same investigation in which he was not a target).

And now, Mueller can use the license of the special prosecutor to probe any other crimes he comes across. Now Donald Trump's entire life and all his business dealings will be open to scrutiny and prosecution by a special prosecutor.

Already, leaks are flowing into the media from what appears to be Mueller's office, so that the president will be tried in the press before any issue gets to Congress.

What a scenario for impeachment. What a way to plan a coup!

JAMES COMEY: LEADER OF THE COUP?

Comey's first time in the spotlight was when he was serving as acting attorney general in 2004, while AG John Ashcroft was hospitalized for severe gallbladder pancreatitis. On the day before the expiration of the NSA program of warrantless eavesdropping that had been instituted after 9–11, Comey refused to sign a reauthorization. The program had been declared unconstitutional by the Justice Department.

Nevertheless, the Bush White House was trying to circumvent Comey and get Ashcroft to sign the reauthorization. To stop them, Comey and his BFF, then–FBI director Robert Mueller III, rushed to Ashcroft's intensive care unit bedside to urge him not to sign it. They were soon joined in the crowded hospital room by White House chief of staff Andrew Card and White House counsel Alberto R. Gonzales, there to lobby the AG to sign the document.

It could have been a brawl, more appropriate for a bar than for a hospital. Mueller, as head of the FBI, dispatched agents to stand outside the hospital room to be sure that Comey was not thrown out and was able to make his case to the attorney general.

Ashcroft didn't sign, and when Gonzales asked Comey to come to the White House to work out a compromise, Comey refused to come without a witness present, a practice he let lapse with President Donald Trump. (Since he didn't have a witness to anything that the president of the United States might say to him, he ran home and wrote up notes about his view of the meetings.)

And he didn't keep his singular championship of good over evil to himself.

When Comey was nominated as FBI director, he no doubt wanted to show his "superhero side."[5] So he spoke to Preet Bharara, a former subordinate in the U.S. attorney's office in Brooklyn, who was now Senator Chuck Schumer's counsel. "Bharara knew . . . that Comey wanted to tell this amazing story about a constitutional crisis in the hospital room of then-Attorney General John Ashcroft. So Bharara arranged for Comey to testify before a Senate subcommittee" about what happened that night.[6]

Although Comey must have known the question would be coming, the video of his testimony shows him seemingly struggling to tell the story, appearing emotionally overwrought at the memory of the story he wanted to tell. Good performance.[7]

Ruth Marcus, writing in the *Washington Post*, describes how Comey came across as "a superhero, able to leap up hospital stairs in a single bound. It was Comey as the resolute public servant, leader of a brave band prepared to quit rather than waver in defense of the rule of law."[8]

Such praise must have felt so good. Who wouldn't embrace that image?

But, by the summer of 2016, British intel operatives told Comey's people that they were picking up evidence of a Russian attempt to interfere in the U.S. election. Wow. What a story!

And, to make it even sexier, there was evidence that the Russian intervention was designed to help elect Donald and defeat Hillary. Then, to add even more fuel to the fire, Christopher Steele, the British ex-spook, produced a dossier that landed on Comey's desk, claiming that Trump had been working with Putin to meddle in the election. Steele had worked with the Bureau before and had done a good job.

Any study of the charges in the dossier would prove it to be mainly fiction, with few—if any—facts wedged in between. For example, a ten-minute phone call from the director of the FBI would have sufficed to prove that Trump's lawyer—who was said to have negotiated the deal with Putin's people in Prague—had never been there.

But, surprisingly, it does not appear that Comey chose to investigate. Why deflate the balloon? Why nip a great story and a massive scandal in the bud?

Instead, Comey seemed to move heaven and earth to get the dossier's charges to Congress and the president, with the inevitable leaks to the media and the public.

In addition to the fanciful stories about Trump's lawyer's secret negotiations, the dossier peddled nutty stories of Trump having orgies with prostitutes in a Moscow hotel room. And it identified the supposed hackers who had invaded the DNC computer system. Again, the FBI could have easily checked and found that the charges were not true.

As noted, without any proof of the sensational charges, nobody would publish the dossier. Not the media. Not the print press. Not the TV or cable stations. Not even a blog or a website. It was only after Comey made sure that the dossier was disseminated to the highest levels of government that there was a news peg to report on the dossier. And then it spread like wildfire.

At first, Comey was too busy announcing the closing of the investigation of Hillary's emails and then announcing its reopening and then another closing. He must have had no time to worry about Russian threats. He appeared as the Master of the Universe—controlling the fate of a presidential candidate. He was in charge.

When Trump won the election, events shifted. When John McCain brought Comey the dossier, it was this transaction that ended up legitimizing it, which, in turn, helped sandbag the president-elect.

Trump would learn fast who was in charge here.

Once the dossier came out, Congress and the media buzzed with speculation and rumor about Trump and Putin. But after Trump took office, there was a danger that the story—fanciful and unproven from the get-go—would begin to fade.

That's when the intelligence agencies leaked a false story saying that the Bureau had phone records and intercepted calls between Trump operatives and Russian spies.

The story—which appeared in the *New York Times* on February 14, 2017—said that "phone records and intercepted calls show that members of Donald J. Trump's 2016 presidential campaign and other Trump associates had repeated contacts with senior Russian intelligence officials in the year before the election, according to four current and former American officials."

The story said that "American law enforcement and intelligence agencies intercepted the communications."[9] That's known as the FBI in these circumstances.

That charge, brazen and bold in black and white, set the predicate for the entire investigation of the Trump team's ties to Russia. And it was false. Comey admitted as much in his testimony before the Senate Intelligence Committee on June 8, 2017—four months after the piece appeared and shaped the discussion of the Russia-Trump liaison.

When that story first appeared, the man of virtue and honesty had kept quiet.

Was it Comey's lie? Whether he originated it or not, he had to know it was false.

Comey was the head of the FBI. When he read a news story saying that "American law enforcement and intelligence agencies intercepted the communications around the same time they were discovering evidence that Russia was trying to disrupt the presidential election by hacking into the Democratic National Committee,"[10] he had to know that it hadn't happened. He hadn't gotten the word and, as director of the agency, he would have had to have been notified. He had to know that it was a false story. Disinformation. Why didn't he round up the four sources and fire them?

And, unbelievably, the false *New York Times* story also tried to prop up the credibility of the dossier, saying that "senior F.B.I. officials believe that the former British intelligence officer who compiled the dossier,

Christopher Steele, has a credible track record, and he briefed investigators last year about how he obtained the information. One American
law enforcement official said that F.B.I. agents had made contact with
some of Mr. Steele's sources."[11]

Like the guy who was supposed to have been in Prague to cut the
deal who had never gone there? He's never heard from the FBI.

When Comey had read the *Times* story on February 14, "he even
called President Trump's Chief of Staff Reince Priebus to assure him
the . . . report was false." But when Priebus "asked [him] if he could
refute the report in public, [he] declined."[12]

It's not easy to track down a leaker, but it can be done. Fox News,
ingeniously, searched the news for stories sourced—anonymously—to
"top FBI or DOJ (Department of Justice) officials" that were written
by Michael S. Schmidt of the *New York Times*. Every pitcher needs a
catcher. And, apparently, when Comey tosses a leak into the air, it is
usually covered by Schmidt.

Like most bullies, when his own career is on the line, Comey folds
like a cheap suit. When he knew that he would have to face media questions—in the middle of the election—about whether the FBI was investigating Hillary for her handling of classified emails on her private
server, Comey went to his boss, Attorney General Loretta Lynch, to get
direction. Lynch told him to release the information, but not to call it
an "investigation." She wanted to save her favored candidate—Hillary
Clinton—from the headline "FBI INVESTIGATING HILLARY." So she told
Comey to call it a "matter"—just like the Clinton campaign was doing.

"Why would I do that?" Comey probed. Lynch just repeated her
instruction: "Call it a 'matter.'" Comey obeyed. Comey did as he was
told, no doubt taking notes on the meeting. He said that the battle over
nomenclature was "not a hill worth dying on."[13]

In other words, it wasn't worth his job.

Longtime career Justice Department officials disagreed with Comey's dismissal of this particular hill's importance. Michael Mukasey,
attorney general under Bush-43, said that Lynch's order and Comey's

acquiescence were "egregious." He said that "the attorney general of the United States was adjusting the way the department talked about its business so as to coincide with the way the Clinton campaign talked about that business." Mukasey added, "In other words, it made the Department of Justice essentially an arm of the Clinton campaign."[14]

But Director Comey apparently did not take well to being told what to do by Lynch. He was boiling inside. The director later said that Lynch's directive to use the euphemism "matter" to describe the Hillary investigation greatly affected him. [15] He must have spotted a chance for revenge in his private rivalry with the attorney general when he learned that, on June 27, 2016, she had met with former president Bill Clinton as their planes stood ready for takeoff on a runway in Phoenix. Many observers said the meeting "immediately raised questions about whether she—or the Justice Department—could be impartial in the Hillary Clinton email investigation."[16]

Comey later testified that the tarmac meeting between Lynch and the former president was a "deciding factor" in his decision to act alone to update the public on the Clinton probe. "Yes, that was the thing that capped it for me," Comey said. "I needed to protect the investigation and the FBI."[17]

Coincidentally, it also put him in the spotlight.

This wasn't the first time that some concluded that Comey exercised power irresponsibly over other people's lives.

Comey's prosecution nearly ruined Martha Stewart's life. In the media, he criticized her sale of about four thousand shares of her company stock in 2001, calling it insider trading. But, as Gene Healy wrote for the Cato Institute, "Comey didn't charge Stewart with insider trading. Instead, he claimed that Stewart's public protestations of her innocence were designed to prop up the stock price of her own company and thus constituted securities fraud."[18] Cato's Alan Reynolds hit it on the head when he said that Martha was prosecuted for "having misled people by denying having committed a crime with which she was not charged."[19]

Why did Comey go after Martha Stewart in the first place? She pocketed about $40,000 in the stock sale under scrutiny while all over the world millionaires and billionaires escape prosecution after blatant insider trading.

Publicity?

When America was rocked after 9–11 by a series of anthrax attacks, the spotlight beckoned again. Opening sealed envelopes laced with anthrax, seventeen people were infected and five of them died.

Comey and Robert Mueller worked together on the case. From the outset, they suspected Steven Hatfill, a former biodefense researcher of the U.S. Army Medical Research Institute of Infectious Diseases at Fort Detrick, Maryland. Despite the fact that Hatfill was a virologist who had never handled anthrax, a bacterium, Comey and Mueller were convinced he was their man.

But they were wrong.

Carl M. Cannon of RealClearPolitics describes the flimsy evidence against Hatfill. The FBI "imported two bloodhounds from California whose handlers claimed could sniff the scent of the killer on the anthrax-tainted letters. These dogs were shown to Hatfill, who promptly petted them. When the dogs responded favorably, their handlers told the FBI that they'd 'alerted' on Hatfill and that he must be the killer."[20]

Hatfill's home was raided, his phone was tapped, and he was kept under intensive surveillance for two years.

Then the real killer surfaced when the FBI identified another military scientist, Bruce Edwards Ivins, as the man solely responsible. Ivins committed suicide. Hatfill sued the government and collected $4.6 million, while Comey and Mueller went on to greener pastures. Paul Wolfowitz, the deputy defense secretary, said that "Comey was absolutely certain that it was Hatfill."[21]

Oops.

Now James Comey is in the ultimate role on the ultimate stage: that of the lone honest man who stopped the president from selling us out to the Russians.

ROBERT MUELLER III: THE BATTERING RAM?

Robert Mueller brings a key qualification to the table as special prosecutor—he is a close ally and friend of James Comey. As Byron York writes in the *Washington Examiner:*

> Comey is a good friend of special counsel Robert Mueller—such a good friend, for about 15 years now, that the two men have been described as "brothers in arms." Their work together during the controversies over Bush-era terrorist surveillance has been characterized as "deepening a friendship forged in the crucible of the highest levels of the national security apparatus after the 9/11 attacks," after which the men became "close partners and close allies throughout the years ahead."[22]

Now Mueller is moving his investigation of President Trump away from whether Trump's associates conspired with Russia's meddling in the U.S. election and onto the issue of whether Trump obstructed justice. He is following the well-trod path other special prosecutors have blazed when the underlying "crime" they are sent to investigate turns out not to have happened.

Just as the investigation of President Clinton was initially about the Whitewater real estate deal and ended up focusing on Monica Lewinsky, so Mueller's investigation has shifted its focus to unrelated crimes that could be pinned on Trump and his associates.

As the president said: "They made up a phony collusion with the Russians story, found zero proof, so now they go for obstruction of justice on the phony story. Nice."[23]

Former House Speaker Newt Gingrich, as usual, said it best:

> "Mueller is now clearly the tip of the deep state spear aimed at destroying or at a minimum undermining and crippling the Trump presidency. Mueller is setting up a dragnet of obstruction, financial

questions and every aspect of Trump's life and his associates' lives. Very dangerous. The brazen redefinition of Mueller's task tells you how arrogant the deep state is and how confident it is it can get away with anything."[24]

Will Comey's public statements calling Trump a liar influence Mueller? Have Mueller and Comey spoken privately about Comey's views? We have no idea.

What we do know is that Mueller has made some questionable choices about the lawyers he's hired to work on the probe, which seems to suggest that he has a blind spot for optics.

It's hard to believe this, but it's true: Of the six lawyers disclosed, half were donors to Hillary Clinton's campaign. One unfathomable choice is Jeannie Rhee, who has given $16,000 to Democrats since 2008. She contributed the maximum to Hillary Clinton in 2015 and 2016.

But that's not her only connection to Hillary Clinton. It gets worse. She was one of the lawyers who defended Hillary Clinton personally, as well as the Clinton Foundation, in a racketeering lawsuit.[25]

Didn't this raise a *big* red flag for Mueller? Can we assume that a lawyer who represented the Clintons and contributed the maximum legal amount to her campaign doesn't have a neutral opinion of Donald Trump? Weren't there any other lawyers in the United States who didn't have that connection?

Because it doesn't inspire confidence in us!

Then there's Aaron Zebley. He represented Justin Cooper, a close aide to Bill Clinton, who set up the infamous Clinton email server in their Chappaqua home. Cooper had a low-level job in the White House, but was invited by Clinton to work as a personal aide. Working from the Clintons' Chappaqua home, he helped write Bill Clinton's first two books and traveled all over the world with him. He also worked on Clinton Foundation and Clinton Global Initiative issues.[26]

Again, wasn't there another lawyer who had no connection to the Clinton world?

Finally, James Quarles, a former Watergate prosecutor, has contributed roughly $30,000 to the Democrats and only $3,000 to Republicans.[27]

THE UNKNOWN LEAKERS ARE THE REAL CULPRITS IN THE COUP

When battlefield monuments are built, they try to include a tribute to those who are missing in action. At Arlington National Cemetery in Washington, DC, it is the Tomb of the Unknown Soldier, with its precisely timed changing of the guard, that attracts tourists.

As the history of the coup d'etat against Trump is written, we must be sure to leave space for the Tomb of the Unknown Leakers.

For it is the anonymous leakers from the FBI, CIA, NSA, Justice Department, and White House who are the spear carriers in this coup. Their leaks are akin to the broadcasts that rebels send after they seize the government's radio station in a military coup.

In Chapter Seven, we will explore who they are and what their motivation is.

They are the bureaucrats left behind by the retreating Obama appointees as they fled the White House before Trump arrived. They are the nameless and faceless saboteurs who are doing the daily grunt work in bringing down a president.[28]

IS CHRISTOPHER STEELE A ROGUE SPOOK?

Christopher Steele was a former MI6 spy in Moscow and is now a private spook in London. He was a longtime British intel operative at the height of the Cold War. During that period, Britain's legendary intelligence agency, MI6, was filled with special agents whose top priority was studying, understanding, recruiting, outwitting, and thwarting the enigmatic Soviet Union.

Those elite spies in MI6, for example, were often embedded undercover in foreign diplomatic posts, engaged in traditional spycraft and physically surveilled Russians in Moscow and St. Petersburg. They were adept at following paper trails, embedding moles in Russian intelligence, identifying moles the Russians had placed in British intelligence, and following up on secret tips.

These spooks had traditionally been the cream of the British intel crop. Russia was the biggest threat to the West, and for decades, Britain did its part—and more—to protect its interests by investing in a highly professional clandestine spy operation. The pivotal role British intelligence played during World War II had cemented its reputation as the best in the world. And, for decades, its ingenuity and excellence were directly focused on Russia.

Recruited by MI6 right out of Cambridge, Steele joined MI6 in 1987, and a friend once introduced him as "James Bond."[29] For a good part of his early years in MI6, he lived the glamorous and exciting lifestyle of a fictional spy.

Steele and his wife lived in Moscow for three years, using his diplomatic position of second secretary in the British embassy as cover for his covert activities.

It was the end of the Cold War and a time of great upheaval in Russia. In August 1991, Steele and his wife watched as rows of tanks rolled across Red Square in the unsuccessful attempt to overthrow Mikhail Gorbachev, who was seen as too pro-democracy. As the world watched along with the Steeles, Boris Yeltsin suddenly jumped on top of one of the tanks and electrified the military, convincing them to support him. That was the Russia Steele knew.

But it's been more than twenty-five years since Steele stepped foot in Moscow, which is light-years in Russian history. The Cold Warriors who became assets for Steele and his fellow spooks at that time were either hard-line Communist insiders or pro-democracy radicals. They would have had no relationship with Putin.

In fact, it's hard to imagine that Steele and Putin ever crossed paths. According to David Hoffman of the *Washington Post*, "Until he was handpicked in August [1999] by then-President Boris Yeltsin to become prime minister, Putin had never been a public figure."[30]

Moreover, Putin had not moved to Moscow until 1996, long after Steele had left the country. Prior to that, Putin worked for the KGB in East Berlin from 1985 to 1990, before moving back to his native St. Petersburg, where he was an assistant to the mayor. Putin became head of the FSB shortly after moving to Moscow.

So Steele did not have the opportunity to build up any relationships with sources within the Putin regime.

Steele left at the changing of the guards, which meant the changing of the spies, too.

Without any ability to travel to Russia, because of his status as a former spy, Steele was certainly operating in the dark. Steele had served British intelligence in the heyday of the Cold War. But all that changed when the Soviet Union collapsed in 1991. After the fall of the Soviet Union and Russia, they were no longer the heroes, the James Bonds of MI6.

As other geopolitical hotspots—Afghanistan, Iraq, Ireland, and Iran—took precedence, the former spooks who obsessed over Russia were in less demand. And there were other factors that contributed to their loss of influence. Starting in 1994, MI6 had drastic budget cuts— more than 13 percent in a three-year period.

Times had changed. The days of glamorous living, travel, entertainment, and posh diplomatic functions were ending. Instead, for the most part, Steele sat behind a desk at MI6, looking out at the Thames. But he kept in touch with his friends from the old days. When MI6 celebrated its hundredth anniversary, "Steele was one of four former British intelligence officers who spoke at [the] black tie gala dinner."[31]

He also kept in touch with Sir Tim Barrow, his former office mate in the British embassy in Moscow. Until recently, Sir Tim was the UK's ambassador to Russia. Now he is the UK's permanent representative to the EU. It's a small world.

And ex-spooks look out for each other. When the story about Steele's role in the dossier was published, the British government issued a "Defense and Security Media Advisory Notice," which requests the media not to publish certain information. The press was asked to hold off until 10 p.m., thus allowing time for the former agent to "make arrangements for personal security."[32]

The Cold War perceptions of those MI6 spies has remained alive, largely in the novels of British authors like John le Carré, Ian Fleming, and Frederick Forsyth. All these authors were former intelligence agents, basing their novels on their own experience in the field.

One thing the former MI6 agents didn't do was forget about what they had witnessed and learned about Russian ambitions and ruthlessness.

Just as these authors based their books on old experiences, Steele refused to let go of his formative impressions of Russia. Obsessed by perceived threats of a return to the Cold War and triggered by increasing evidence of a revival of Russian imperialism and of Putin's desire to upend Western democracies, it would be understandable if Steele was getting frantic. When those concerns combined with a growing suspicion of Trump's inexplicably glowing compliments of Putin, did he decide to take things into his own hands?

He knew just how to do it. Or did he?

Isn't Steele the man who wrote the infamous anti-Trump dossier?

We now know, of course, that actually he didn't.

What we don't know is who the real author is. And apparently neither does Steele—at least for a good part of it.

As we described, Steele's reports are filled with statements that were never verified or investigated, and are perhaps simply rumor or gossip. That's the best-case scenario. It is also possible that the allegations are nothing but imaginary scenes featuring phantom sources—complete fakes.

Much of the material in the reports that make up the dossier is unsupportable. And much more is simply fiction—bad fiction. We know that not just by his admission but because the fiction has been exposed.

Who made up these tales is still a mystery. Was it the Russians playing Steele? Or someone else entirely? Did Steele have anything to do with the fake stories? Did he realize they were fake?

By all accounts, prior to the publication of the dossier, Steele was a highly touted agent at MI6 and a successful consultant in his private intelligence company. He was a patriot, a believer in democracy and order. There was never a single rumor about unorthodox behavior or questionable reports. He maintained close relationships with the top levels of the British intelligence community and appeared to have always operated within the rules.

Until he didn't.

In fact, it was the trustworthiness of Steele's previous work with the FBI that apparently gave his unverified dossier credibility with U.S. officials. They accepted it as credible simply because it came from him. He had successfully worked with the Bureau on the FIFA (Fédération Internationale de Football Association) international soccer scandal and, from 2013 to 2016, had also shared valuable intelligence about Russia and Ukraine uncovered while working for a "private client."[33] (It's safe to assume that the private client was pro-Ukraine, because there is no chance that Steele was working for the Russians.)

When the U.S. intel chiefs decided to give President Obama a two-page summary of the unsubstantiated dossier—despite its blatant inaccuracies—they explained that they relied on the high quality of Steele's past work with the FBI in deciding to pass on the contents of the obviously flawed document.

The intelligence community was quick to tout Steele's credibility. The *New York Times* reported that "Senior F.B.I. officials believe that the former British intelligence officer who compiled the dossier, Christopher Steele, has a credible track record."[34]

CNN reported that U.S. officials found Steele's "past work . . . credible."[35] And the *Guardian* joined in the praise for Steele: "And the answer to that [decision to include a summary of dossier] lies in the credibility of its apparent author, the ex-MI6 officer Christopher Steele, the quality of the sources he has, and the quality of the people who were prepared to vouch for him."[36]

John Sipher, a twenty-eight-year veteran of the CIA who ran the Agency's Russia program for three years, described Steele as having "a good reputation and 'some credibility.'"[37]

One of the most public champions of Steele's work was Sir Andrew Wood, former UK ambassador to Russia, who helped arrange for Senator McCain to get a copy of the dossier. He said that Steele was a "very competent professional operator."[38]

Sir Andrew is an associate at the company that Steele founded after he left the secret service. He volunteered to CBS that Steele was "an honest professional. And nobody in his position would wish to make this sort of stuff up because, after all, it's a potentially dangerous problem."[39]

So if Steele didn't make it up, who did?

Regardless of how wonderful Steele's earlier work for the FBI had been, the fact remained that although the FBI had been receiving Steele's reports since July 2016, it was still unable to verify his allegations by the time the dossier was released in January 2017.

Why did the FBI still pay any attention to the dossier, and why didn't it find the false claims as quickly as the media did when it was released? Media sources immediately discovered, for example, the totally phony allegations about Michael Cohen in Prague. Why couldn't the FBI do the same? The Bureau had more than ample resources and manpower and could have either spoken to Michael Cohen or checked passenger manifests. They apparently did neither.

So why would the FBI give a second thought to the dossier? And why would it leak parts that would humiliate Trump, then president-elect?

What was going on here? Why was the FBI so invested in the still-unverified dossier? Was FBI director Comey looking for a new cause and anxious to play the role of the honest FBI chief who was fighting evil—wherever it came from? He sure slipped easily into the role.

And what was it that made Steele, an old-school, traditionalist ex-spy, turn into a rogue spook? Did he honestly believe the material he sent to his American client? We don't know.

Blame it on Donald Trump.

Alastair Sloan, a British journalist specializing in human rights, commented on the phenomenon of ex-spooks, suggesting that Donald Trump was the catalyst that turned them: "the case of Chris Steele highlights a growing movement within the intelligence services of highly motivated officers and former agents, who are willing to take extraordinary, but personal, steps to prevent Donald Trump from taking office." Sloan emphasized that they were not doing this with the support of the British government.[40]

We call these men and women the "rogue spooks"—former and current high-level spies, intelligence operatives, diplomats, and politicians who decided to take things into their own hands, sometimes working outside the rules, outside the norms, to accomplish what they saw as an urgent and necessary goal.

And Christopher Steele seems like he was one of them.

Steele seems to have become more and more obsessed with Putin— and more and more enraged by him—over the past few years.

And people noticed.

Nigel West, a friend of Steele and European editor of the *World Intelligence Review*, suggested that Steele had "a deep dislike of Putin and his Kremlin for ignoring accepted rules of espionage. . . . He feels very strongly that the Putin Kremlin tore up the rule book and the convention by which intelligence agencies do not attack each other's personnel."[41]

That was undoubtedly a reference to the brutal radiation poisoning of former Russian FSB officer Alexander Litvinenko in 2006—at Putin's direction. After publicly accusing FSB superiors of ordering the murders of political opponents of the Kremlin, Litvinenko escaped Russia and was granted asylum in Britain. He reportedly became an asset of MI6, consulting with them on what he named the Moscow Mafia.

Steele was designated as MI6's Litvinenko handler and kept in regular touch with him for about three years before his death. On the day before he was poisoned, they supposedly met at the Watermark bookstore in Piccadilly. According to the BBC, "the handler" visited him in the hospital, where he would have seen Litvinenko's agony.[42]

Steele witnessed the last twenty-three days of Litvinenko's life, lived in excruciating pain after the poisoning. So Steele had a personal involvement in the most appalling assassination of a British agent in history. That would have turned anyone against Russia and Putin.

Published reports indicate that Steele was also responsible for investigating the poisoning and quickly concluded that it was a Russian hit. There's no doubt that Steele was terribly traumatized by the brazen poisoning—"the only recorded example of deliberate plutonium poisoning anywhere in the world."[43]

A formal inquiry found evidence that it was a direct assassination order by Putin. According to Nigel West, Litvinenko's death inevitably colored Mr. Steele's view of Russia and turned him into a "man with a mission."[44]

So what exactly was Steele's mission that was discussed? While those Hillary donors who hired him did so in the hopes of using his talents to destroy Trump, it would make sense that Steele's motivation was also to undermine Putin, breaking up his emerging bromance with Trump and showing him in the worst possible light to the American people.

Any person in Steele's place would certainly have been outraged by Putin's barbaric disregard for human life. But it appears that, by 2016, Steele's simmering rage against Putin may have reached a boil and led him to action that, for him, was well outside the box. His sinister view of the Kremlin, not easily disputed, could easily have merged with what must be his deep concerns about Trump.

At the time, some associates of Steele told Sloan that "he was privately very concerned about civil unrest on the streets, and was also deeply worried, as many serving intelligence officers were, about Trump's stance on NATO, and his sympathies for Vladimir Putin."[45] No one would blame him for that.

Sloan postulated that Steele's strongly anti-Putin views may have influenced what he wrote in the dossier. He believed that Steele had some assistance from "some former colleagues at MI6." Sloan added that "begins to look very much like a transatlantic deep state stitch up—in which profit and political motives align perfectly for Steele to produce a dossier that is dirtier than the facts allow."[46]

Wow.

Sloan was not alone in his view that the dossier may have gone over the top. Steele's friend Nigel West wrote an opinion piece about the dossier for the *Telegraph*. The headline screamed:

CHRISTOPHER STEELE FELT THE KREMLIN BROKE
THE RULES WHEN THEY MURDERED LITVINENKO.
THAT COULD HAVE CLOUDED HIS JUDGEMENT.[47]

West criticized the "unsubstantiated, some quite lurid, allegations" in the sixteen reports as well as the questionable sources, even disclosing the "surprise" of "professional intelligence officers" about the poor quality of the report. And he accused Steele of "jaundice" in analyzing Putin's regime after Litvinenko's poisoning and found that Steele's report was biased.[48]

West concluded: "Intelligence analysts are taught not to trim their sails to suit their paymasters, but this may indeed be the exception."[49]

West is correct, but Steele seems to have gone even further than simply slanting his reports. He also shared his intel with MI6. (Or were they the ones sharing with him?) Was he under contract with them, too?

It's a rather small point in this very large picture, but Steele was not the owner of the reports that he produced; his American client who paid for them was. Yet he repeatedly made the material available to intelligence agencies without telling his client.

Steele definitely had a mission. Why else would he continue working on the dossier after election day? It makes no sense otherwise. Obviously, that would not help the Hillary Clinton supporters who had hired him.

What his mission was, we can't be sure of. But the dossier was the beginning of the White House crisis that is unfolding around us. It would help to know the names of the Hillary Clinton supporters who paid for the project. And it would also be helpful to know whether anyone else was paying him at the same time to work on the dossier. Until we know his motives, we can't really be sure whether he is a rogue spook or not.

ANOTHER FRIEND WHO HELPED OUT: MEET SIR ANDREW WOOD

Sir Andrew Wood is a former UK ambassador to Russia and Yugoslavia. He spent ten of his thirty-three years in the British Foreign Service in Moscow. He also worked on foreign intelligence matters in the Cabinet Office for the prime minister, analyzing raw intelligence sent by field officers. He was a lifer.

Sir Andrew is now a frequent lecturer and writer on Russia and the Ukraine, appearing on TV shows to discuss Russia and Crimea. Since retiring from the Foreign Service, Sir Andrew has been a fellow, specializing in Russian Eurasia, at Chatham House, a prominent British think tank. According to his Chatham House biography, Sir Andrew is also a "consultant to a number of companies with an interest in Russia . . . [and] an expert on Russia's domestic and foreign policies."[50]

And he is an associate at Orbis Business Intelligence.

It was Sir Andrew who spoke to Senator John McCain about the dossier and arranged for his associate to get a copy from Steele. Other than that, we don't know anything else about any other role he might have had in producing the dossier and its publication. We know that Steele said that Sir Andrew was aware of the investigations, but nothing further.

He is an old friend of Steele's and, like Steele, had a long history of involvement with Russia before and after he became the UK ambassador. Sir Andrew and Steele had more in common than their focus on Russia. Both were Cambridge graduates, both served in Moscow, and both were considered to be experts on Russia. But the most important thing that they had in common was their fervent belief that the intentions of the Russian regime were malevolent—especially as they related to the Ukraine.

They also shared a personal and poignant experience. While still young and serving at their posts, each had lost his wife and been left with small children to care for—Steele had three, Sir Andrew had one.

That terrible trauma may have bonded them.

Sir Andrew was twenty-four years older than Steele. Right out of Cambridge, he got a job in the Foreign Office and was immediately immersed in achieving fluency in Russian. After a lengthy language training course, the agency sent him to Paris to live with an "elderly Russian lady" to learn more about Russian culture and mores. After a few months, he was ready to go to the then Soviet Union.[51]

He frequently commented on timely events regarding Russia. In March 2017, for example, Sir Andrew warned that "the Kremlin could interfere in a second Scottish independence referendum as it seeks to destabilize the West," and insisted that Russia posed a "'widespread set of risks' to British democracy."[52]

"In the Russian perspective," Sir Andrew said, "if you've got the chance [to disrupt Western democracy] you will do it and they are doing it and they have done it. They threaten the French elections and the German elections too."[53]

In describing the threat that Russia represents, Wood recently said that Russia's aim is "to encourage splits and divisions in Western Alliance."[54]

Sound familiar? Steele also used those exact same words in the dossier.

Sir Andrew helped get the dossier to McCain, who then brought it to Comey's attention. He was a player, but that's all we know about his involvement in the dossier.

HELP FROM FOREIGN SPOOKS

Starting more than a year before the U.S. election, official British spooks repeatedly warned the United States about Russian hacking and "suspicious contacts" between Russians connected to the Kremlin and persons connected to the Trump campaign.

The British signal agency, GCHQ, which intercepts digital and satellite intel, reported directly to the CIA in August 2016 about Russian plans to intervene in the election. Robert Hannigan, its director, traveled to New York to meet directly with John Brennan, the CIA director. Brennan then passed on the information to the president and leaders of Congress.

Was this simply information that was gathered in the ordinary course of business, or were Donald Trump and his campaign a high priority for the Brits?

Two weeks after Trump's inauguration, Hannigan, a popular reformer of the agency, abruptly resigned, giving his staff only six hours' notice.

Was there a problem with the new Theresa May administration about his activities?

The Brits' involvement is explored in detail in Chapter Four. Stay tuned.

WHAT IS THE INTELLIGENCE COMMUNITY?

The Intelligence Community (IC) was established on December 4, 1981, when President Ronald Reagan signed an executive order reorganizing the agencies into a new framework. Reagan created a federation of sixteen different agencies, including:

Defense Intelligence Agency
National Geospatial-Intelligence Agency
National Reconnaissance Office
National Security Agency
Military Intelligence Corps

Office of Naval Intelligence

Twenty-Fifth Air Force

Marine Corps Intelligence

Coast Guard Intelligence

Office of Intelligence and Analysis (Homeland Security)

Central Intelligence Agency

Bureau of Intelligence and Research

Office of Terrorism and Financial Intelligence

National Security Intelligence (DEA)

Intelligence Branch (FBI)

Office of Intelligence and Counterintelligence (Energy Department)

The *Washington Post* reports that its combined budget is about $50 billion. It performs its work through 1,127 government agencies and 1,931 private companies in 10,000 locations in the United States. It employs 854,000 people. Twenty-nine percent of its workforce is employed by private contractors, who account for about half of its budget.[55]

TWO

GETTING THE DOSSIER OUT . . . WITH A LITTLE HELP FROM JOHN McCAIN

WHEN THE BALLOTS WERE COUNTED ON ELECTION NIGHT AND DONALD TRUMP was officially the president-elect, most of Washington was caught off guard. But one man, across the ocean, was positively ready: Christopher Steele.

Donald Trump's unexpected victory made it even more urgent that Steele get the dossier in front of top law enforcement officials and get it out to the public. He was on a mission and he needed results. Fast. People needed to know what he had on Trump. As he told David Corn of *Mother Jones* a week before the election, "This story has to get out."[1]

But he was thwarted at every turn.

The FBI was not giving Steele the attention that he felt his findings deserved. In fact, he was "increasingly frustrated that the FBI was failing to take action on the intelligence from others as well as him. He came to believe there was a cover-up, that a cabal within the Bureau blocked a thorough inquiry into Mr Trump."[2]

And, on top of that, the press would still not publish his unverified dossier.

Over his years as a private spook, Steele had built up a good relationship with the FBI and had worked extensively with the Bureau on its investigation of the FIFA World Cup scandal. From 2013 to 2016, he had provided them with information on Russia and the Ukraine that he had found in his work for private clients.[3] Who were these private clients? We don't know. But, based on what we know about Steele, it seems impossible that he would ever work for Putin's people and gather information on the democratic regime in the Ukraine. So, while Steele was working for the Hillary backers, could it be possible that he may also have been working for a pro-Western, Ukrainian private client?

The motivation of the Hillary supporters to pay for Steele's work obviously ended on election day. But Steele continued to work on releasing the dossier well after election day had passed and long after he stopped getting a paycheck. Why was he doing this? Was some other anti-Trump or anti-Russian entity paying him? Or was something else going on? Because it really doesn't make sense that he would become a volunteer, pro bono spook long after his contract expired.

This was apparently not simply a cut-and-dried project for Steele. He spoke to *Mother Jones* about feeling "duty bound to share information he deemed crucial."[4] Duty bound? Who was this duty to? Certainly not to the American clients who were paying him and apparently didn't know he was also working with—and getting paid by—the FBI. He described his view of Putin in cataclysmic terms, telling Corn that he "believed Russian intelligence's efforts aimed at Trump were part of Vladimir Putin's campaign to disrupt and divide and discredit the system in Western democracies."[5] That quote from Steele to Corn is, interestingly, a direct paraphrase of the language used in the first memo in the dossier:

> Russian regime has been cultivating, supporting and assisting TRUMP for at least 5 years. Aim, endorsed by PUTIN, has been to encourage splits and divisions in western alliance.[6]

So who is speaking—the sources or Steele? Are they one and the same voice?

As election day approached, Steele had been pressuring the FBI, without success, to investigate and publicize Trump's ties with Russia, which Steele believed to be something of huge significance, way above party politics.[7]

Since Steele had given his initial report to his FBI contact in July, he had kept sending them regular reports but heard nothing back about any investigation. In August, they had questioned him on the reports, asking for details. He had continued to bombard the FBI with his reports, but the story continued to remain confidential. Then, in October, the FBI asked him to come to Rome and bring his reports. It seemed like the FBI was now paying attention. But his trip to Rome came and went and still nothing seemed to be happening.

GETTING THE DOSSIER OUT

So, prior to the election, here's where things stood: The dossier had not been published anywhere and the FBI did not seem particularly aggressive in attempting to verify it. It was at this point that Steele appears to have taken steps to bring the dossier to the attention of the highest level of the FBI.

But how to get it there?

How could he accomplish that? Nothing was working. He needed to switch gears. If the sensational charges against Trump in the dossier didn't get out, Steele's apparent mission would fail. That's why, in retrospect, it seems that, at this moment, there was a dramatic shift in strategy. Instead of approaching journalists and media outlets, a series of events were set in motion to bring the dossier to the attention of a prominent U.S. senator, then to the director of the FBI, and, eventually, to the president of the United States.

How did they do it?

Did Steele—and whoever he was working with—decide that it was necessary to enlist someone with irrefutable political gravitas to take it to the highest level of the FBI and get those in charge to take it seriously? It looks like they did.

Because one week after the election, the first steps to accomplish this began.

INTRIGUE AT THE HALIFAX CONFERENCE

The Halifax International Security Conference in Nova Scotia, Canada, November 17–20, 2016, attracted dozens of anti-Trump diplomats, intelligence community leaders, anti-Russian activists, Ukraine militants, elected and appointed officials from around the world, as well as NATO officials, high-level U.S. military, ex-spies, and U.S. politicians.[8] Almost everybody who participated had likely rooted for or voted for Hillary, and, looking over the list of attendees, the conference may have been scheduled two weeks after election day in order to celebrate her anticipated victory.

These folks were definitely not Trump's people—they were horrified by his comments on NATO and dumbfounded by his comments on Russia and Putin.

The keynote speaker was Senator Tim Kane, Clinton's nominee for vice president. Other American politicians attending were Howard Dean, former chairman of the Democratic National Committee, and Senator Jeanne Shaheen—both diehard Hillary Clinton supporters.

But they had nothing to celebrate.

Donald Trump had changed everything on November 8. Hillary Clinton was over. Now the buzz was all about the new president-elect. One newspaper wrote that there was little doubt that "the delegates would speak about little else than the billionaire and his impact on foreign and defense policy."[9]

That prediction became true in more ways than one.

While pro-Hillary participants consoled each other, sharing their shock at the election of Donald Trump, others worried about the likely policies of the new administration, particularly concerning NATO. Since its inception in 1949, NATO had provided a collective defense against Russian aggression aimed at the United States or Europe. But Trump had specifically criticized the unacceptably high cost of American involvement and called for changes at NATO,[10] sending the participants at the Halifax conference—for whom the alliance was gospel—into a tizzy.

Trump was the big elephant in the room. Although none of the panel discussions focused specifically on the new Trump administration, the image of the incoming president did furnish a little fun. One of the workshops at the symposium reportedly put an empty stool on stage with a red hat on it bearing the logo MAKE DEMOCRACY GREAT AGAIN, a jab at Trump's signature baseball cap and its MAKE AMERICA GREAT AGAIN logo.[11] (It seems unlikely that they were trying to make the point that Trump had been invited and turned them down. More likely, they were celebrating his absence and mocking his personal style and unabashed nationalism.)

Many of the delegates were trying to understand and predict what Trump's foreign policies might be. Janice Stein, the founding director of the Munk School of Global Affairs at the University of Toronto, said: "For them, whatever else they're worrying about, top of mind right now, is what will Donald Trump's foreign policy be? What will his security policy be? Will it be disruptive of the existing order?"[12]

A disruption of the existing order was exactly what they feared.

But while those questions dominated the public discussions among the delegates, a completely different agenda was playing out in private.

ENTER JOHN McCAIN

One of the most prominent attendees was Senator John McCain, a regular speaker at the Halifax conference each year. McCain made no secret of his utter contempt for Donald Trump.

Many might argue that he was entirely justified. During the presidential campaign, Trump cruelly disparaged McCain's war record and time as a POW in Vietnam: "He's not a war hero. He was a war hero because he was captured. I like people who weren't captured."[13]

McCain spent five and a half years as a POW, enduring constant torture and beatings after the plane he had been piloting was shot down by the North Vietnamese. He spent two years in solitary confinement. The injuries caused by his brutal torture permanently damaged his arms and legs.

Todd Purdum recounted this torture in a profile of McCain in *Vanity Fair:*

> Despite the injuries he had already suffered, upon capture he was promptly bayoneted in the ankle and then beaten senseless. The North Vietnamese never set either of his broken arms. The only treatment of his broken knee involved cutting all the ligaments and cartilage, so that he never had more than 5 to 10 percent flexion during the entire time he was in prison.[14]

Offered early release in 1968, McCain refused to leave his fellow POWs behind. Then "his captors went at him again; he suffered cracked ribs, teeth broken off at the gum line, and torture with ropes that lashed his arms behind his back and that were progressively tightened all through the night."[15]

For his bravery and service to his country, McCain earned the Silver Star, the Bronze Star, the Purple Heart, the Legion of Merit, the Distinguished Flying Cross, and the Prisoner of War Medal.

Despite Trump's insensitive and outrageous comments about McCain's service, McCain initially supported him as the Republican nominee, but he publicly withdrew his support for Trump before election day, citing his vulgar comments about women.

So it was no secret that there was undisguised hostility between the two men.

At the Halifax conference, McCain further fueled that animosity by publicly challenging Trump. In his speech, he declared, "I don't give a damn what the president of the United States wants to do. . . . We will not waterboard." He threatened that anyone who sought to bring back that torture would find themselves in court "in a New York minute."[16]

Them's fighting words!

McCAIN LEARNS ABOUT THE DOSSIER

It was at the Halifax conference that Sir Andrew Wood, a former UK ambassador to Russia, spoke to McCain and his associate David Kramer about the dossier. Soon after, a bizarre and clandestine scenario to eventually deliver a copy to McCain in Washington unfolded.

McCain had come to the conference already very concerned about where Putin was taking Russia and where Trump would lead America. A constant and forceful critic of the Russian regime, McCain was accompanied at the conference by David Kramer, the senior director for human rights at the McCain Institute for International Leadership and a respected former assistant secretary of state, who, like Senator McCain, is vehemently anti-Russian, pro-Ukraine, and pro-democracy. Also joining them was Kurt Volker, the equally respected former deputy assistant secretary of state and former U.S. permanent representative to NATO, who is the executive director of the McCain Institute. All three men are tireless advocates for the Ukraine—writing and speaking about the importance of a democratic Ukraine, the Russian menace in Crimea, and the Putin regime's absence of any regard for human rights. Volker's firm, BGR Group, has a $600,000 lobbying contract with the pro-Western Ukraine government.[17] These men care passionately about the future of NATO and the preservation of Europe. And, given that, it would be natural for them to be horrified by Trump's comments about Putin, NATO, and the Ukraine.

And Ukraine was certainly on the minds of the people at the Halifax conference and the private group discussing the dossier.

Sir Andrew was there as a panelist on the subject of "Maidan, Crimea, and the Obstacles to Democracy in Ukraine." Maidan was, of course, the name of the famous square in Kiev where 104 protesters were brutally murdered in clashes with Ukrainian government security forces in February 2014. The protests were sparked by pro-Russian Ukrainian president Viktor Yanukovych's refusal to sign an EU association agreement and had endured for months.[18]

The dossier included allegations about Trump's former campaign manager, Paul Manafort, who, as noted earlier, had been Yanukovych's political consultant for years. Those charges no doubt interested the unabashedly pro-Ukrainian trio.

This was not the first meeting between Sir Andrew and David Kramer. Two and a half months earlier, Sir Andrew had been invited to help organize and speak at a conference put together by the McCain Institute for International Leadership in Tbilisi, Georgia, a former Soviet Republic. Among the issues listed for discussion at the conference were "democracy under attack and outlook for the region, the upcoming presidential elections in the United States." No doubt there was plenty of discussion among the delegates about what a Trump presidency might mean for the region.[19]

We don't know for sure whether the McCain–Sir Andrew meeting in Halifax was arranged beforehand, but it's probably safe to assume that it was, given Steele's efforts to get the attention of the FBI and the known antipathy of McCain and his associate to Trump's policies.

Steele may not have been able to arrange the meeting himself. He admittedly operated "in the shadows" and might not have wanted to approach McCain directly.[20] Unlike Sir Andrew, he did not participate in the anti-Russian, pro-Ukraine conference circuit. So he likely had turned to his colleague Sir Andrew to work it out. The existing collegial relationship between Sir Andrew, Kramer, and McCain made it easy. And the Halifax conference was the perfect time and place to talk to McCain.

The men discussed the dossier and Sir Andrew "arranged for Steele to meet Mr. Kramer as McCain's representative to review the sixteen pre-election memoranda on a confidential basis."[21] A hard copy was to be delivered to the DC opposition research firm that had originally hired Steele. Fusion GPS would then deliver it to McCain, via Kramer—all done very hush-hush. It looked like the dossier was on its way to the FBI.

UNDERCOVER OPERATIONS TO GET THE DOSSIER OUT

But it wasn't as simple as it sounded. For reasons that are not at all obvious, things got complicated and convoluted.

And somewhat comical.

The story of how McCain eventually got a copy of the dossier was very close to a caricature of a scene from a James Bond movie. Kramer arranged to go to Heathrow on November 28, 2016, to meet Steele, and was instructed to look for a man reading a copy of the *Financial Times*.[22] Once Kramer saw the man, they "engaged in an exchange of word code"[23] to assure that they were the proper parties. (What a comment on the limited daily print circulation of the vaunted *Financial Times* that there would be only one man reading it at baggage claim in a major airport in Britain.)

Why the spook antics? Couldn't McCain have easily gotten a copy of the dossier by email, fax, or DHL? What was the reason for all of the drama?

Was there some reason to carefully add layers of distance between McCain and the transfer? Why would that have been important?

Is it possible that Sir Andrew wanted to keep his distance from the dossier?

Sir Andrew claimed, erroneously, that the dossier had been "pretty much public" since the autumn. But it wasn't.

Sir Andrew also insisted that he had nothing to do with getting the dossier to John McCain: "I would like to stress that I did not pass on any dossier to Senator McCain or anyone else and I did not see a dossier at the time."[24]

He may not have actually handed the dossier to McCain physically, but media accounts and a sworn statement by Steele indicate that he was the one who arranged for Steele to give the document to Kramer.

It was Sir Andrew who arranged for him to meet Kramer in London. Otherwise, McCain would have never received the dossier. There's no question that after they spoke, a covert James Bond–like scenario was put into place that led a trusted McCain associate to London to meet Steele and get the dossier for McCain.

Afterward, when his role became public, Senator McCain, too, was extremely circumspect about his involvement in the dossier project.

At first, McCain seemed to be trying to keep the British role confidential. The *Guardian* reported that he "was informed about the existence of the documents separately by an intermediary from a western allied state" and "dispatched an emissary overseas to meet the source."[25] Sounds like military spook babble. What was going on here?

But then McCain denied that he had sent an emissary. "Media reports that I dispatched an emissary overseas to meet the source of the information I received are false."[26]

McCain suggested that he was just being a good citizen when he handed it over to the FBI:

> "I did what any citizen should do, I received sensitive information, and then I handed it over to the proper agency of government and had nothing else to do with the issue."[27]

But McCain had everything to do with the issue, because he personally brought it to the FBI.

But when asked on CNN why he thought that he had been given the dossier, he replied, "No idea."[28] Here's a hint, Senator: It wasn't for your reading pleasure.

But, of course, he did know exactly why it was given to him, and he went to great lengths to get it, probably hoping, all the while, to keep his role secret.

THE DOSSIER COMES OUT

At first, McCain was apparently worried that any involvement he had with bringing the dossier to FBI attention might appear as simply a vindictive move against Trump. He may also have been loath to break so publicly with the newly elected president. After all, they were both Republicans. But, despite his reservations, McCain handed over the dossier to FBI director James Comey on December 9, 2016, six weeks before Trump would be sworn in.

Even as he did so, he confirmed his lack of knowledge about the dossier's credibility.

Mission accomplished.

The story of how the dossier came to be published is as bizarre as its allegations.

Once McCain gave the dossier to Comey, as the *Washington Post* reported, "the nation's top spies . . . faced an excruciatingly delicate question," should they tell the president?[29]

As we reported earlier, they decided to tell President Obama by appending a two-page summary of the dossier to one of his regular intelligence briefings.

Why did they choose to do it? The spooks said they had no choice. "'You'd be derelict if you didn't' mention the dossier, a U.S. official said. To ignore the file, produced by a private-sector security firm, would only make the supposed guardians of the nation's secrets seem uninformed, officials said, adding that many were convinced that it was only a matter of time before someone decided to publish the material."[30] This response is certainly puzzling. Why would there be any obligation to pay attention to any document created outside U.S. intelligence agencies that could not be verified? Why would anyone be derelict in *not* releasing a completely unverified document?

While director of national intelligence James Clapper insisted that "The [intelligence community] has not made any judgment that the information in this document is reliable," he said it had to be released anyway to give policy makers "the fullest possible picture of any matters that might affect national security."[31]

These protestations that the top spooks were protecting national interests are absurd. They had gone rogue. Anyone could see how bogus the dossier was after an hour of examination and a few phone calls.

Then, likely to assure that the dossier would, in fact, be leaked, the spooks sent it to the congressional leadership. They might as well have issued a press release.

The only purpose in releasing it was to embarrass, hobble, ensnare, and weaken Donald Trump as he prepared to take the oath of office.

It was as close to an assassination attempt as you can get without a gun or a knife.

To lend an appearance of fairness, Comey also privately briefed President-elect Trump about the dossier. Everything about the confidential briefing was leaked by officials in the Obama administration. NBC reported that "a senior U.S. official said that it was FBI Director James Comey himself who pulled Trump aside after the briefing and spoke with him one-on-one about the so-called 'dossier.'"[32]

Donald's reaction must have been something to see.

It didn't take very long for the classified material to be leaked by rogue spooks, holdover Obama appointees, and congressional staff or members. CNN admitted that its sources in preparing the story about the dossier included "multiple high ranking intelligence, administration, congressional and law enforcement officials, as well as foreign officials and others in the private sector with direct knowledge of the memos."[33]

Of course, the dossier spread like a gasoline fire all over the capital. Now there was a presidential imprimatur on a document so outlandish, phony, and fabricated that no journalist had dared publish it on his own. Christopher Steele's wish had finally come true—the story did get out.

Liberal, left-wing publications, always eager for headlines, readers, and ratings, had refused to print the dossier in what was perhaps the most stellar—and unique—example of following the ethics they had been taught in journalism school.

If even these folks—who would print anything and stop at nothing—wouldn't touch the dossier, what conceivable business did the FBI and the president have in letting it out and legitimizing it?

And so the dossier hung out there for months. It's still out there, unrefuted, unquestioned, and unverified, for all to read about their new president. The fact that it is false seems not to have diminished its circulation in any way.

It is easy to understand why committed liberals and partisan Democrats would not flinch when it came to peddling dirt about a conservative Republican president. But why were a British ex-spy (and possibly current ones?), the directors of the FBI, CIA, NSA, and national intelligence, a former UK ambassador to Russia, and a U.S. senator so interested in doing so? Who, exactly, wanted it out there?

THREE

THE DOSSIER

The "dossier" refers to the questionable thirty-five-page document produced by British ex-spook Christopher Steele. It included seventeen separate reports, written between June and December 2016. Steele was hired by an American opposition research firm, Fusion GPS, in June 2016 to dig up dirt about Donald Trump and his businesses in Russia. The project was originally funded by unknown supporters of Hillary Clinton.[1] But after election day, after the Americans were no longer paying him, Steele inexplicably continued to update the dossier with purportedly new information and worked overtime to get the attention of the FBI.

THIS DUBIOUS DOCUMENT BELONGS IN A SPECIAL CATEGORY—RIGHT NEXT TO the intel fabrication that Saddam Hussein had weapons of mass destruction, an invention that misled the entire world and sent us scrambling down a blind alley. Here's how the same caliber of fake news unfolded in the case of this anti-Trump dossier.

It started on Tuesday, January 10, 2017—just ten days before President-elect Donald Trump's inauguration, when CNN reported that he had been briefed by top U.S. intelligence sources about an explosive dossier alleging that Russian spies had amassed compromising material about his personal, financial, and political activities in Russia.[2] Within hours, BuzzFeed had published the entire document.[3]

Trump vehemently denied the reports, calling its author a "failed spy" and denouncing the claims as "phony."[4]

He got that right. The dossier's claims about him were based on fake reports, phantom sources, and make-believe events—deception, dishonesty, and disinformation all rolled into one big fiction.

But it was this bombshell dossier that spawned the widely published rumors about Trump's supposed liaison with Putin. And, galvanized by its contents, the FBI and both houses of Congress launched serious investigations. FBI director James Comey announced the scope of his agency's inquiry, saying that:

> "[T]he FBI . . . is investigating the Russian government's efforts to interfere in the 2016 presidential election. . . . That includes investigating the nature of any links between individuals associated with the Trump campaign and the Russian government, and whether there was any coordination between the campaign and Russia's efforts."[5]

What Comey didn't tell Congress—or the president—was that he knew, better than anyone else, that the scurrilous dossier was not reliable and could not be verified. His agency had been scrambling to do just that for six months and had come up cold.

We now know why. On April 4, 2017, in defense to a defamation lawsuit based on the dossier, Christopher Steele admitted in a signed sworn statement filed in the High Court of Justice, Queen's Bench Division, that claims made in at least two of his reports were based on "unsolicited intelligence."[6]

Steele added that he had concluded "correctly" that "raw intelligence" in at least one of the dossier's memos—the one dated December 13, 2016 (the only one at issue in the lawsuit)—"needed to be analysed and further investigated/verified."[7]

Wasn't that supposed to be his job?

It wasn't surprising since many of the most serious claims against Trump had already been debunked and exposed as fiction.

Think about that and what it says about the dossier's "sources." As late as April, Steele couldn't verify that the sensational charges about the president of the United States are true or that the people who made them are authentic. That seems to be a rather low bar for a document that could destroy and humiliate the president of the United States. But that never stopped Steele from marketing his claims to the FBI, MI6, and the media.

And what is truly astounding is that the lack of authenticity never caused the FBI to reject the dossier and reach the inescapable conclusion that it was a deliberate fabrication designed to crush Donald Trump.

A few months later, James Clapper, the former director of national intelligence, left no doubt that he couldn't vouch for this document. "Without respect to the veracity of the contents of the dossier, that's why it was not included as part of our report because much of it could not be corroborated. . . . and, importantly, some of the sources that Mr. Steele drew on, the second- and third-order assets, we could not validate or corroborate."[8]

That says it all, doesn't it?

There was one item that Clapper was able to verify. He found the statement that Putin hated Bill and Hillary Clinton to be true.[9] Thank goodness for our intelligence agencies!

Other than that obvious fact, the only thing that could be easily verified was that everything in the dossier about the conspiracy between Putin and Donald Trump and his close associates is false: a concoction. A fabrication.

BuzzFeed made the thirty-five-page dossier available online in its entirety, freely admitting the uncertainty about its truthfulness. In releasing it, Ben Smith, BuzzFeed's editor, included a disclaimer, admitting that "It is not just unconfirmed: It includes some clear errors." Smith subsequently defended his decision to publish it anyway, saying,

"We are now in a media environment where you have to engage in false statements."[10]

Someone needs to get this man a libel lawyer. Immediately.

Fortunately, the rest of the press corps did not share Smith's bizarre analysis. Veteran journalist John Podhoretz of the *New York Post* warned of the inherent absence of trustworthiness in information from intelligence sources: "In my experience, there is no source of whom you need to be more skeptical, and whose information you need to verify to the letter before you can even begin to think of publishing it, than an 'intelligence' source."[11]

That is certainly good advice to follow in this case.

Perhaps the lesson in all of this is that we should never confuse "intelligence" with intelligence.

They're not the same.

WHAT'S IN THE DOSSIER?

disinformation, noun: *false information deliberately and often covertly spread (as by the planting of rumors) in order to influence public opinion or obscure the truth.*[12]

There is only one plausible conclusion that can be reached about the reliability of the Steele dossier: It is unreliable.

Much of it appears to be a hoax, a fake that was designed to entice U.S. intelligence agencies, manipulate the press, and hoodwink American voters into believing that Donald Trump was in a secret conspiracy with Vladimir Putin.

In spook talk, that tactic is called disinformation—and that's exactly what filled the dossier—a catalog of false information designed to appear as if it came from authentic intelligence sources.

Where did it come from? That's the big question. We have no idea.

Steele admits that much of it came from "unsolicited material." Who sent it? And how did they know who to send it to? Was it rogue spooks trying to defeat Trump? Or was it the Russians peddling information so patently false as to discredit anyone who used it to accuse them of interfering in the U.S. election? Did it come from Hillary Clinton supporters who loathed Trump? Or was it someone else entirely, some other anti-Trump zealot who wanted to defeat him?

Regardless of where it originated, it was anything but authentic, an annoying fact that didn't stop Steele from giving it to the FBI and MI6 or from passing it along to a U.S. senator—likely in the hopes of legitimizing it. And it didn't stop Steele's American employer, Fusion GPS, from peddling the claims in the dossier to the press,[13] just as the rogue spooks had done before the election.

It wasn't until months after the dossier was published that Steele had anything to say about it—and that was in a statement in a court filing. He had disappeared for several weeks after he was outed and had been unavailable to any reporters since then.

It turned out that in large parts of the dossier, Steele had simply summarized "intelligence" that someone had gratuitously passed on to him, and he apparently had never independently scrutinized it or probed the information for its accuracy. It looks like he had no knowledge of whether the intel was true or false.[14]

Neither did the FBI. It started receiving information about the conspiracy in July 2016 and frantically tried to verify it before election day—with no success. That's because lies—and there were many of them—cannot be verified.

That's what is in the dossier about Donald Trump—unverified, uninvestigated, unsourced, and untrue accusations.

Its thirty-five pages purportedly chronicle a secret collusion between Trump and Putin to undermine the U.S. presidential election, documented by sources such as "Kremlin insiders" and "a former senior Russian intelligence officer."[15]

There's also a lurid depiction of Trump's unorthodox sexual encounters in a Russian hotel room, which, it says, could become the basis for potential blackmail.[16]

There was a tipoff that the document was a ruse right on the face of it: The dossier cast Michael Cohen as the star of its imaginary drama.

THE MYTH OF MICHAEL COHEN, CONSIGLIERI, SECRET AGENT IN PRAGUE

According to the dossier, Michael Cohen was at the epicenter of the Putin-Trump collaboration.

Why was this important? Because Cohen is a longtime confidant and personal lawyer to Donald Trump, whose office was only thirty feet away from him at Trump Tower. His involvement in this intrigue would have signaled that Trump was up to his ears in the scheme. Without the complicity of a trusted lieutenant, the story wouldn't be believable. That's why the dossier targeted Cohen for the tallest tale of all.

The dossier carefully placed Cohen at the helm of the conspiracy—attending meetings in Prague with his Kremlin counterparts to direct payoffs and cover-ups. With appalling specificity, the fake report details the fake meetings, the fake agendas, the fake attendees, and their fake locations.[17]

But there is one mind-boggling problem with this fable: *Cohen has never been in Prague!* Immediately after the dossier was published, Cohen presented his passport to the president-elect, at Trump Tower, which confirmed that he had not traveled outside the United States at all during the period in question. The closest he got to a clandestine encounter was a meeting with his son and a college baseball coach in California.[18]

(NOTE: A painstaking search of California cities reveals none named Prague.)

Jake Tapper of CNN confirmed that the information about Trump's lawyer was not at all true. Tapper reported that "intelligence officials believed that it was another Michael Cohen with a passport from another country who traveled to Prague."[19]

Another Michael Cohen? Are they kidding?

This wasn't a mistake, it was an invention that leaves no doubt that the entire dossier is a fraud. The fictitious activities of Mr. Cohen, "Trump's lawyer," go on for pages and pages in great detail. It's all lies. Because once there's no Michael Cohen, "Trump's lawyer," at the pretend Prague meetings, everything that supposedly happened there must be dismissed—the entire Kremlin conspiracy, the payoffs, the hacking, the cover-ups. Everything.

How can we believe anything in this dossier when it is clear that so much of it has been proven to be completely false—perhaps fabricated in order to advance the fiction that Donald Trump and his closest associates were conspiring with Putin? We don't know exactly who fabricated the fictions in the dossier—or why—but somebody did. Was it the Russians, the British, or somebody else who wanted to stop Trump?

The only Michael Cohen they were interested in was in California, not Prague.

Michael Cohen—the real one—first heard about his inclusion in the dossier when he was "bombarded by calls."[20] He recalled, "I must have received sixty or seventy calls that afternoon from reporters inquiring about the story. Specifically, each one asking if I had been to Prague or the Czech Republic—all I could do was laugh."[21]

But it was no laughing matter. Suddenly he found himself propelled into the middle of the fiercest of controversies through no action of his own.

But then the important call came, the only call he truly cared about. The "boss," Donald Trump, called Cohen and asked, "Have you seen the story? Were you ever in Prague?"

"No, Mr. Trump," Michael answered. "You know where I was. I was in California at USC with my son Jake taking a look at the school."

"I forgot to ask you, how did it go?" Trump inquired.

"Very well," Cohen replied. Then he turned to the matter at hand: "Mr. Trump, I've been with you for a decade. I have never lied to you. I would never lie to you. And I am not lying to you now. This story is a fake news story. An absolute lie."

Trump probed further. "Michael, this is very important. A very serious accusation. Think carefully. Is there any element of it that might be true? Any at all?"

Cohen assured him that it was completely false and then asked Trump if he wanted to see his passport to confirm that he'd never been to Prague.

Trump liked the idea and asked him to come back to Trump Tower, where he was having a meeting with his aides—Reince Priebus, Steve Bannon, Kellyanne Conway, Jared Kushner, and others.

When Cohen arrived, he handed his passport to the future president. Trump opened it and scrutinized it carefully, turning each page. He looked up and told the gathering: "He's never been to the Czech Republic. He's never been to Prague."

The aides passed the passport around, each in turn examining it and agreeing that Michael was right.

The false narrative had been carefully woven to demonstrate Michael Cohen's importance to the secret Kremlin-Trump operation. The first reference to Cohen in the dossier is in "Company Intelligent Report 2016/135," dated October 18, 2016, when Cohen's "key role" is highlighted:

> a Kremlin insider with direct access to the leadership confirmed that
> a key role in the secret TRUMP campaign/Kremlin relationship
> was being played by the Republican candidate's personal lawyer,
> Michael COHEN.[22]

Once he was established as a conspirator by the "Kremlin insider," a story about Cohen's cover-up activities was fabricated:

COHEN was now heavily engaged in a coverup and damage limitation operation in the attempt to prevent the full details of TRUMP's
relationship with Russia being exposed. In pursuit of this aim,
COHEN had met secretly with several Russian Presidential Administration (PA) Legal Department officials in an EU country in
August 2016.[23]

Later on, the dossier gets more specific and puts Cohen in Prague
for these clandestine meetings.

Report 2016/166, dated December 13, 2016, provides extraordinary
details about an ostensible meeting with Cohen and high-level Russian
government officials in August 2016.

According to the report, well-connected sources had exposed exactly what Cohen was up to:

> speaking to a friend and compatriot on 19 October 2016, a Kremlin
> insider provided further details of reported clandestine meeting/s
> between Republican presidential candidate Donald Trump's lawyer
> Michael Cohen and Kremlin representatives in August 2016.[24]

In addition to the uncontroverted evidence that Cohen was *not* in
Prague and did *not* direct any payments or cover-up, new evidence that
emerged on April 4, 2017, puts to rest any pretense that anything in the
dossier about Cohen is reliable.

Apparently the highly sensitive nature of the dispatches between
Cohen and his Kremlin contacts made it necessary to carefully disguise
their true content—in true spook fashion. But, even so, the enigmatic
correspondence left no question that the meeting was held in Prague:

> Although the communications between them had to be cryptic for
> security reasons, Kremlin insider clearly indicated . . . that the re-
> ported contact *took place in Prague.* . . .[25]

There was amazing specificity about the fantasy Cohen meetings in Prague. According to Memorandum #166 Cohen was reportedly "accompanied to Prague in August/September 2016 by 3 colleagues for secret discussions with Kremlin representatives and associated operators/hackers."[26]

The three phantom colleagues were, of course, never identified, because they, too, were illusions. Or perhaps apparitions.

Nevertheless, the report meticulously described the particular items of the agenda that Cohen discussed at the make-believe Prague meetings:

> questions on how deniable cash payments were to be made to hackers who had worked in Europe under Kremlin direction against the CLINTON campaign . . . and various contingencies for covering up these operations and Moscow's secret liaison with the TRUMP team more generally. . . . what was to be done in the event that Hillary CLINTON won the presidency. It was important in this event that all cash payments owed were made quickly and discreetly and that cyber and other operators were stood down / able to go effectively to ground to cover their traces.[27]

To underscore the seriousness and high-level Kremlin involvement in the bogus Cohen meetings, the Kremlin source implicated the head of the Duma Foreign Relations Committee in the upper house as the host and catalyst for the meeting:

> Kremlin insider went on to identify leading Pro-Putin Duma figure Konstantin KOSACHEV (Head of the Foreign Relations Committee) as an important figure in the TRUMP campaign-Kremlin liaison operation.[28]

(Note to Kremlin insider: Kosachev might be a powerful principal in the Russian legislature, but he never hosted a meeting with Trump's associate Michael Cohen. Not in Prague, not anywhere.)

The dossier also identified Oleg Solodukhin as "one of [the alleged Cohen team's] main interlocutors . . . operating under cover . . . of the Russian Center of Science and Culture in Prague."[29] Solodukhin was supposedly the liaison between Cohen and his three make-believe companions.

But according to Radio Free Europe, Solodukhin denied any such meeting and insisted that he did not know Cohen.[30]

So how could anyone possibly come up with the harebrained idea to embroil Michael Cohen in the scam in the first place? To malevolently place him in compromising meetings in Prague?

Whoever it was did it with impunity because of their overwhelming, unbelievable arrogance and certitude that they would never be caught. They probably also believed that they had a paper trail to cover them. But, instead, that would turn out to be exactly what exposed them.

The most feasible explanation for this caper is that government intelligence agencies—or rogue agents—probably reviewed digital records listing the comings and goings of people identified with the Trump organization and campaign on the one hand and FSB operatives or Kremlin bigwigs like ambassadors and legislators on the other. It was a simple matter of finding whether their paths had crossed and then taking it from there.

Or maybe it wasn't so simple.

Because they got it wrong. Really wrong. Obviously the intel about Cohen wasn't based on a sighting of him in Prague—because he was never there. So, some enterprising spook probably noticed that in August 2016 someone named Michael Cohen traveled to Prague at the same time as Konstantin Kosachev, the head of the Upper House Foreign Affairs Committee in Russia.

Someone then leapt to the conclusion that it was the Michael Cohen who was Trump's associate. Seizing on the coincidence of their unrelated visits, someone then invented a series of meetings between the two and imagined a very detailed and incriminating agenda.

Inspector Clouseau must have personally overseen this investigation.

Because whoever was doing this carelessly failed to check if they had the right Michael Cohen on the manifest—the Michael Cohen who worked for Trump. And they didn't. It wasn't him; it was another Michael Cohen entirely (at least that's what's claimed). So their fiction was easily exposed and, as a consequence, all of the additional fake information that flowed from it was debunked as well.

Oops.

Fully a third of the dossier is based on the travels and supposed statements of the wrong Michael Cohen. There's more.

There were other false statements about Cohen. Report 134 lied about Cohen's family and suggested there were strong ties to Russia, perhaps to bolster his credentials as the lead delegate to the fake Moscow-Trump alliance:

> Kremlin insider highlighting the importance of TRUMP's lawyer, Michael COHEN in covert relationship with Russia. COHEN's wife is of Russian descent and her father a leading property developer in Moscow.[31]

Once more, the claims were a figment of someone's imagination and were absolutely not true. Cohen denied them, noting that his wife was born in Ukraine and that he didn't believe that his father-in-law had ever been to Russia in his entire life.

All of this disinformation about Cohen was nothing but a spook's canard.

But it didn't stop there.

THE HACKERS WHO COULDN'T HACK IT

U.S. and UK intelligence believe that Russia was behind the hacking of the Democratic National Committee (DNC). But the dossier goes further and says that it was a joint project between Putin and Trump. Apparently, while Michael Cohen was at the phony meetings in Prague, he was arranging for payoffs to the hackers and trying to move them to Bulgaria to keep them quiet. A kind of spook witness relocation program.

(Remember that Cohen was actually in California at that time.)

The dossier pretended to answer the question that has been buzzing around Washington for months: Who were the people who actually hacked into the DNC computers?

The ones Cohen was supposedly arranging payoffs for?

The dossier claims that one hacker was a tech company, XBT, run by Aleksej Gubarev, a Russian-born Cypriot. The other was a Russian hacking expert, Seva Kapsugovich.[32]

But once more, the dossier was wrong. In fact it was so wrong that after BuzzFeed published the dossier, one of the supposed hackers sued the online site and its editor, Ben Smith, for defamation. BuzzFeed had to apologize and retract the false charge from the online version of the dossier.[33] (This is the same Ben Smith who, we noted earlier, said that "We are now in a media environment where you have to engage in false statements."[34] We told you he needed a libel lawyer!)

Originally the dossier had charged that:

[Name redacted] reported that over the period March-September 2016 a company called [redacted] and its affiliates had been using botnets and porn traffic to transmit viruses, plant bugs, steal data and conduct "altering operations" against the Democratic Party leadership. Entities linked to one [Alexei GUBAROV since redacted] were involved and he and another hacking expert [Seva KAPSUGO-VICH, since redacted], both recruited under duress by the FSB were significant players in this operation. In Prague, COHEN agreed to contingency plans for various scenarios to protect the operation.[35]

There goes that Michael Cohen again—making agreements in Prague, a place he's never been to, in order to protect an "operator" who never operated.

Because just as Michael Cohen was never in Prague, Gubarev had nothing whatsoever to do with the DNC hacking. And, FYI, he never moved to Bulgaria.

Gubarev has also filed suit against Christopher Steele in London and BuzzFeed in Florida. His Florida lawyer, Brady Cobb, told the *Daily Caller* that he expects to get critical information through discovery in the lawsuit. Using interrogatories and depositions, he intends to find out who paid for the dossier, the identities of the sources, and what efforts, if any, were made to verify the information.[36]

And, in the meantime, Steele admitted that the claims were unverified. Stay tuned.

Interestingly, Gubarev says he was never contacted by Steele or the FBI or anyone else to discuss the totally false allegations. Was that because they knew he wasn't connected with the DNC hacking so there was nothing to talk to him about?

That wasn't the last of the cooked-up tales in the dossier. It turns out that the second hacker was a delusion, too.

According to Kevin G. Hall of McClatchy DC, the second hacker, Seva Kaptsugovich, is actually a convicted Russian pedophile who could not possibly have been involved in the hacking.[37]

McClatchy confirmed that Kaptsugovich has been serving an eighteen-year prison sentence in a Russian penal colony more than 600 miles from Moscow since April 2014. An official human rights activist told McClatchy that Kaptsugovich "does not have access to the internet, a computer or a mobile phone. He only has access to the landline phone."[38]

No way he was hacking from the prison landline.

It wasn't easy to track him down in prison and that's probably why he was blamed for the hacking—because anyone trying to verify the dossier wouldn't be able to question him in jail.

Perhaps to throw any would-be verifiers off his trail, the authors of the dossier misspelled his name as "Kapsugovich" instead of "Kaptsugovich," the correct spelling.

The McClatchy DC team searched for "alternate spellings of 'Kapsovich' in Cyrillic, the alphabet of the Russian and other Slavic languages."[39] That's when they found online "references to Kaptsugovich and Russian media accounts of his prior convictions, which matched the description laid out in the dossier."

Needless to say, Kaptsugovich, like Gubarev, didn't relocate to Bulgaria.

So the dossier has a man who wasn't there (Cohen) arranging payments to two supposed hackers—one who didn't do it (Gubarev) and another who couldn't have done it (Kaptsugovich).

That's one more reason that we know that everything in the dossier about Michael Cohen is a fake.

THE ALLEGED PERVERSE SEX ACTS IN MOSCOW

Predictably, it was the accusations of bizarre sex with prostitutes in a Moscow hotel that were most prominently featured in the news stories about the dossier. It was in the very first report in the dossier, 2016/080, that the dossier's alleged sources made these claims:

> Former top Russian intelligence officer claims FSB has compromised TRUMP through his activities in Moscow sufficiently to be able to blackmail him. According to several knowledgeable sources, his conduct in Moscow has included perverted sexual acts which have been arranged/monitored by the FSB.[40]

The "source" explains that the Kremlin planned to exploit Trump's personal obsessions and sexual perversion in order to obtain compromising material:

> According to Source D, where s/he had been present, TRUMP's (perverted) conduct in Moscow included hiring the presidential suite of the Ritz Carlton Hotel, where he knew President and

Mrs. OBAMA (whom he hated) had stayed . . . and defiling the bed where they had slept by employing a number of prostitutes to perform a "golden showers" (urination) show in front of him. The hotel was known to be under FSB control with microphones and concealed cameras in all the main rooms to record anything they wanted to.[41]

Let's go through the evidence here:

Source D, now identified as Sergei Millian, allegedly claimed that he was physically present in the Moscow hotel room with Donald Trump while the perverse sex acts were going on.

Think about that one.

Is Millian really saying that he personally witnessed the spectacle that he described? That Donald Trump somehow asked him to join him for a viewing?

How likely do you think that is?

This was not Donald Trump's first rodeo. Like other observant people who have visited the Russian capital, he must have seen the omnipresent muscular men on every corner—with visible Bluetooths—a not-so-gentle reminder of the very obvious likelihood that Big Brother is watching.

And Trump has emphatically stated that whenever he went to Russia, he warned his staff about the dangers of surveillance lurking in every corner, every restaurant, every hotel room, every car, elevator, hallway, restroom. He knew what the Russians were all about.

So knowing that, would he really ignore his own warnings and go so far off the reservation? That's really unlikely. Donald Trump is a man who is always in control. A man who has never had an alcoholic drink, has never tried drugs.

And a man who is not an idiot.

And, as he has openly admitted, he is germophobic. He is not a touchy-feely guy. So would he really get involved in any of this?

Trump has vehemently denied that any of this story ever happened. And, after the dossier was published, Millian also denied having any negative information about Donald Trump. Seems like they are in complete agreement. It never happened.

Millian appeared on Russian television and contradicted the disclosures attributed to him in the dossier:

> "I want to say that I don't have any compromising information, neither in Russia nor in the United States, nor could I have," he said, speaking in Russian. "Without a doubt it is a blatant lie and an effort of some people—it's definitely a group of people—to portray our president in a bad light using my name."[42]

Considering that he now says that he only met Trump once, in 2008, it seems rather unlikely that they were chitchatting about prostitutes in 2013. Like the rest of the claims in the dossier about Donald Trump, the sex story is nothing but a fantasy. A big one.

There's one more thing to consider about the claims of Donald Trump's alleged crazy sexual stuff. The dossier suggests that there *might* be an audio- or videotape of the festivities. But it does not categorically claim that any such tape exists—or that anyone has ever seen it. Instead, the dossier merely suggests that if the FSB wanted to, it could have created a tape.

Does anyone believe, for a New York minute, that if a salacious tape actually existed—showing Donald Trump and his invited guests enjoying a "golden shower" in a Moscow hotel room—that it wouldn't have been released by now?

But there's been no sign of any tape or audio. And, to quote former MI6 spy Frederick Forsyth, without any such tape, there's no "actionable evidence."[43]

And it's not like there wasn't an inducement to come forward with a tape or audio of Trump. You might recall that at the time the dossier was circulating in September 2016, there was an offer of substantial cash for a copy of any unpublished audio or video demeaning Trump.

David Brock, the wacky Hillary-hater turned Hillary BF, announced a new program called "Trumpleaks" and offered cash for "unreported video or audio of Donald Trump so voters can have access to the Donald Trump who existed before running for president and before his recent affinity for teleprompters."[44]

Was he looking for the Moscow video? Brock didn't say how much he would fork out, but in an earlier offer, he had promised to pay up to $5 million in legal fees to anyone who would produce damaging tapes about Trump's comments and actions during his tenure at *The Apprentice*.[45] The legal fees would presumably be for violating a confidentiality agreement.

That's a lot of money! Was his PAC going to pay it? We don't know if Brock—or his PAC—ever paid anyone. But his offer raises a serious question: Would either of the offered payments violate campaign finance laws?

Here's another question: Did he or his organizations have anything to do with funding the Steele project? We don't know who put up the money. Disclosure is not required so we only know that it was "donors" or "supporters" of Hillary Clinton.

Brock is currently recovering from a heart attack and is temporarily sidelined from politics.

As for the lurid sexual claims, the deplorable accusations simply cannot be proven. But reward or not, the tape never surfaced, and Source D (whom the dossier also identifies as Source E) disavowed all negative statements about Trump that were attributed to him. In addition, Trump indicated his full awareness of the likelihood that the Russians might try to lure him and his associates into a compromising sexual situation that could be filmed or taped for use as future blackmail,[46] a practice called "honeypot."[47]

No one has ever called Trump stupid.

THE DOSSIER ACTUALLY BACKS OFF ITS OWN
CLAIMS ABOUT CARTER PAGE

The dossier assigns a secondary role to an American investment banker, Carter Page, saying that he met with senior Russian officials as an emissary of the Trump campaign.

Page, unlike Cohen, really did go to Russia, but he'd been doing that—on private business—for twenty-six years. The dossier claims that he "discussed quid-pro-quo deals relating to sanctions, business opportunities and Russia's interference in the election."[48]

Page did visit Russia in July 2016, when he delivered a commencement speech at the New Economic School in Moscow that was critical of U.S. policy. At the time, Trump advisor Hope Hicks issued a statement clarifying that Page was in Moscow "in a private capacity and was not representing the campaign."[49] CNN reports that the "trip drew the attention of the FBI and raised concerns about Page's contacts with suspected Russian operatives."[50] The FBI used his trip to Russia as the basis for seeking—and getting—a warrant from the FISA court for surveillance of Page.[51]

We don't know what Page talked about in Russia. For what it's worth, dossier report 2016/134, dated October 18, 2016, says that "Page . . . confirmed [at a meeting with a close associate of Putin] if Trump elected president, then sanctions on Russia would be lifted."[52]

Then, the dossier retreats, saying that Page "had not stated . . . explicitly [that Trump would lift sanctions but] he had clearly implied that in terms of his comments on Trump's intention to lift Russian sanctions if elected president, he was speaking with the Republican candidate's authority."[53]

The problem with the dossier's account of Page's role is not one of mistaken identity this time. They had the right Carter Page. But there is no evidence of any close relationship between Page and President Trump.

They have never even met, even though Page twice asked for an appointment. Page was a volunteer member of a large committee of foreign affairs specialists who were said to be advising Trump. He only saw Trump at rallies, along with thousands of other people.

And, in December 2016, Trump's lawyer Donald McGahn ordered Page to stop holding himself out as an "advisor" to Trump:

> "You were merely one of the many people named to a foreign policy advisory committee in March of 2016—a committee that met one time," he lectured Page. "You never met Mr. Trump, nor did you ever 'advise' Mr. Trump about anything. You are thus not an 'advisor' to Mr. Trump in any sense of the word."[54]

Sounds like the rogue "advisor" met the rogue spooks.

The dossier's last entry about Page is in the December 13, 2016, report that Steele has already admitted was unverified and needed further investigation, so it can probably be ignored. Once again, the dossier summons the ghost of Michael Cohen to establish Page's role in the supposed Trump-Kremlin liaison:

> We reported earlier that the involvement of political operative Paul MANAFORT and Carter PAGE in the secret Trump-Kremlin liaison had been exposed in the media in the runup to Prague and that damage limitation of these also was discussed by COHEN with this Kremlin representative.[55]

Since we know Prague never happened, then those discussions about "damage limitation" with the "Kremlin representative" never happened, either.[56]

As for Manafort—his work as a consultant in Ukraine from 2004 to 2014 to former president Viktor Yanukovych was years before he joined the Trump campaign, where he worked from March until August 2016. Whatever his work entailed in Ukraine, it had nothing to do with Donald Trump. Manafort and Trump were casual acquaintances and were never friends, confidants, or business partners.

The dossier claims that Manafort was Trump's personal representative in the conspiracy with the Kremlin before he left the Trump campaign and that Michael Cohen took his place, but it describes nothing at all about what Manafort did in that supposed role.

We know that everything it says about Michael Cohen isn't true. The only other claims about Manafort relate to well-published details associated with his work in Ukraine. No new information, except that his name comes up when Steele reports on a confidential meeting between Putin and Yanukovych near Volgograd on August 15, 2016.

During the "secret" meeting, Yanukovych allegedly confided in Putin that he had authorized "substantial kick-back payments to MANAFORT," but assured Putin there was "no documentary trail left behind that could provide clear evidence."[57]

Let's look carefully at this one. At that point, Yanukovych was a fugitive. He was forced to flee the Ukraine on February 22, 2014, after the parliament voted unanimously to remove him from office, citing human rights abuses and other crimes. Since then, he has been in exile.[58]

Government officials eventually found logs that precisely detail his involvement with over $2 billion in bribes—a stunning $1.4 million for each day he was in office.[59] Many bribes were to government officials and many went to election commissioners to make sure that he would remain in office. Prosecutors are still investigating this.

In November 2016, Yanukovych was indicted for high treason, and his trial on the matter began in early May 2016. He refused to return to Ukraine and is being tried in absentia.[60]

But all he talked about with Putin was a supposed bribe he paid to Manafort. That's odd, isn't it?

And who else sat in on—and reported—this secret meeting in which Yanukovych incriminated himself while he was under investigation for massive corruption? The source is described as a "well-placed Russian figure."[61] What does that mean? If no one else was there, did

Putin report this to someone himself? And whoever he might have trusted then passed it on to the British spies? That's doubtful, too. And, if someone else were there, would Yanukovych really describe his criminal activity in front of other people? That's doubtful, too.

And if Putin did repeat his conversation with the Ukrainian to an associate, did that person really tell the rogue spooks about it? And is this person still alive? That's really far-fetched.

THE DOSSIER'S IFFY SOURCES

Let's cut to the chase. The sources in the dossier were about as reliable as its intel—which is to say they were unreliable. And we don't know if Steele corroborated anything that was given to him, regardless of how outlandish it was.

In fact, had he sought corroboration about a Trump-Kremlin collusion, he would not have found any, because the intel itself about that was not true—it was totally false. No amount of examination or review could change that.

Here's the cast of characters who supposedly provided the source material to Steele:

Source A, a senior foreign ministry figure

Source B, a top-level former intelligence agent

Source C, a senior Russian financial officer still active in the Kremlin

Source D, a close associate of Trump's who had organized Trump's recent trips to Moscow

Source E, hotel employee

Source F, woman, an ethnic employee of the hotel

Source G, Kremlin official

an ethnic Russian associate of Donald Trump

two "well-placed and established sources"

another Kremlin insider

Even when we try to look through their cloak-and-dagger descriptions to imagine the real people behind them, none of these vaguely described characters seem terribly authentic or threatening.

There is no context to them, no credible indication of past experience, no analyses of their possible motives or truthfulness. In fact, we now know that many of them simply don't exist, and their supposed juicy intelligence tidbits were easily proven to be nothing but fake news.

What we also know now is that Steele has no relationship with them. He could not simply call them and discuss the information they offered. They were faceless, their information coming to him in unsolicited reports.

But here's the gnawing question: Why would anyone close to Putin ever speak to Steele or any of his paid sources? (If there actually were any, which is a BIG "if.")

Are we to believe that there are actually people who are so intimate with Putin that they know his important thoughts and beliefs who would dare to share them with a British ex-spy or his surrogate? It's pretty unlikely. And, if they were tempted, they would surely know that the consequences, if they were caught, would be severe and could even lead to death. So the likelihood of a Putin confidant providing this kind of information is not very high.

We have already debunked many of these sources connected to the fake Cohen meeting in Prague that underlies so much of the story about Donald Trump. So we know that the sources are dubious, at best.

So where did the unsolicited "raw intel" come from? He didn't disclose that, so we don't know. Steele merely offered that he received the unsolicited intel and passed it on.

Some intelligence professionals say they were concerned about the sources for the dossier even before Steele admitted that many of the claims were unverified. John Sipher, a CIA agent for thirty-four years, attributed "the uproar over Steele's dossier to the fact that 'no one truly knows his sources.'"[62]

That's certainly true.

Steele seems to have acted like a post office drop. "Unsolicited" raw intelligence just landed in his lap, thrown in over the transom.

Even though he said it needed further investigation, did he do anything at all to probe the allegations? Did he do any independent investigation? What exactly was Steele paid for?

We know, for example, that the claims about the alleged hacker Gubarev were never investigated. Gubarev was never contacted by anyone about the hacker claim.[63]

Who was it that sent Steele the unsolicited intelligence?

What made the credibility of his distant sources even more problematic is that, in many cases, he may have had to pay them for the information they offered. That was suggested in Howard Blum's article in *Vanity Fair* about the dossier and Steele. But even that might not be true.[64]

Former acting CIA director Michael Morell, who publicly endorsed Hillary Clinton, criticized Steele's use of sources "who were paid intermediaries who in turn paid sources for the information he used in the report. . . . And that kind of worries me a little bit because if you're paying somebody, particularly former FSB officers, they are going to tell you truth and innuendo and rumor, and they're going to call you up and say, 'Hey, let's have another meeting, I have more information for you,' because they want to get paid some more."[65]

In spook worlds, payment always raises questions about how honest informants are and how trustworthy their information is.

John le Carré, the well-known British author of spy thrillers, including *The Spy Who Came in from the Cold,* spent twenty years as a spy for MI6. Not long ago, he warned of the dangers of relying on paid sources.

There's huge money in the secret world now, too—money for fabricators who put together brilliant pieces of intelligence. We saw that with the forged documents suggesting Saddam Hussein tried to buy yellowcake uranium in Niger. Somebody was paid a fortune for that nonsense. Huge money is now being paid out to informants, a lot of it for hokum.[66]

Morell also raised concerns about the dossier, noting that the fact that the information came from second- and thirdhand parties and was not directly conveyed to Steele raised "red flags."[67]

"Unless you know the sources," Morell said, "and unless you know how a particular source acquired a particular piece of information, you can't judge the information—you just can't."[68]

Morell told NBC categorically that "he had seen no evidence that Trump associates cooperated with Russians." On the question of the Trump campaign conspiring with the Russians, he said, "there is smoke, but there is no fire, at all."

Those were strong words from a well-known Clinton ally who might have been considered for CIA director had Hillary Clinton won.

Morell was not alone in his skepticism about Steele's sources. Craig Murray, former UK ambassador to Uzbekistan, questioned how a small private company like Steele's Orbis Business Intelligence, with limited resources, could possibly manage a large number of highly connected sources and consistently get unique information that eluded government intelligence sources with endless resources and billions in budgets:

> A private western company is able to run a state level intelligence operation in Russia for years, continually interviewing senior security sources and people personally close to Putin, without being caught by the Russian security services. . . . They can continually pump Putin's friends for information and get it, . . . which the CIA/NSA/GCHQ/MI6 did not have, despite their specific tasking and enormous technical, staff and financial resources amounting between them to over 150,000 staff and the availability of hundreds of billions of dollars to do nothing but this.[69]

We, too, wonder how they were able to pull this off.

The *Independent* (UK) reported on a "business intelligence consultant" (same title as Steele) with experience similar to Steele's in Russian matters who questioned the genuineness of the Steele dossier: "with its extremely highly placed sources and lurid details, [the dossier] was simply 'too good to be true.' . . . It would have meant that whoever was writing the report was far better than any British or CIA agent since the Russian revolution."[70]

Then there is the fact that Steele, who lived in Russia for three years but left in 1992, did not travel to Russia to investigate Trump's activities. The Russians knew of his history and he had spoken out about their brutal poisoning of the oligarch Litvinenko. Without the diplomatic cover that he had when working in the British Embassy in Moscow, he would not have "diplomatic immunity" if he were arrested. So, he could not have personally interviewed the main sources for the dossier. It had to be second- and thirdhand. He could not look those giving him information in the eye, question them, and evaluate their honesty and motives, as spies are trained to do.

Other criticisms of the dossier were more blunt. Respected investigative reporter Bob Woodward of Watergate fame—who has written extensively about the CIA—described Steele's dossier as, simply, "garbage."[71]

And another twenty-year veteran of MI6, former spy Frederick Forsyth, who is also a famous author of spy thrillers, including *The Day of the Jackal*, called the dossier "dubious." Speaking to the BBC, Forsyth said he found "no evidence of workable evidence, no tapes, no intercepts . . . and without that, there is nothing but allegations."[72]

Another government official, who was familiar with his work, noted that Steele was not always impervious to disinformation: "Sometimes he would get spun by somebody. [But] it was always 80% there."[73]

But the most devastating dismissal of Steele's dossier and sources came from an odd source, General James Clapper, the former director of national intelligence. Remember, he stated, "some of the sources that

Mr. Steele drew on, the second- and third-order assets, we could not validate or corroborate."[74]

Those ex-spies are certainly coming in from the cold.

CONTRADICTIONS WITHIN THE DOSSIER

In addition to the outright lies in the dossier, the document actually contradicts its own talking points in many cases. For example, while claiming, on the one hand, that the Russians have been cultivating Trump for many years, the memos also clearly describe Trump's lack of interest in any of the bribes that were offered.

Again, here's what the dossier says:

Russian regime has been cultivating, supporting and assisting TRUMP for at least 5 years. Aim, endorsed by PUTIN, has been to encourage splits and divisions in western alliance.[75]

But see its contradictory words:

So far Trump has declined various sweetener real estate business deals offered him in Russia in order to further the Kremlin's cultivation of him.[76]

And more:

The Kremlin's cultivation operation on Trump had also comprised offering him various lucrative real estate development business deals in Russia, especially in relation to the ongoing 2018 World Cup Soccer tournament. However, so far, for reasons unknown, TRUMP had not taken up any of these.[77]

So apparently the cultivation was a one-way street, with Donald Trump nowhere on the block.

MISSPELLINGS IN THE DOSSIER

There were some clues that Steele may not have written all of the reports himself. There are glaring misspellings of the names of supposedly key actors in his narrative. As a Cambridge graduate, Steele would be expected to have a somewhat more polished writing style and at least know how to spell.

For example, Paul Manafort was a frequent focus of the dossier, yet his name is misspelled as "Mannafort" many times, once even in the title of a report.[78] Did someone else write it, or did Steele not even read over what he ostensibly wrote?

Likewise, when discussing Alfa-Bank, the largest commercial bank in Russia, the dossier refers to Alfa as "Alpha" ten times in a two-page document.[79] This error is like an American referring to "Citybank." Did Steele, considered one of Britain's leading experts on Russia, not even notice the mistake? And, by the way, Alfa Bank has filed a defamation lawuit against BuzzFeed and its editor, Ben Smith.[80]

There was another notable spelling error. Mikhail Kalugin, a "leading" diplomat working in the British embassy in Washington, was incorrectly identified as Mikhail Kulagin.[81] Was this "leading" diplomat so unimportant that the writer didn't know how to spell his name correctly?

Spies at his level don't repeatedly misspell names that are familiar to them—unless they are just passing on other people's work, barely glancing at it as they add it to their file.

As longtime Trump associate Roger Stone noted: "If 007 wants to be taken seriously, he ought to learn how to spell."[82]

But the troubles with the dossier did not end with the misspellings. A combination of concerns about many unknown sources—paid informants often contacted by second- and even third-party go-betweens, as well as obviously contradictory information and blatantly fictionalized reports, made the document highly suspicious.

The wholesale invention of key people, the blatant misidentification of others—along with the naked contradictions and inexcusable misspelling of key names within the document itself—expose this dossier for the unreliable document it is.

FOUR

WHAT WERE THE BRITS UP TO?

WHY IS IT THAT BRITISH INTELLIGENCE AGENCIES WERE SO FAR AHEAD OF THE United States in detecting Russian intrusions into our presidential election? Britain's GCHQ originally notified the FBI about Russian hacking into the DNC in September 2015. The FBI had missed that completely and did virtually nothing about it, allowing the Russians to quietly continue burrowing into the computers of one of our major political parties. The Brits had to be wondering why the U.S. spooks didn't consider it as critical as they did.

Then, in late 2015, the Brits passed on information about "suspicious 'interactions'" between Trump associates and "known or suspected Russian agents."[1]

Again, for the third time, in the summer of 2016, the Brits came to us with further intel. Robert Hannigan, then the head of GCHQ, traveled to the United States to meet with CIA director John Brennan and passed material to him. "The matter was deemed so sensitive it was handled at 'director level.'"[2] The Brits "acknowledge" that GCHQ played a "prominent role in kickstarting the FBI's Trump-Russia investigation" by sharing surveillance and electronic interceptions.[3]

So was it that the British were much more skilled at gathering intelligence than U.S. agencies? Or was it that their tracking of Russian targets was a much bigger priority for them than it was for us?

It's probably both.

But was there something else? Did British intelligence want to stop Donald Trump? Given some of his provocative statements, about Russia and Putin, they would have had good reason to do so—especially when they saw how unconcerned the FBI was about their reports about hacking and suspicious contacts.

The Brits had daily reminders of the threat of Russian imperialism. They had watched the annexation of the Crimea with escalating fear, and they were revolted by the Kremlin's defiant disregard for democracy and human rights; Putin was right in their face.

But so was Donald Trump.

While all eyes have been focused on Russia's intervention in the U.S. election to try to help Donald Trump, there is increasing evidence that Britain's interest in electing Hillary Clinton may have led to actions that were equally—or even more—important.

The United States might well have been played by a foreign power in the 2016 election—but was it by the Russians, who wanted to defeat Hillary Clinton, or by those in Britain who wanted to defeat Donald Trump?

Or was it both?

Could it be that in the hopes of fatally weakening their respective American bête noires, the Russians *and* the British each took matters into their own hands? The Russians resorted to covertly hacking the email accounts of the DNC and Hillary's campaign chairman, John Podesta, releasing them to the public to embarrass Hillary.

At the same time, British intelligence secretly tracked and shared classified data concerning the movements and communications of Donald Trump's campaign associates. (The Brits claim that it was just incidental intel picked up as they monitored Russians with whom the Trump people were supposedly speaking, but what difference does that make?)

Did they do so just to be helpful, or was it part of a plan to use their own intel findings to injure Trump?

There's no question that the British establishment and the UK intelligence community feared Donald Trump.

Current and former MI6 agents believed that Donald Trump's unorthodox positions on NATO, the United Nations, and Brexit created an existential threat to Britain. So some rogue British ex-spooks—and perhaps some current ones?—decided to act to stop him from becoming the leader of the free world.

Certainly Trump's disparagement of the UN and NATO would be alarming to a nation that had relied on these twin supports to defend their freedom against a rapacious Soviet Union for over fifty years.

And Trump left no doubt that he intended to radically decrease U.S. funding of both organizations because of what he said repeatedly was an unfair burden on the United States. During the campaign, he articulated his intentions in no uncertain terms, telling the *New York Times:*

> "If we cannot be properly reimbursed for the tremendous cost of our military protecting other countries. . . . We're talking about countries that are doing very well. Then yes, I would be absolutely prepared to tell those countries, 'Congratulations, you will be defending yourself.'"[4]

He described NATO as "obsolete"[5] and criticized its limited role in battling terrorism. He repeatedly pointed out that twenty-three of its twenty-eight member states—including Germany—had failed to live up to the requirements of the treaty regarding military spending, leaving the United States to bear the burden.

He made similar arguments about the UN, saying: "we get nothing out of the United Nations other than good real estate prices [in Manhattan]. We get nothing out of the United Nations. They don't respect us, they don't do what we want, and yet we fund them disproportionately again. Why are we always the ones that funds everybody disproportionately, you know?"[6]

He promised to revoke U.S. support of certain UN treaties that he believed interfered with U.S. sovereignty, treaties that the British actively supported.

And when it came to Brexit, Trump uttered nine words that sent chills down the spines of the entire British establishment: "I think Brexit is very good for the UK."[7] Trump has been so identified with Brexit that he once bragged to a U.S. audience that the British would "be calling me Mr. Brexit soon."[8]

The British political establishment did not understand "Mr. Brexit." Just like they didn't understand the attraction Brexit held for so many of their countrymen.

But it was, in fact, the same populism that animated Trump's shocking U.S. victory that was also a key factor in the equally surprising success of Brexit in the United Kingdom. Prominent British writer Jonathan Coe, writing in the *New York Times,* spoke to the establishments on both sides of the Atlantic when he wrote of the parallels between Trump's "surprise campaign and Britain's populist-fueled decision to leave the European Union: In both cases, so the received wisdom goes, simmering resentment among a forgotten, disparaged section of the public was stirred up by canny populists and visited defeat and humiliation on the complacent, smug political establishment."[9]

It was an article of faith among the UK establishment that Brexit was a disaster, cutting the island nation off from the rest of the continent and casting it adrift economically.

The *Guardian* reported that former intel chiefs were worried that national security would be compromised if Britain left the EU. And apparently the former spooks announced that they were speaking for serving officers, too.[10]

Alex Younger, head of Britain's spy agency MI6, gave a speech that warned that future intelligence sharing with Europe "could prove disastrous" because of Brexit.[11]

Nigel Inkster, a former director of MI6, said British intelligence agencies would be "concerned" that leaving the EU would undermine intelligence sharing with the continent, "notably over information on suspected terrorists or violent extremists."[12]

And the former head of MI5 (the British internal security service), Lady Eliza Manningham-Buller, mirrored Inkster's concerns. Another former head of MI6, Sir John Sawers, equated an anti-Brexit vote with patriotism and declared that, as a "lifelong patriot," he would vote to "Remain."[13]

The UK establishment had good reason to fear that the election of Trump would upend the status quo and injure the historically cordial relationship between Britain and the United States.

But the British intelligence community also had reason to fear the Russians and to be alarmed by any indication of a relaxation in America's vigilance in the cause of freedom.

The British operatives were motivated by a number of factors, not the least of which was their collective history of service in Russia during and after the Cold War. Their firsthand experience left an indelible memory of the atrocities and disregard for civilized society that the communists and their successors evidenced. Recent events stoked their fears. When Russia annexed Crimea, encroaching on Europe, the operatives became very worried. When Donald Trump's positive public statements about Putin and Russia and his negative comments about NATO and the EU were added to the mix, the British spooks got spooked.

And suddenly, it once again felt like the old days of the Cold War. This time, its epicenter was not Berlin but the British capital—its symbol not the Brandenburg Gate but Wellington Arch.

It wasn't just Putin's aggressive stances that led to the feeling. It was a physical sense of change, too. Looking around London, there were Russians everywhere. In 2001 there were only about 15,000 Russians living in the city. By 2014, that number had swelled to almost 150,000.[14]

As scores of Russian oligarchs fled Putin's Russia, many chose the relative safety of London. Those oligarchs were among the enemies Putin feared most. They were phenomenally wealthy and unused to the power and opportunities that such immense wealth brings, and their shifting allegiances—inside and outside of Russia—made them a perpetual source of instability for the Kremlin.

In large part because of them, London is now home to more billionaires than any other city in the world. There are 117 billionaires in the United Kingdom, 80 of whom live in the capital city. (New York City ranks a poor second with 56 billionaires; Paris has only 21.) The combined wealth of the billionaires in London is 325 billion pounds. And many of them are Russian oligarchs.[15] For the most part, these relatively new arrivals are not afraid to flaunt their riches, and their mind-boggling spending is often on full display, giving new meaning to the French phrase "nouveau riche."

They had neither inherited nor really earned their newfound wealth. When Russian president Boris Yeltsin decided to privatize vast portions of the economy, his advisors hit on a novel way of doing so. They issued one share of the privatized industries to each Russian, for free. The idea was to foster capitalism and a sense of free enterprise. But the Russian peasants didn't know what to do with the stock certificates. So clever Russian entrepreneurs would go to the bars and hangouts and offer a glass of vodka in exchange for a certificate. In that way, a few people amassed a large share of the industries and immense wealth, particularly in Russia's energy sector.

They literally did not know what to do with their money. When Valery Kogan, one of the Russian billionaires, wanted to throw a bash for his nineteen-year-old granddaughter's wedding, he paid singers Elton John and Mariah Carey $4.2 million to come to London to sing as part of a nine-hour program, sharing the stage with lots of other performers and celebrities.[16]

It was folks like Valery Kogan who had fled to London, with their wealth, as Putin began to crack down on pro-democracy advocates. When Putin imprisoned the best-known and richest oligarch—Mikhail Borisovich Khodorkovsky—in 2003 on trumped-up charges and left him to rot in a Siberian cell for a decade, the other oligarchs got the message very quickly and left for new homes in the United Kingdom.

It was not just the Russian oligarchs who were populating London. The long arm of Putin's security services reached out to follow them. Along with the many new Russian émigrés came an increased number of Russian FSB agents, keeping tabs on the former citizens.

With the long-distance assassination of former KGB agent Alexander Litvinenko, Putin had brought the new Cold War right up to Britain's doorstep. The increased number of Russian spies arriving in London to track the oligarchs drew the attention of MI6. They, in turn, assigned more MI6 agents to track the FSB.

When Putin subsequently invaded Crimea and Ukraine, a direct challenge in the heart of Europe, it was even clearer that the Cold War was back on. And Litvinenko's assassination made it obvious that London had become a frontline battlefield.

Suddenly, the British government began to wake up, blaming Moscow for "concerted attempts to undermine the UK through fake espionage, misinformation, cyber attacks and fake news."[17]

At a high-level meeting in the UK cabinet office in October 2016, "intelligence officers and senior civil servants across government voiced their concern about the growing scale of the Russian threat." The *Telegraph* reported that "Whitehall officials have for the first time acknowledged that Russia is waging a 'campaign' of propaganda and unconventional warfare against Britain."[18]

The British were up to their eyeballs in Russians and were, understandably, extremely upset about Trump's positive words about Putin and his disdain for the EU and other institutions considered vitally important to the Brits.

Perhaps that's when U.K. rogue spooks, in office and out, might have decided to do whatever they could to stop Russia's interference on behalf of Trump.

British fingerprints—of both official and unofficial spooks—are all over the efforts to keep Donald Trump out of the Oval Office.

Consider the following pieces of evidence (some have been explained above but are repeated to show the extensive reach of British involvement):

1. It was Britain's Government Communications Headquarters (GCHQ) that first warned the United States that the Russians had hacked the Democratic Party's computers. Back in September 2015, long before the FBI and CIA knew anything about it or showed any interest in it, GCHQ was waving warning flags about Russian hacking. For a long time, the U.S. intel agencies did nothing about it.[19]

2. During the campaign and even after, both MI6 and GCHQ routinely passed along classified intelligence information to the U.S. intelligence community about Trump's associates.[20]

3. It is Christopher Steele, an ex-MI6 spy, who was responsible for the dossier that contains unsubstantiated, unreliable, but nevertheless explosive material about Donald Trump. Was Steele only a *former* MI6 agent? Bear in mind what the Russian embassy said, shortly after details of the dossier were released: "MI6 officers are never ex."[21]

4. It was Steele who went to the FBI, without telling his American client, in July 2016 to tell them about his dossier and urge them to investigate Trump and his associates.[22]

5. It was former UK ambassador to Russia Sir Andrew Wood—a business associate of Steele's—who first alerted Senator John McCain about the dossier and warned him about the danger that Trump might be vulnerable to Russian blackmail if the dossier was actually true.

6. It was to London that an associate of McCain's traveled for a prearranged meeting under clandestine circumstances to obtain the dossier.

7. Numerous uncontradicted published reports indicate that Steele shared his intelligence with MI6. And he admitted that

he received "'unsolicited intelligence' and 'raw intelligence'"—could that perhaps have come directly from British intel sources?[23]

8. It was former colleagues of Steele who, along with Wood, offered a virtual echo chamber of comments to the press about Steele's credibility. None of them had seen or verified the document.

9. The director of MI6, Alex Younger, used notes from Steele's dossier in his first public speech since being appointed.[24]

10. Two weeks after the dossier containing all the negative information about Trump was published—and three days after President Trump's inauguration—Robert Hannigan, the popular director of GCHQ, abruptly resigned, citing family illnesses, giving only six hours' notice. The media reported that "his sudden resignation . . . prompted speculation that it might be related to British concerns over shared intelligence with the US in the wake of Donald Trump becoming president."[25]

11. MI6 issued a D-Notice when the dossier was published and Steele's identity was revealed.[26] A D-Notice is a government directive that can prevent publication for national security reasons, including protecting the identity of former and current British spies. In Steele's case, the D-Notice requested that all media refrain from reporting anything at all about Steele for nine hours—enough time for him to escape from London.[27]

12. UK prime minister Theresa May and several government ministers were briefed on the Trump dossier before the U.S. inauguration and decided to stay quiet about it.[28]

All of the British involvement leads to a key question. Which caused more damage:

- Russian hacking of the Democratic National Committee and Hillary Clinton's campaign chairman John Podesta on the one hand; or
- The constant flow of British intelligence material to the FBI and other government agencies documenting the depth of Russian involvement in the U.S. election as well as the production and publication of the unverified and incendiary dossier about the purported vulgar and criminal conduct of Trump and his associates and their improper coziness with Russia on the other?

It's hard to tell with any precision. But it is quite obvious that the exposure of a possible Trump-Moscow link has done and continues to do Trump immense harm.

Undoubtedly, the hacking of the DNC and Podesta emails hurt Clinton's campaign. Hillary was already drowning in her own email scandal. She did not need the additional daily drumbeat of Podesta's emails coming out also. If it was the Russians who did it, their intervention was embarrassing, especially since the emails were published the day before her convention was to start. But it was certainly not a knock-out punch.

The hacking clearly hurt the Clinton campaign and provided bursts of unwelcome news as Hillary tried to give her campaign needed momentum. But, ultimately, the damage done to her by the Russian hacking was contained and the campaign moved on from there. Debbie Wasserman Schultz, the DNC chairman, resigned. The Sanders voters were initially alienated by the conclusive evidence the hacking provided that the DNC had worked hand in glove with Hillary's campaign to defeat the Vermont senator, but after a few weeks they, too, came back into the Clinton fold. The disruption caused by the email release faded, and Hillary's convention proceeded nicely. She left Philadelphia—the convention site—ahead of Trump in the polls and stayed there until questions about her health cost her the lead in early September.

Although the publicity the hacked emails received certainly exacerbated the tear in the fabric of the Democratic Party that separated the Sanders wing from the mainstream, it did not spark a widespread rebellion against Hillary's candidacy.

But, while Hillary was fending off email releases that might have been arranged by Moscow, she was on the offense, raising the issue of Russian efforts to help Trump. Undoubtedly she was privy to the secret dossier that her own supporters had paid Steele to generate starting in June 2016.[29]

The charge of a Trump-Putin axis became a big part of the 2016 campaign. It made its way into the debates and was a mainstay of Hillary's accusations against Trump. The Steele dossier indicates that Putin was worried that Russian involvement might backfire and help Hillary. He was probably right.

THE TRUMP-PUTIN ISSUE LIFTS HILLARY

Hillary used the debates with Trump to trumpet (pardon the pun) charges that Putin was intervening in the U.S. election to stop her and to elect the Republican. In the second and third TV debates, Hillary berated Trump for his positive comments about Putin and made them a key issue.

"Our intelligence community," she declared, "just came out and said in the last few days that the Kremlin, meaning Putin and the Russian government, are directing the attacks, the hacking on American accounts to influence our election. And WikiLeaks is part of that."[30]

She pounded the issue. "We have never in the history of our country been in a situation where an adversary, a foreign power, is working so hard to influence the outcome of the election. And believe me, they're not doing it to get me elected. They're doing it to try to influence the election for Donald Trump."[31]

Then she said that Trump may be in the Russian dictator's pocket. "Now, maybe, because he [Trump] has praised Putin, maybe because he says he agrees with a lot of what Putin wants to do, maybe because he wants to do business in Moscow, I don't know the reasons. But we deserve answers."[32]

She flatly accused Russia of backing Trump, saying the Russians have "decided who they want to see become president of the United States, too, and it's not me. I've stood up to Russia. I've taken on Putin and others, and I would do that as president."[33]

Throughout October, Hillary raised the bogeyman of Russian intervention in the campaign. Refusing to let go of what had become a potent issue in her arsenal, Hillary dredged up Putin any chance she got in the third and final debate with Trump.

"What is really important about WikiLeaks is that the Russian government has engaged in espionage against Americans. They have hacked American websites, American accounts of private people, of institutions. Then they have given that information to WikiLeaks for the purpose of putting it on the internet. This has come from the highest levels of the Russian government, clearly from Putin himself."[34]

Hillary even accused Trump of being Vladimir Putin's puppet, saying that Putin "would rather have a puppet as president of the United States."[35]

So while Hillary suffered as the Russians hacked her party's computers and revealed her campaign chairman's emails, the charge that Trump was too close to Putin hurt Trump just as much or even more.

If the Russians tried to hurt Hillary by leaking, the British tried to hurt Trump by exposing and perhaps embellishing the extent of Russian activity.

THE BRITISH USE RUSSIAN MEDDLING TO GET OBAMA TO BE TOUGH ON PUTIN

As the U.S. elections approached, British intelligence became increasingly worried about renewed Russian expansionism. As in 1945, when a complacent United States had to be jolted awake by Churchill's warning about an "iron curtain"[36] that was descending across Europe, the Brits worried that America was not taking Russia's territorial ambitions seriously.

Before 2015, Obama didn't see the Russians as a major threat. In fact, during the 2012 presidential election, Obama famously mocked the Republican nominee Mitt Romney for calling Russia the "number one geopolitical foe" America faced.[37]

In their debate on foreign policy, Romney spoke of the threat al Qaeda posed. Obama replied with all the sarcasm he could muster: "Governor Romney, I'm glad that you recognize Al Qaeda as a threat because a few months ago, when you were asked what's the biggest geopolitical threat facing America, you said Russia. Not Al Qaeda, you said Russia," Obama repeated. Then, turning to Romney, he quipped: "The 1980s are now calling to ask for their foreign policy back because you know, the Cold War has been over for 20 years." He added, "when it comes to our foreign policy, you seem to want to import the policies of the 1980s, just like the social policies of the 1950s and the economic policies of the 1920s."[38]

But when Russia invaded Crimea and Ukraine in 2015, the pressure on Obama to toughen up mounted. The *National Review* called him "Putin's Poodle" and wrote that Obama was letting Russian aggression go unpunished: "If Vladimir Putin is the dominant alpha male in the new international pecking order, Barack Obama has emerged as his highly submissive partner."[39]

Obama ruled out a military response to Putin's invasion of Ukraine, saying that "Russia is a regional power that is threatening some of its immediate neighbors, not out of strength but out of weakness." He said that "the fact that Russia felt it had to go in militarily and lay bare these violations of international law indicates less influence, not more."[40]

Europeans did not share Obama's benign view of Russia and worried about continued Russian aggressions. But Obama stayed his course.

So Britain had its hands full in trying to summon the anger in Obama necessary to get the United States more involved in what

London saw as the increasingly urgent task of reining in Moscow. The British lion couldn't fight the Russian bear if the United States remained only a "poodle."

Moreover, the Brits had reason to believe that Obama didn't like them much. In his best-selling book *Dreams from My Father*, the future president wrote bitterly of British colonial rule in Kenya.[41] When President Obama took office, he moved into the hall the famous bust of Winston Churchill that British prime minister Tony Blair had loaned to the White House after 9/11.[42] But President Trump has brought the bust back into the Oval Office.

So did the British hatch a plan to alienate Obama from Moscow and make him see the extent of the Russian threat? Did they want to show Obama that Putin and his government were a threat to his legacy and to the future of his party?

It was one thing for Russia to threaten U.S. and British national interests. It was another for Moscow to interfere with Obama's plans for his own country. If London could make Obama believe that the Russians were intervening in the U.S. election to forestall a Hillary victory, did the British believe that Obama might rise to the bait and take the threat more seriously?

It was one thing for Putin to hurt the United States and the Western alliance, but quite another—in Obama's partisan-obsessed mind—for him to hurt the Democratic Party.

When Britain has run into trouble—as it did in both world wars and the Cold War—its immediate, instinctive reaction is to turn to the United States for help.

But the United States it turned to in the fall of 2016 was not the United States of FDR or JFK or Ronald Reagan, but the United States of Barack Obama. This America was passive, lethargic, and slow to realize the threat that Russia posed. The United States might have to be nudged.

And nudging the United States by influencing an American election was not exactly unprecedented.

There is a long history of covert British intervention in American politics to benefit the United Kingdom's national interests.

Many Americans came to believe that the United States was tricked into intervening in World War I on the British side by propaganda emanating from London—propaganda that represented the German kaiser as a rampaging ape (Hun) ravaging a beautiful young woman (Belgium).

British intelligence worked overtime to get us into World War II. Christopher Woolf, in Public Radio International's *The World*, wrote that "the Brits used wiretaps to get dirt; recruited journalists to plant favorable stories; invented fake stories; used dirty tricks to try to destroy opponents; and funded and coordinated pro-British activist groups."[43] All to get us into the war.

They even tried to fix the 1940 presidential election. (We might even say they "hacked" the election.)

Britain's fate—and that of western civilization—hung in the balance as Roosevelt sought an unprecedented third term. The U.S. president had been tiptoeing toward greater assistance to Britain, battling to modify and, eventually, repeal the Neutrality Acts that barred American aid.

The British knew that if Roosevelt was defeated in the election of 1940 and one of the Republican Party's early front-runners—Senator Robert A. Taft (R-Ohio), Senator Arthur H. Vandenberg (R-Mich), or District Attorney Thomas E. Dewey of New York (isolationists all)—won, they could expect little help from America.

So the British decided to get their own candidate—Wendell Willkie—nominated by the Republicans instead. An unknown former utility executive, Willkie ran as a former Democrat, promising not to dismantle FDR's New Deal programs and to give Britain "all aid short of declaring war."[44]

If Willkie became the GOP nominee, the Brits figured they were covered. If Roosevelt won, so much the better. If Willkie pulled it off, at least he was no isolationist.

Two of Britain's closest allies in America, Ogden Reid, the owner of the *New York Herald Tribune* (the most influential Republican newspaper in the country), and his wife, Helen, became outspoken backers of Willkie, running a front-page editorial in the paper supporting his nomination. With aid from Henry and Clare Boothe Luce, owners of Time-Life magazines, they propelled Willkie into contention.

Through propaganda films like *London Can Take It,* which showed how ordinary Londoners were bearing up under the German bombers, they fanned the support for "bundles for Britain."

Behind the scenes, the British waged what historian Nicholas John Cull says was "one of the most diverse, extensive, and yet subtle propaganda campaigns ever directed by one sovereign state at another."[45] All with the goal of bringing America into the war by getting the Republican Party to nominate Willkie.

Just as the Republican delegates were gathering in 1940 at their convention, a polling organization called Market Analysis issued a survey that showed that 60 percent of the delegates supported helping Britain. (It later came out that the company was owned by the British.)

The poll's findings received massive publicity in the *New York Herald Tribune,* and William Allen White, the influential columnist, wrote that the poll had made it clear that the other three candidates were out of touch with the party's rank and file.

Governor Harold Stassen of Minnesota, the party's keynote speaker, came out for Willkie. A million telegrams deluged the delegates urging Willkie's nomination, spurred on by ominous news of German advances deep into France. A Gallup poll, released after the convention, showed that by the time the balloting had started, Willkie led among Republican voters by 44 percent to Dewey's 29 percent.

Willkie, starting out in third place on the convention's first ballot, swept to the nomination after five ballots while the galleries chanted, "We Want Willkie."

It had been the most overt—and most successful—intervention by a foreign power in an American election.

Were the British trying to repeat history now by injecting the issue of Russian involvement into the heart of the U.S. campaign as it approached its final months?

The British gambit worked in 1940 and it worked again in 2016. President Obama went from treating the Russian threat lackadaisically to imposing sanctions that hurt Moscow. The accusation of Russian meddling in the U.S. election enraged the president and brought Moscow-Washington relations to their lowest point in decades. Obama even used the hotline between the Kremlin and the White House to warn Russia to back off.

As in 1917 and in 1940, Britain succeeded in jolting an American president back to reality and persuading him to stand by our closest ally.

Were they trying that strategy again?

FIVE

HOW THE INTELLIGENCE COMMUNITY WENT FROM RED TO BLUE

THE CIA AND THE FBI HAVE ALWAYS BEEN BASTIONS OF THE RIGHT. IT WAS THE FBI that was filled with anti-communist zealots who hunted down those they considered to be "disloyal." And the CIA patrolled America's borders, intervening to stop any other country from falling under Moscow's or Beijing's spell.

So they should have been in the cheering section saluting a Trump victory with all they had.

But, instead, they recoiled so violently against Trump that they became the key participants in the virtual coup mounted by the rogue spooks to stop him from governing.

The transformation of the intelligence community from red to blue may stand as one of the most enduring achievements of the Obama presidency—or at least one of the hardest to erase.

When Obama and his liberal allies saw Trump about to enter the White House, they decided to deploy their weapon of choice against him: leaks from the intelligence community. Having taken care to scrub the intelligence agencies to expunge any taint of conservative thinking, these agencies were perfectly positioned to do Obama's will.

And, in the media, he had a compliant, liberal/radical institution only too happy to print the leaks his people would be handing out.

The intelligence community has long realized that it has two ways to influence public policy in Washington. It can go legitimately up the chain of command to the president, arguing the merits of its case. Or it can go outside the process entirely—go rogue—and leak information—or disinformation—to a media willing and eager to do its bidding.

As the abomination of a Trump presidency neared the Oval Office, they decided to kill Trump by leaking.

THE INTELLIGENCE COMMUNITY SENTENCES TRUMP TO DEATH BY A THOUSAND LEAKS

Veteran *New York Times* Washington correspondent James Reston once said, "The ship of state is the only known vessel that leaks from the top."[1]

Every president is as frustrated and tortured by leaks as a dog is by his fleas. President Clinton told Dick Morris, one of the authors of this book, that he decided never to say anything of substance in front of more than one person. That way there would be no leaks. And, if there were, it would be obvious who the leaker was.

Most Washington leaks are designed to burnish someone's reputation or to steer the debate over an issue in a certain direction. Others are to embarrass an opponent and many are simply to curry favor with an influential journalist or to save the credit for future use.

Leakers keep their names secret so that they won't antagonize their bosses or let their enemies see their fingers on the knife as they plunge it in.

But the leaks that bedeviled the Trump transition team and continued into the early months of his administration were different, and their goal was much more important. These leakers were seeking to destroy a president as he was taking office.

Everybody knew where the leaks came from. It was right there in the news stories, which would usually cite "sources in the intelligence community" or use some such attribution to satisfy their editors, but protect their informants.

But leaking is a risky business. The federal government recognizes no legal protection for leakers and contends that it has the right to force a reporter to reveal his sources.

New York Times reporter Judith Miller spent eighty-five days in jail for refusing to "out" her source who identified a CIA agent in violation of federal criminal law. A special prosecutor, hired to find the leaker, asked her to identify him under oath. When she refused to do so, she went to jail.

But there was no similar risk to these former Obama employees savaging Trump, since the leaks had been scripted—choreographed—in private deals among the leaker, his federal agency, the reporter, and the news organ. It was a closed loop that gave the leaker a de facto carte blanche to proceed.

Of course, when Trump actually became president, it was a different story since he could, obviously, prosecute the leakers. But the problem was identifying them. The leaker, typically an Obama holdover, was usually embedded in an agency amid like-minded people. The liberal/left ethic that motivated the leaker also helped him or her hide in plain sight, surrounded by supportive colleagues and conspirators. (And, on June 5, 2017, a woman named Reality Winner was arrested for mailing classified material to a news outlet, the first arrest for leaking in the Trump era.[2])

The FBI and the Department of Justice, charged with outing the leakers, were themselves compromised by eight years of ideological cleansing by Attorney General Eric Holder. The liberals who manned the desks shared a vision and approved of a holy war against the incoming president. War by leaks.

But the question remains: How did Obama change the intelligence community from red to blue, a feat of ideological alchemy without parallel in recent history?

The saga begins in the late Clinton years, after the CIA and the FBI had been buffeted by two decades of criticism and attacks.

The CIA failed to realize that the Soviet Union was about to fall and that the Shah was doomed in Iran. It missed these two key calls by a mile. Both the CIA and the FBI were bedeviled by the exposure of dozens of spies and traitors within their ranks, who had been successfully selling our vital national secrets—including the names of our agents—to the Russians for more than a decade.

But, oddly, it was their successes more than their failures that doomed them to irrelevance. Once the Soviet Union fell, both agencies lost their sense of purpose.

Former CIA director Richard Helms put it best: "with espionage you've got to be motivated. It's not fun and games. It's dirty and dangerous. There's always a chance you're going to get burned. In World War II, in the OSS, we knew what our motivation was: to beat the goddamn Nazis. In the cold war, we knew what our motivation was: to beat the goddamn Russians. Suddenly the cold war is over, and what is the motivation? What would compel someone to spend their lives doing this kind of thing?"[3]

A congressional investigation during the Clinton years concluded that the CIA lacked the "depth, breadth, and expertise to monitor political, military, and economic developments worldwide."[4]

Both the CIA and the FBI are proud agencies. There are no other federal departments that have a comparable sense of their own history or their mission. They were the civilian equivalent of the Marine Corps, and it was not uncommon for men and women to be willing to give their lives to serve these two agencies. You don't find that spirit in any other agency. Nobody is going to lay their lives on the line for the Department of Labor or the Department of Housing and Urban Development.

But the shattering experiences of the closing decades of the twentieth century brought the survival and relevance of both agencies into question. How were they to survive? This institutional vulnerability would linger and animate the concerns of the leaders and staff of each agency as Trump, the unknown, came to power.

BUSH-43: NEW LIFE TO INTELLIGENCE

President George W. Bush took office with two corpses on his hands: the CIA and the FBI.

Clinton's first-term CIA director, George Tenet, who served from 1997 through 2004, said that, at the time he took over, "dollars were declining." He said the CIA's "expertise was ebbing" and that the organization was "in disarray."[5]

James R. Schlesinger, his predecessor as director, said, "The agency is now so battered that its utility for espionage is subject to question."[6]

By 1999, 20 percent of the CIA's top spies and experts had left and another 7 percent retired every year thereafter.

The Agency's culture was infected. While it employed 17,000 people, the majority stayed behind their desks and never got their hands dirty. Only about one thousand worked overseas in the clandestine service. The bulk of the staff lived comfortable bourgeois lives within the confines of Washington, DC.

Then came 9/11.

All bets were off. Suddenly, the CIA was the hottest ticket in town. The wraps were off. Though 9/11 was the ultimate failure of intelligence, for the CIA it was also the beginning of a new lease on life.

A week after 9/11 President Bush issued a directive to the CIA to hunt, capture, imprison, and interrogate terror suspects around the world.

In the following days, Bush began laying out new rules for the intelligence community, giving it the power, in the words of John C. Yoo, then deputy assistant attorney general, "to take whatever actions he deems appropriate to pre-empt or respond to terrorist threats from new quarters,"[7] whether or not they can be linked to the specific terrorist incidents of September 11.

A September 25, 2001, Justice Department memo declared that under the Constitution, decisions regarding the "'amount of military force to be used' in response to the terrorist threat, as well as 'the method, timing and nature of the response,' are 'for the President alone to make.'" And a January 2002 Justice Department memo argued that "customary international law has no binding legal effect on either the President or the military."[8]

The *New York Times* writes that "President Bush secretly authorized the National Security Agency to eavesdrop without obtaining a court order on calls and e-mail messages sent from the United States to other countries. He has issued a steady stream of signing statements, signaling his intent not to comply with more than 750 provisions of laws concerning national security and disclosure, most notably one that questioned Congress's authority to limit coercive interrogation tactics."[9]

The administration also claimed that "the president's war powers gave him the authority to detain people indefinitely and deny them access to lawyers and the courts, a policy that it would later be forced to modify in response to legal challenges."[10]

The handcuffs were off.

And the CIA went to town!

Critics like Frederick A. O. Schwarz, Jr., senior counsel at the Brennan Center for Justice at NYU Law School, called the president's actions "monarchist claims of executive power" unprecedented "on this side of the North Atlantic."[11]

A lot of liberals and Democrats felt that these extraordinary usurpations of authority by the president weren't particularly in response to 9/11 but rather were how conservatives like Vice President Dick Cheney thought the country should work anyway.

But lingering behind this broad assertion of executive power lay the pivotal issue of torture of prisoners to extract information.

In the new war on terror, could techniques euphemistically called "enhanced interrogation"—like sleep deprivation, slapping, nudity, and, ultimately, waterboarding—be permitted?

It seemed so. In February 2002, President Bush signed an order declaring that "none of the provisions of [the] Geneva [convention] apply to our conflict with al Qaeda in Afghanistan or elsewhere throughout the world."[12]

In 2003, the Justice Department issued a very narrow definition of what constitutes torture, saying it was the causing of "intense pain or suffering" akin to that which is "ordinarily associated with 'serious physical injury so severe that death, organ failure, or permanent damage resulting in loss of significant body function will likely result.'"[13]

Knowing that the American public's appetite for such practices was limited and fearing exposure of their use to public view, the Bush administration set upon the practice of "rendition," where terrorist interrogation was farmed out to other—largely third world—countries that could operate in assured secrecy. Bush's order to "kill, capture, and detain al Qaeda operatives" included, the intelligence people said, the authority to create these so-called "black sites."[14] Contracting out interrogation of prisoners had drastic—intended or unintended—consequences.

As part of the residue from the Church Committee (the Senate committee investigating intelligence activities—called the Church Committee after its chairman Senator Frank Church [D-Idaho]), the Foreign Intelligence Surveillance Act of 1978 established special "FISA" courts to control, limit, and supervise spying on American citizens.

But, in 2002, Bush's order specifically permitted the National Security Agency (NSA) to conduct surveillance without a court-approved warrant, circumventing the FISA statute.

While U.S. intelligence operatives had been pretty rough in their interrogations in the past, the new Bush order gave them the power to turn suspects over to foreign intelligence services for questioning.

Writing in the *New York Times*, Tim Weiner said that "American intelligence may have to rely on its liaisons with the world's toughest foreign services, men who can look and think and act like terrorists. If someone is going to interrogate a man in a basement in Cairo or Quetta, it will be an Egyptian or a Pakistani officer. American intelligence will take the information without asking a lot of lawyerly questions."[15]

Many felt that the CIA had crossed a line and was becoming a global military police. Under Bush's order, the CIA began to function that way as it sent prisoners to secret jails in Afghanistan, Thailand, Poland, Egypt, Pakistan, Jordan, and Syria.

And then there was the Patriot Act, which, among other things, let the CIA examine banking and other financial records of American citizens and companies. The CIA could now spy on Americans.

Jammed through amid the post-9/11 hysteria, the Patriot Act passed the House by 357 to 66 and the Senate by 98 to 1. Bush signed the Patriot Act six weeks after the World Trade Center towers collapsed.

It authorized indefinite detention of immigrants in terror investigations. Law enforcement officers got the authority to search homes or businesses without the consent or even knowledge of the owner or occupant. In a transaction eerily reminiscent of the lettres de cachet of royalist France—permitting summary arrest and detention without trials—the act expanded the use of National Security Letters, which allowed the FBI to search telephone, email, and financial records without a court order, and expanded access of law enforcement agencies to business records and libraries.

The act succeeded in thwarting dozens of terrorist attacks on American soil, and it is notable that none took place for the balance of Bush's two-term presidency. But its provisions ran afoul of the norms in which people believed and led to ever greater fears of government encroachment.

INTEL OVERREACHES

It was the best of times but also the worst of times for government spies. The restrictions under which they had been required to labor vanished and they got a carte blanche instead.

But the CIA and the FBI both needed to be careful of what they wished for, because when they got these enormous new powers, the price was public skepticism and hostility.

So it was the worst of times for the intel community, too. One after another all the secrets came out as Americans who worked for intel agencies or their contractors, or just saw what was going on, leaked to the media.

Bush was powerless to stop the leaks. His formal authority did not extend to the individual consciences of Agency employees.

Chief among these hyperactive consciences was that of Edward Snowden, a former CIA employee who, while working for a contractor to the NSA, copied and leaked classified information detailing how far Agency surveillance had intruded into the lives of the American people.

Charged with amassing electronic intelligence from foreign sources, it turned out that the NSA routinely scooped up intel about the phone calls, emails, and texts of ordinary American citizens through the collection of metadata.

Normally, a wiretap yields the full text of a phone call. But metadata did not record what was being said, rather who was calling whom, from where, and when. The why could be derived easily once you knew the answer to the broader questions.

When information on American citizens was gathered inadvertently while tapping the phones of foreigners or amassing their metadata, the NSA was at best careless and at worst negligent in how it handled the intelligence.

As the details of waterboarding and other forms of torture became the subject of public debate and the rendition of prisoners to third world jails became widely known, many Americans had cause to regret the blank check they had given the president in the weeks and months after 9/11.

The CIA's name was further blackened when its assurances that Iraqi dictator Saddam Hussein had weapons of mass destruction were found to be false. Since it was this so-called "intelligence finding" that led to the U.S. invasion of Iraq and the subsequent war in which 4,491 American soldiers died, the CIA and the entire intelligence community became a national object of scorn.

Based on CIA intel, Vice President Dick Cheney told America, on August 26, 2002, that "there is no doubt that Saddam Hussein now has weapons of mass destruction." The VP continued to force his foot further down his mouth: "There is no doubt he is amassing them to use against our friends, against our allies, and against us."[16]

Secretary of Defense Donald Rumsfeld said: "We know they have weapons of mass destruction. . . . There isn't any debate about it."[17]

CIA chief George Tenet told the Senate Intelligence Committee on September 17, 2002, that "Iraq provided al Qaeda with various kinds of training—combat, bomb-making, and chemical, biological, radiological and nuclear."[18]

On October 7, 2002—on the eve of the congressional vote authorizing military action in Iraq, President Bush said that Iraq "possesses and produces chemical and biological weapons." He went on to warn that "Iraq could decide on any given day to provide a biological or chemical weapon to a terrorist group or individual terrorists."[19]

Only Saddam didn't have any such weapons. Once Iraq had been fully conquered and was in our grip, the forces of the United States and its allies searched all over for WMDs but came up empty.

The invasion revealed the grim truth that the CIA had made a big, big mistake. Oops. To save face and salvage a mission now transparently based on a falsehood, Bush kept at the war and body bags piled up at American ports.

This was the CIA's war and the Agency had been wrong.

Disillusionment swept the land. The nation, once united in its purpose after the 9/11 attacks, became sundered by accusations and political attacks. While Bush won re-election after a tough campaign in 2004, the credibility of the president, the intelligence community, the military, and the American government itself was now at the lowest ebb ever.

The CIA, the NSA, the FBI, and the entire panoply of intelligence agencies were under the harshest form of investigation and censure, even mockery. These dedicated men and women had all thought they represented a united nation in its battle against the terrorists who had struck with such devastation on 9/11. But, as the political support for the more extreme of their policies faded—and the absence of WMDs in Iraq cost them their credibility—the intelligence agencies became a political piñata to be kicked around by liberals, Democrats, and dissenters of all stripes.

Foremost among them was Senator Barack Obama.

Obama's very path to the 2008 nomination was opened because his chief opponent, Hillary Clinton, had voted for both the Iraq War and the Patriot Act in Congress. One beat behind her constituents, she was still a vigorous defender of the war in Iraq even after no WMDs were found. Newly elected as the senator from New York—where most of the 9/11 attacks hit—and aspiring to become America's first female commander in chief, Hillary Clinton felt she could not be caught out in left field questioning American policy but needed to stand in the middle of the national consensus—even if it turned out to be wrong.

That left Obama with a clear shot.

His campaign was based on what he said were the extreme policies of the CIA and the FBI. He attacked the CIA prison at Guantanamo, the rendition of terror suspects, waterboarding, and degrading or enhanced interrogation, saying that they were not in conformity with our values. His favorite phrase was "that's not who we are."[20]

Elected in a landslide, he set about to reverse the anti-terror policies that were the sum and substance of the Bush administration. The reversal was a mortal threat to the entire intel community.

But the intelligence community had been through rough times before. It was not laid low by Harry Truman's distrust. It lasted through Eisenhower's planning and plotting of anti-communist coups. It even survived JFK's use of its resources to keep his personal scandals at bay. It had weathered the tidal wave of criticism showered on it for helping

President Lyndon Johnson attack and suppress domestic dissenters. Even after Nixon tried to hide behind the intel community to cover up Watergate, the agencies had survived. The Iran-Contra scandals besmirched their reputation but did not destroy them. They had survived despite the double agents and intelligence failures of the eighties and nineties. And, even when they were almost totally ignored by President Clinton, they kept their power. Indeed, under Bush-43, they expanded it exponentially.

So why should Obama's criticism be a unique threat?

Part of the problem was that Obama was dramatically altering the nation's course. In all the previous scandals, the intelligence community had been doing the bidding of the incumbent president and, after he left office, they found that his successor was of a similar mind. At the very least, each new president was loath to expose the intrusiveness of the intel agencies under his predecessor.

Kennedy was not going to expose Eisenhower for plotting coups. He had some of his own in mind.

Nixon, the pot, could not call Johnson, the kettle, black for the massive intrusion on American civil liberties as the FBI and the CIA did all they could to muzzle dissent under both presidents.

Bush-41 and Clinton followed similar agendas on intelligence and terrorism. And the only criticism Bush-43 had of the agencies was that they had not gone far enough.

But now, a president—overwhelmingly popular and elected with a solid majority—had run on a platform of dismantling the intelligence community and its methods. He had a mandate to go as far as he wanted. Nobody in the hallowed halls of any intel agency was safe or immune.

The very essence of Bush's intel policies was reversed. Large parts of the Patriot Act were not renewed when they sunsetted (although some key parts were). Waterboarding, torture, and enhanced interrogation were out. Now terror suspects had to be Mirandized and eagerly used their right to counsel. One hundred ninety-six of the 242 Guantanamo prisoners (whom Cheney had described as "the worst of the worst"[21]) were released to other countries (where they usually shortly went free).

THE LEFT TAKES OVER INTEL

But the policy changes were only the tip of the iceberg. The most significant changes were in *people* not just in *policies.*

Frank Gaffney, former acting assistant secretary of defense for international security affairs under Reagan, said that Obama "cut through the entire federal bureaucracy—including the intel community—with a sharp and wide scythe, replacing career intelligence people with liberal political appointees."[22] Even the career people veered left as the new heads of the intel agencies sought to bring like-minded people into the fold.

Throughout the administration, more with each passing year of his term, Obama filled the government with leftists and liberals dedicated to his extreme agenda. The EPA, FBI, CIA, NSA, IRS, FCC, FTC, FEC, SEC, ICE, and the departments of State, Justice, and Treasury came to be hotspots of leftist activity. It was as if the leftist ideology of America's campuses had spilled all over Washington.

Obama did not try to pour new wine into old bottles. With the new policies came new people.

It was vitally important to Obama to make changes that reached down into the very bowels of the intel agencies. It was not enough to bring on new cabinet secretaries and new deputies. The changes had to go much, much deeper.

Obama was seeking not just to adopt some liberal policies and programs but to change the very culture of American governance, particularly when it came to the two traditional bête noires of the left: the FBI and the CIA.

The FBI had been the scourge of the left for decades. It was the agency presidents had used to keep tabs on domestic communists and to ward off what it assured Americans was the perpetual threat of overthrow of our democracy by fifth-column communists. It was the FBI that kept files on dissidents and conducted background checks on presidential appointees.

Abroad, the CIA had come to represent the extreme anticommunism of Kissinger and Nixon, plotting coups and fixing elections at will to tell other countries how they should be governed.

But now there was a special urgency about bringing new people into these two agencies and throwing out the longtime career civil servants: The new technology of spying and surveillance made it imperative that this capability was firmly in liberal hands.

The CIA and the FBI knew too well how to bring down a president or an entire government. They did so in the Watergate scandal of 1974 and abroad in dozens of countries. Now, with the NSA's tools of surveillance, these two traditionally right-wing agencies packed an especially powerful punch. They had become too dangerous to remain out of control.

BRENNAN MAKES THE CIA BLUE

Nobody more typified this new generation of leftists than John Brennan, chosen to head the CIA throughout Obama's second term (2013 to 2017).

Even before Brennan was officially appointed to head the CIA, Michael Hayden, Bush's CIA director, said that Brennan was, de facto, the "actual national intelligence director"[23] throughout both of Obama's terms.

How far left was Brennan? He was not just a Democrat or even a socialist; he had actually voted for the Communist Party in the elections of 1976.

He explains his curious decision: "I voted for the Communist Party candidate. As I was going to college, [my vote was a way] of signaling my unhappiness with the system, and the need for change."[24]

But this was no youthful indiscretion. Brennan was twenty-one years old at the time, no callow child.

When he came to head the CIA, the *American Spectator* reports that he brought with him a coterie of political radicals and left-wing academics and gave them plum positions from which to leak to the press.[25]

Bill Gertz of the *Washington Times* explains how Brennan did it: He says that Brennan turned his left-wing hires into "operatives" by fiddling with standards at the Directorate of Operations. These political hacks disguised as apolitical operatives had no more business receiving high-security clearances than Brennan himself did.[26]

Brennan even encouraged the recruitment of the families of liberal CIA employees as vacancies opened up. "He trusted that they would be easier to control," one expert said. "He figured family loyalties would run deep and that he could be sure he was getting the liberals he wanted in office."[27]

His liberalism ran deep. As an attorney, Brennan's law firm had, pro bono, represented many of the Guantanamo inmates he was now demanding be freed. He enthusiastically backed reading terror suspects their rights, including telling them, helpfully, that we would pay for a lawyer for them if they wanted.

Brennan so deeply opposed waterboarding terror suspects to extract information about possible forthcoming attacks that he said he would resign rather than allow it on his watch. "I can say that as long as I'm director of CIA," Brennan said, "irrespective of what the president says, I'm not going to be the director of CIA that gives that order [to water-board]. They'll have to find another director."[28]

Even on social issues, his liberalism was apparent. In particular, he advertised his commitment to gay rights and the LGBT community. The Daily Caller reports that he was "known for walking around [CIA] headquarters wearing a rainbow lanyard to show support for the LGBT community and signal his commitment to diversity."[29]

Brennan told the *Wall Street Journal*, "I just think that having those varied perspectives really adds great color and dimension and diversity to how we look at problems."[30]

Diversity became the watchword for new hires under Brennan. In 2011, he developed a program specifically to recruit gays for the Agency. But his agenda was not merely social; he thought that gays could be counted upon to be ideologically leftist when it came to intra-agency battles.

When Brennan took over as CIA director, he initiated a total reorganization of the Agency. In the past, the bureaucracy was stratified by function. The National Clandestine Service oversaw spying and covert operations. The Directorate of Intelligence provided insights on global developments to policy makers. Other Agency employees were organized into a third directorate that focused on science and technology and a fourth that worked on logistics.

But Brennan wanted to organize the Agency along the same lines as the U.S. military, where all those focused on a certain geographic area were pooled in one command regardless of the specific role they played.

His move was widely seen as a denigration of the field operatives, who had always been the elite of the CIA. Many quit. Much of the cream of the old guard at the top of the CIA moved on rather than live under the new organization. Brennan had more vacancies to fill with liberals.

But some see a more sinister motivation in Brennan's actions. A person intimately familiar with the CIA and its top officials says that Brennan's reorganization bleached out the best intelligence at the Agency. Important information was diluted as the critical mass of intelligence gatherers were dispersed throughout the Agency.

This source deeply believes that the very purpose of the reorganization was to dumb down the intelligence we got so as to make it more malleable by the top officials of the Obama administration. Particularly where Iran was concerned, this source believes, Brennan wanted to downplay the bad intentions of the Ayatollah to facilitate public acceptance of any deal the president would negotiate.[31]

In fact, on February 23, 2012, the intelligence community published an assessment of Iranian intentions saying that Iran was not actively trying to build an atomic bomb. It "concluded that Iran halted efforts to develop and build a nuclear warhead in 2003." The report was represented as the consensus of sixteen intelligence agencies.

The assessment said that while Iran was pursuing research that "could put it in a position to build a weapon, it has not sought to do so."[32]

Anyone with a smidgen of knowledge would know that Iran is so determined to build a bomb that it has weathered crippling sanctions, assassinations, and malware to do so. Its conduct since that CIA assessment—and even since the Iran nuclear deal was signed in 2015— makes it perfectly clear that building a bomb is the top priority in Tehran.

But reorganizing the CIA is not the only way in which Brennan weakened its ability to gather important intelligence. Part of the impact of Brennan's outspoken opposition to enhanced interrogation, detention, and Guantanamo has been that it is increasingly difficult logistically to capture and interrogate a terror suspect. If a suspected terrorist were questioned in the United States, he would be protected by the rights guaranteed by our Constitution, even if he was not a citizen. It's hard to imagine a successful interrogation with a lawyer watching every question and whispering in the suspected terrorist's ear before each answer. And Obama pledged not to ship him to another country for questioning. And Obama barred further incarcerations in Guantanamo. So, if we captured a terrorist and wanted to interrogate him, where could we do so?

Indeed, when Ahmed Abu Khatallah—the mastermind of the Benghazi attack that killed our ambassador—was captured, he was placed aboard a U.S. ship that cruised around the Indian Ocean while he was interrogated. He could not go to Guantanamo. He couldn't be turned over to another country, and we didn't want him to be able to consult with an attorney, so questioning on U.S. soil was out. So the Navy took him for weeks on end on its own version of a cruise to nowhere.

The result of Brennan's and Obama's restrictions on interrogation was that the United States pretty much stopped capturing terrorists, preferring to kill them with drone strikes rather than deal with the messy business of extracting information. As a result, our ability to detect and deter future terror attacks declined. Under Bush-43—after 9/11—there were no lethal terror attacks on U.S. soil. Under Obama, there were dozens.

The *American Spectator* explains how Brennan's personal leftist agenda, his liberal hires at the CIA, and the anti-Trump leaking from high up in the Agency combined to assure that Trump inherited a hostile intelligence apparatus. Brennan's people, it said, "marched through the institutions, stayed long enough to find the exits, and now booby-trap them as they file out. The trail of McGovernite liberalism ends as it began, in lawlessness, with a departing CIA director who behaved no differently than Daniel Ellsberg."[33] (Ellsberg was one of the authors of the Pentagon Papers and was responsible for its release in 1971. It was a classified history of the Vietnam War.)

The *Spectator* continued: "Now those aging radicals break the law out of hatred for a Republican president."[34]

"Nested within intelligence agencies," the magazine wrote, these Brennan operatives "have fed a series of criminal leaks to a press corps that functions like an anti-Trump dirty tricks operation."[35]

As soon as Trump was elected, Brennan probably did his share of the leaking that aimed to destabilize the new presidency.

President Donald Trump, himself, has publicly speculated that Brennan might be one of the criminal leakers who has been using his high position in the outgoing Obama administration to try to spread negative disinformation about the incoming president. In January 2017, he tweeted, singling out Brennan, "Was this the leaker of Fake News?"[36]

Former CIA analyst Tony Shaffer also suspects Brennan as one of the leakers. He said on Fox Business Network that the leaks that forced Michael Flynn out can be laid "squarely at the feet of"[37] Brennan, among other embittered Obama aides.

White House chief of staff Reince Priebus responded with a veiled threat, telling *Fox News Sunday* that Brennan was responsible for many of the negative stories about friction between the incoming president and the intelligence community. "I think that John Brennan has a lot of things that he should answer for in regards to these leaked documents,"[38] he said.

Even during the 2016 campaign, Brennan did nothing to hide his aggressive leftism. The *Spectator* reports that even though it was a government agency, "John Brennan's CIA operated like a branch office of the Hillary campaign, leaking out mentions of this bogus investigation to the press in the hopes of inflicting maximum political damage on Trump. An official in the intelligence community tells *TAS* [*The American Spectator*] that Brennan's retinue of political radicals didn't even bother to hide their activism, decorating offices with 'Hillary for president cups' and other campaign paraphernalia."[39]

While John Brennan was trying to fill the CIA with liberals who would do his bidding, Eric Holder, Obama's attorney general, was trying to drive out the right-wing career intelligence people who had controlled the CIA.

HOLDER DRIVES THE INTEL COMMUNITY TO THE LEFT

Reflexively, we have come to identify the Federal Bureau of Investigation with J. Edgar Hoover, communist hunting, and right-wing, law-and-order G-men.

But that was before Obama appointed Eric Holder attorney general. Called "Obama's enforcer" by authors John Fund and Hans von Spakovsky,[40] Holder radicalized the Department of Justice and the FBI to an extent no liberal ever dreamed could happen.

Fund and Spakovsky write that Holder "filled the career ranks of the Justice Department with political allies, cronies, and Democratic Party donors, in clear violation of civil service rules."[41]

One of the longtime Justice Department officials said that the Obama-Holder administration "racialized and radicalized the [department] to the point of corruption. They embedded politically leftist extremists in the career ranks who have an agenda that does not comport with equal protection or the rule of law; who believe that the ends justify the means; and who behave unprofessionally and unethically. Their policy is to intimidate and threaten employees who do not agree with their politics, and even moderate Democrats have left the department, because they were treated as enemies by administration officials and their lackeys."[42]

Holder has particularly politicized the Civil Rights Division of the Department of Justice (DOJ).

With a budget of $145 million, it is one of the DOJ's largest divisions. Holder has vastly expanded the Civil Rights Division and has gone out of his way to hire new people in civil service slots—so they can't be removed—who are radical, liberal lawyers. Byron York, of the *National Review,* says the division is "bigger, richer and more aggressive than ever, with a far more expansive view of its authority than at any time in recent history."[43]

Holder, a strong backer of choice, has used the DOJ to go after pro-life activists. But, on education, where he opposed school choice, he came down hard on voucher plans to give parents a choice as to which school their child attends. A strong backer of gay rights, he has attacked schools whose dress codes don't allow boys to come to school dressed in drag.

He has been especially vehement in attacking election laws designed to stop voter fraud as well as those that require verification of citizenship in order to vote.

Central to his view of civil rights is the doctrine of disparate impact, which says that even if no actual discrimination can be found or proven, if minorities get shorter shrift in employment, pay, or benefits, illegal discrimination can be inferred.

Bob Driscoll, a former chief of staff in the Civil Rights Division, says that today's Justice Department "is more like a government-funded version of an advocacy group such as the ACLU or the NAACP Legal Defense Fund than like government lawyers who apply the facts to the law."[44]

Holder's own inspector general—appointed by President Obama—said the DOJ is rife with "polarization and mistrust."[45]

Fund and Spakovsky write that in the DOJ, career civil service employees who their colleagues feel are conservative or Republican—or who simply believe in racially neutral enforcement of the laws—"are subjected to racist comments, harassment, intimidation, bullying, and even threats of physical violence."[46]

Above all, Holder worked to assure a staff that is radical and extremely left wing. "The career lawyers in the Civil Rights Division are overwhelmingly liberal and have always manipulated the hiring process to ensure that the staff remains that way."[47]

According to a 2013 inspector general report, Holder told his DOJ section chiefs he would personally "take control" of the hiring process if slots were not filled quickly (by liberals). The IG reports that the chiefs "got the message loud and clear."[48]

Holder set up a hiring system designed to maximize the number of liberals brought on board. No longer did it matter much if the job applicants went to top law schools or scored high on proficiency tests; the key new requirement was that they had worked for a civil rights group, invariably liberal.

Fund and Spakovsky write that "100 percent of all of the lawyers hired by Eric Holder for career civil service positions in the Civil Rights Division have been Democratic activists or ideological liberals and firebrands."[49]

The 2013 inspector general report found that in the voting section alone, 56 percent of those hired since 2009 came from only five organizations: the American Civil Liberties Union, La Raza, the Lawyers'

Committee for Civil Rights, the NAACP, and the Mexican American Legal Defense and Educational Fund. The IG report says that the "Voting Section passed over candidates who had stellar academic credentials and litigation experience with some of the best law firms in the country, as well as with the Department" in order to hire those they considered to have a "commitment" to "traditional" civil rights (liberals who support quotas and ethnic and gender entitlements).[50]

Bob Popper, a former deputy chief who finally left the division in 2013 out of frustration, says he was "routinely excluded from hiring decisions" starting in 2009 because he was perceived as a "conservative."[51]

Retired lieutenant colonel Tony Shaffer, the former analyst for the CIA, described how the Obama administration staffed the FBI and the CIA with its own liberal people.

> The problem is this: you have a lot of folks who are either career members of the intelligence community who are skeptical of the current situation or who were at one point political appointees who have burrowed themselves into the infrastructure who are now career intelligence officers.

Shaffer said that many of these people have retained loyalties to the Obama administration. He said this "causes them to [judge] for themselves what they should or should not do regarding intelligence."

Shaffer explained that some of the career members were selected because of their political orientation.

"What we've seen over the past eight years is a manipulation of the intelligence community," Shaffer said. He blames the manipulation on the tendency of people like the former director of national intelligence James Clapper, and the former director of the CIA John Brennan, to hire "people like themselves." He says that "some of those professionals were selected because of their [political] reliability, not because of their professional ethics."[52]

On becoming attorney general, Eric Holder also reached across to the CIA to threaten those who had always been our best defense against terrorism with dismissal, disgrace, and prison.

During Obama's campaign, Holder railed against the CIA for its overaggressive interrogations and use of rendition, charging that the "government authorized the use of torture" under Bush and vowing that "we owe the American people a reckoning."[53]

His day of "reckoning" came in August 2009 when he asked a special prosecutor, Assistant U.S. Attorney John Durham, to reinvestigate the CIA's handling of about one hundred high-value terrorists captured by American forces on the battlefield. Bush's administration had already charged a team of long-term, career Justice Department prosecutors with that task. Their painstaking investigation of each agent concluded that the CIA had only followed the rules laid out by the Justice Department on how to interrogate terror suspects. The investigators published hundreds of pages of evidence to bolster their findings, called declination memos (in which they explained their reasons for declining to prosecute the intelligence officers).

But Holder wanted a do-over. In fact, he revealed that he had not read many of the declination memos he was seeking to overrule.

Seven former CIA directors who had served from the sixties onward protested Holder's decision to reopen the cases. They said it would create "an atmosphere of continuous jeopardy" for CIA employees and would "seriously damage the willingness of many other intelligence officers to take risks to protect the country." As they pointed out, "Those men and women who undertake difficult intelligence assignments in the aftermath of an attack such as September 11 must believe there is permanence in the legal rules that govern their actions."[54]

Leon Panetta, the director of the CIA at the time, was so upset over Holder's decision that he engaged in a "profanity-laced screaming match" with the attorney general at the White House.[55] Panetta was so upset that the cases were being reopened that he offered to pay the legal expenses of the agents Holder had ordered be investigated.

But Panetta and the former directors had it wrong. It was precisely Holder's intention to create "an atmosphere of continuous jeopardy" by reopening the investigations. Holder wanted to drive the interrogators out so he could put his own radicals in their places.

Fund and Spakovsky put it well when they say that the decision to launch a new investigation was part of an "ideological crusade" against the CIA.[56]

Eventually, Holder found nothing. Nobody was prosecuted or even dismissed, but the cloud of doubt and fear hung over the CIA for years.

But still, Holder's gambit worked. The reign of terror wore on our career intelligence officers and they left their jobs.

Marc Thiessen, a former speech writer for Bush-43, said that the lives of the CIA employees who were investigated—twice—"will never be the same. They have spent much of the decade since Sept. 11 under threat of prosecution, fighting to defend their good names even as they worked to keep us safe." As a result of Holder's "witch hunt,"[57] talented, capable counterterrorism officials have left the CIA and others have chosen wiser, safer careers, free from political backbiting by those they tried to serve.

Holder even went to great extremes to bring into the intelligence community those who had fought, tooth and nail, on behalf of the inmates at Guantanamo. These attorneys who had volunteered their time to try to free the inmates now held sway over the jailers of their former clients. It was as if the world had turned upside down and those who had vigorously prosecuted terrorists found themselves under the gun for serving their country.

Of those Guantanamo inmates these volunteer attorneys succeeded in freeing, over one hundred have been confirmed by the director of national intelligence to have taken up arms against us again, and another seventy-four are suspected of doing so.

Holder, for example, hired Jennifer Daskal in the National Security Division that oversaw counterterrorism operations and prosecutions. While Daskal's resume was devoid of any experience as a prosecutor, she was a left-wing activist who had represented al Qaeda terrorists at Human Rights Watch before joining the DOJ. The fox was hired to guard the henhouse.

The *New York Post* wrote that "Daskal never missed a chance to give Gitmo detainees the benefit of the doubt while assuming the worst about US government intentions."[58]

The *Post* explained that she never accepted the guilt of 9/11 mastermind Khalid Sheik Mohammed and four of his fellow terrorists, despite the outburst from one of the five at the end of his hearing: "I hope the jihad will continue and strike the heart of America with all kinds of weapons of mass destruction."[59]

Omar Khadr was a special object of Daskal's sympathy. A terrorist, he was caught in Afghanistan after he killed Sergeant First Class Christopher Speer. Daskal, Khadr's lawyer, objected to his prosecution, saying that it would violate his rights as a child since he committed the murder at the tender age of fifteen.[60]

Holder's own firm defended eighteen enemy combatants and successfully urged the federal court to extend to them new rights under the Fifth Amendment and the Geneva Accords.

While law firms are supposed to offer pro bono aid to indigent clients, the decision to specialize in accused terrorists likely indicates a mind-set not altogether welcome in the future head of the Department of Justice.

Fund and Spakovsky liken it to hiring a mob lawyer at the Organized Crime Task Force or a lawyer for the Klu Klux Klan to work at the Civil Rights Division.

THE LEAKING BEGINS

So when Trump unexpectedly won the election, he was interrupting a transformation of American government almost without precedent in our history. Particularly in the intelligence community, the FBI and the

CIA, long stalwarts of conservatism, had now become home to hundreds of activist liberals determined to remake their agencies.

Trump was anathema to them and all they stood for. He took office as president presiding over a nest of vipers determined to destroy him.

But these were not ordinary political vipers with whom Trump had to contend. They were experts in the fine arts of propaganda, media leaks, character assassination, and even manipulation of the political process.

The agencies they worked for—the CIA and the FBI—had honed their skills by destabilizing and, ultimately, overthrowing democratically elected governments in Chile, Iran, Guatemala, and dozens of other countries.

These folks knew how to screw up an incoming president in his early, most vulnerable days.

The anti-Trump partisans had already amassed a dossier purporting to show compromising material—"kompromat"—that was shown to be totally phony and unverifiable. Now, they also proceeded to use the vast skills their agencies had evolved over the years in overthrowing elected governments—combined with the latest technology—to discredit the new president.

And they were ably assisted in this task by a sycophantic media corps equally determined to bring down the Trump presidency.

The CIA/FBI playbook for bringing down governments they didn't like centered on using a compliant media to publish anonymous leaks to create a narrative—a facade—of incompetence, corruption, infighting, and treachery around the new administration.

Any thorough play-by-play discussion in a new administration is not likely to inspire confidence. During the dry run, plenty of mistakes are made and the ship of state needs frequent adjustment and repair.

Otto von Bismarck, ruler of Prussia, once said (and Mark Twain echoed): "Laws are like sausages. It is best not to see them being made."[61]

But Donald Trump did not have the luxury of taking his shakedown cruise in private. Instead, his every move—and every mistake—was broadcast clearly around the world by an intelligence community and a media that hated him.

And always the leaks tried to keep the issue of Russia front and center. The slightest whiff of any doubt of Trump by any Republican senator was magnified into a life-and-death challenge to the president. Speculation became headlines. And, when Trump fired FBI director James Comey, the media positively boiled over with speculation that it was to derail the investigation of Russian meddling.

But before they could get to Trump in their efforts to destabilize and destroy his administration, they chose a lesser target—former general Michael Flynn, whom Trump named as his national security advisor.

SIX

IN LIKE FLYNN . . . OUT LIKE FLYNN

HE WAS THE POSTER BOY FOR WHAT THE ESTABLISHMENT MOST FEARS ABOUT President Donald Trump. General Michael Flynn was a maverick who was able to detect the layers of baloney that were piled high on the desks of U.S. intelligence operatives. He knew how to cut through it and get at the facts.

When President Trump appointed him to be his national security advisor, it sent tremors through the alphabet soup of intelligence agencies and the diplomatic community.

He'd been in intelligence agencies before and the wreckage was plain to see all around him.

It began in 2004 when he became director of intelligence at the Joint Special Operations Command (JSOC), the military's hunter-killer force that includes the Army's Delta Force and the Navy's SEAL teams.

There, he pushed the idea that the purpose of raids was not just to kill terrorists but to gather intel. As *Wired* reported, he focused on "getting [the military's] elite commandos to believe that collecting crucial clues from raids on terrorists was central to their missions." Years later the strategy paid off when "the Navy SEALS leaving bin Laden's Abbottabad compound took with them hundreds of thumb drives, cellphones and hard drives."[1]

Based on his brilliant performance, Flynn was promoted in 2010 to be the director of intelligence for the International Security Assistance Task Force operating in Afghanistan. On arrival, General Flynn gave his colleagues an example of his bluntness and insight. Flynn wrote: "Eight years into the war in Afghanistan, the U.S. intelligence community is only marginally relevant to the overall strategy."

Flynn's remedy, as recounted in wired.com, was to "stop looking so much at the Taliban, since its presence and activities were lagging indicators of the war's fates; understand instead the 'pivotal Afghan districts that would determine the war's outcome.'"[2] A kind of swing state focus transferred from political strategy to combat intelligence.

Flynn felt that too many of his agents were comfortably ensconced in their cubicles in the Washington office. He proceeded to send them out into the field to gather actual intelligence. Not a good way to make friends.

Besides, Flynn had committed the cardinal sin in the intel community: He made his critical remarks in public, writing for the Center for a New American Security, a key DC think tank.

Promoted to be the director of the Defense Intelligence Agency (DIA) in 2012, he again raised hell, demanding that the Agency send "more employees overseas, being more responsive to regional U.S. military commanders, and turn analysts' attention from the war zones of Iraq and Afghanistan to a broader array of emerging national security threats."[3]

Asked in an interview how he would treat employees reluctant to embrace his agenda, he said he would "move them or fire them."[4]

In fact, Flynn was the one to get moved and fired when he was forced to resign as DIA in 2014 by James Clapper, the director of national intelligence.

A former Pentagon official who worked with Flynn said that "his vision in DIA was seen as disruptive." He wanted to push DIA analysts and operators "up and out of their cubicles into the field to support war fighters or high-intensity operations." The former official said, "I'm not sure DIA sees itself as that."[5]

But Admiral Michael S. Rogers, who served as head of the National Security Agency (NSA) under Obama, was more fulsome in his praise of Flynn. Speaking when Flynn "retired" (that is, was forced out of the DIA job), Rogers said that Flynn is one of a "very few of us who can say that we have made a difference that spans an entire organization. . . . And, for intelligence, Mike [Flynn] has done just that."[6]

Rogers is far from alone in his praise of Flynn. Retired four-star general Barry McCaffrey, one of the most decorated officers of his generation, who is no fan of Trump (calling him a "willful and abusive braggart"[7]), said, "Mike Flynn is the best intelligence officer of his generation." He went on to say that "he and [General] Stan McChrystal are the principal reason we have not suffered a half-dozen 9/11-type attacks since 2001."[8]

McCaffrey says that Flynn's anger against the conventional thinking of the Obama era stems from the fact his people "ignored Flynn's input on the nature of the threat because it stepped on their narrative and he got fired. Now Mike is filled with anger." The general said, "I find the situation very sad."[9]

Flynn was the bête noire of the intelligence establishment, but he was just what Donald Trump was looking for. It was love at first sight.

Flynn had been consulted on national security policy by most of the Republicans running for president: Carly Fiorina, Scott Walker, Ben Carson, Ted Cruz, and . . . Donald Trump.

As Trump surged in the early primaries, criticism mounted that he had no foreign policy or national security experience. Eager to counter the emerging attack, the Trump campaign turned to Flynn and asked him to become a formal advisor.

It is easy to see how the general's bluntness and willingness to confront the establishment would appeal to Trump. Flynn's reputation for independent thinking could only have excited admiration in the like-minded candidate.

Trump unleashed Flynn during the Republican National Convention, where the general gave a full-throated denunciation of Hillary Clinton and the Obama administration.

"We are tired of Obama's empty speeches and his misguided rhetoric," Flynn declared. "This has caused the world to have no respect for America's word nor does it fear our might." Flynn said that Obama chose to conceal the actions of bin Laden and ISIS members, refusing to label them as radical Islamic terrorists.[10]

General Flynn, egged on by the crowd chanting "U-S-A! U-S-A!," urged his listeners to "get fired up! This is about our country."[11] Then he led the crowd in a chant of "Lock her up!" aimed at Hillary Clinton. "Damn right! Exactly right! There is nothing wrong with that!"[12] He added, "If I did a tenth of what she did, I'd be in jail today."[13]

General Michael Flynn had painted an even bigger target on his back.

The next step in the general's courtship of presidential candidate Trump came in September, when the Donald was eager to push back on accusations that he didn't know what he was doing on foreign and national security policy. Trump's team, working with Flynn, recruited eighty-eight retired generals and admirals to tout his candidacy and extol his credentials. Not to be outdone, Hillary promptly released her own list of ninety-five generals and admirals who endorsed *her*.

Right after Trump's unexpected, climactic win on November 8, pressure built for Trump to name his national security team. Even before he selected the rest of his cabinet, Trump needed to name the officials who would handle his interface with the rest of the world.

During the campaign, Trump had sent shock waves through the international community with his radical suggestions and possible policy departures. At one point, he suggested that NATO, the vaunted North Atlantic alliance that brought down communism, was obsolete and implied that the United States might not keep its commitment to protect its allies unless they raised their own contributions to the collective defense. At another, he mused that perhaps we should encourage

South Korea and Japan to get nuclear weapons to deter North Korean aggression.

Nobody took him too seriously because everyone was confident that Hillary would win and that Trump's wild ideas would be swept aside. They wouldn't even live long enough to qualify for what Russian revolutionary Leon Trotsky called the "ash heap of history."[14]

But when Trump won, the international telephone wires were buzzing: Did he really mean what he said? Who will he be listening to? Can anyone come in and straighten him out?

The answer came back quickly. On November 18, ten days after the election, Trump chose the man whose advice he most valued on foreign affairs—General Michael Flynn—to be his national security advisor. The prospect of Flynn as advisor—traditionally a job almost equal in stature to the secretary of state—scared the establishment to death.

The *Washington Post* reported the appointment under a headline that read: "DONALD TRUMP'S MOST TERRIFYING APPOINTMENT."[15] "There may be no more dangerous choice Trump has made so far than picking Michael Flynn to be his national security adviser. . . . If we contemplate how President Trump might handle an international crisis—which he will face, probably before long—we see just how troubling Flynn's appointment is."[16]

The *Washington Post* summed it up by saying, "to put it plainly, Michael Flynn is a crackpot."[17]

The newspaper reflected what had become the prevailing opinion in the global establishment, noting that Flynn's "staff got so used to him believing things that were obviously false that they began referring to them as 'Flynn Facts.'"[18]

But paramount among the general's sins was the fact that he said that Islam is a "malignant cancer" and a "'political ideology' that 'hides behind this notion of being a religion.'" He had the audacity to say that "fear of Muslims is rational."[19]

Flynn also made no secret of his opposition to the nuclear deal Obama had negotiated with Iran.

As usual, he was blunt: "The U.S. gets nothing but grief [out of the deal]. . . . The U.S. and others were too anxious to get any deal. We gave up all our leverage. We had poor assumptions about what we would get and we were too ambitious to be successful. We got beat by a nation of expert negotiators who got everything they wanted and needed from the deal for only making promises of allowing future observations."[20]

Many of the deal's supporters worried that he would be hostile to it and could even kill it as national security advisor.

The Iran deal had passed into law only by the barest of margins. While normally a treaty needs a two-thirds vote of the Senate to be ratified, Republican Senate Foreign Relations Committee chairman Bob Corker (R-TN) got so hornswoggled by Obama that he agreed to let it become law if no more than one-third of the Senate *opposed it*, the precise opposite of the constitutional provision.

Deputy National Security Advisor for Communications Ben Rhodes (brother of David Rhodes, president of CBS News) was most responsible for getting the deal approved. He constructed what came to be called an "echo chamber" to create a favorable reaction to the agreement from so-called experts, many on the payroll of supporters of the deal. Along with a slavish media that reported their opinions as objective, Rhodes built a base of support for the deal. Bloomberg News reports how Rhodes's "campaign sought to portray skeptics of diplomacy as 'pro-war,' and to play down the dangers of the Iranian nuclear program before formal negotiations started in 2013 only to emphasize those dangers after there was an agreement [and ratification was pending] in 2015."[21]

Now, with Flynn looming ahead as Trump's go-to guy on foreign policy, Rhodes ginned up his echo chamber again to get Flynn out.

Flynn only stoked Rhodes's fears when, on February 2, 2017— barely two weeks into the new administration—he told Iran that he was putting them "on notice" for their recent ballistic missile test launch.

CNN wrote that Flynn did not say whether the United States would take action beyond a verbal warning. Three "senior administration officials, speaking on background," said "we are considering a whole range of options. We're in a deliberative process."[22]

Flynn's apostasy for calling out Iran, after Obama had so frequently refused to do so, underscored a key point for Rhodes and his allies: Flynn had to go.

The Washington Free Beacon recounts how they did it, saying that Flynn's resignation was the "culmination of a secret, months-long campaign by former Obama administration confidantes to handicap President Donald Trump's national security apparatus and preserve the nuclear deal with Iran . . . [by planting] a series of damaging stories about Flynn in the national media."[23]

That effort, said to be led by Ben Rhodes, according to the Free Beacon, "included a small task force of Obama loyalists who deluged media outlets with stories aimed at eroding Flynn's credibility."[24]

The newspaper said that one key reason the Obama loyalists wanted Flynn out was because they were worried about the "Trump administration's efforts to disclose secret details of the nuclear deal with Iran that had been long hidden by the Obama administration."[25]

A member of the National Security Council told the Free Beacon that "leaks targeting the former official were not the result of a series of random events. . . . The drumbeat of leaks of sensitive material related to General Flynn has been building since he was named to his position."

Another Free Beacon well-placed source said that "The Obama administration knew that Flynn was going to release the secret documents around the Iran deal, which would blow up their myth that it was a good deal that rolled back Iran. . . . So in December [of 2016] the Obama NSC started going to work with their favorite reporters, selectively leaking damaging and incomplete information about Flynn."[26]

Whether because of the Iran deal or for other reasons, the combination of Trump and Flynn sent shivers down the spines of the establishment.

And one part of the establishment, in particular, was in shock at the appointment: the intelligence community. At the International Security

Assistance Task Force from 2010 to 2012 and thereafter at the DIA, Flynn had wreaked havoc wherever he went. He refused to follow the rules, was contemptuous of conventional thinking, and was insensitive to the ideas and career needs of his colleagues.

But now the bull was in the china shop. No telling what he'd do.

The intelligence bureaucracy doesn't take to wave-makers easily. They want go-along, get-along guys. They are the "deep state," and they have very potent ways of getting rid of outsiders.

Just ask former JFK aide Ted Sorensen. Appointed to head the CIA in 1977 by President Jimmy Carter right after he entered the White House, Sorensen had been a noted critic of the extreme practices of the intel operatives throughout the 1970s. Back then, hearings conducted by Idaho senator Frank Church uncovered an agency that was out of control. In the Nixon-Kissinger-Ford era from the late sixties to the mid-seventies, the CIA had a hand in coups throughout Latin America, toppling leftist regimes—even those that were democratically elected—and installing military dictatorships in their place.

The national revulsion about CIA tactics scarred the Agency's reputation, but, under Republican presidents like Richard M. Nixon and Gerald R. Ford, the spooks were confident that no harm would come to what they fondly called "the company."

But when Democrat Jimmy Carter was elected in 1976, their sense of security began to fray. Carter had criticized the CIA, and his appointment of a noted liberal like Ted Sorensen sent a signal that he wanted to clean it up.

Sorensen seemed untouchable. Drenched in stardust from his time as JFK's top aide, he was said by some to have ghostwritten *Profiles in Courage,* Kennedy's best-selling book that propelled him into prominence. And everyone gave him credit for many of the most stirring lines in Kennedy's inaugural address. Now, the man who may have written "ask not what your country can do for you, ask what you can do for your country" was appointed to clean out the CIA. (When he was asked if he wrote those lines, he replied with a smile, "ask not.")[27]

But Sorensen wasn't in office yet. The spooks knew that Sorensen would have to be confirmed by the Senate, and they were waiting for him. Sorensen had had two messy divorces, he was a conscientious objector to military service in his youth, and he had spoken out in favor of the release of the Pentagon Papers—the Edward Snowden leak of the time.

Behind the scenes, CIA operatives worked to bend senators to their will and reject Sorensen. We will never know what negative information—"oppo-research"—they dug up to cow senators and make them toe the line against Sorensen.

Seeing that the jig was up, Sorensen withdrew his nomination before it could be voted down.

If they could get rid of Sorensen, it should be no problem to sidetrack Flynn. But there was one problem: The post of national security advisor did not require Senate confirmation. Once the president appointed Flynn, he was in. In like Flynn?

But not so fast. The spooks had a surprise of their own cooking.

They decided to focus on Flynn in an elaborate game of "gotcha" as they combed through their various intelligence sources to find "kompromat," compromising material on the former general. It made no difference that he was now the incoming national security advisor and a presidential appointee. The hunting season was open.

The first target involved the consulting and lobbying firm that he set up after leaving the Defense Department, Flynn Intel Group Inc. A Turkish businessman, Ekim Alptekin, hired Flynn in 2016, charging him with a specific mission: promote the extradition of Fethullah Gülen, a Muslim cleric who was alleged to have masterminded an attempted coup d'etat that sought to oust Turkish president Recep Tayyip Erdogan in 2016. Gülen, currently holed up in rural Pennsylvania, has escaped extradition, and Erdogan, who had moved Turkey closer to the radical Islamist orbit, wasn't happy about it.

Alptekin paid Flynn $530,000 to lobby for Gülen's extradition. At the time he received the money, Flynn was a top advisor to candidate

Donald Trump, who had yet to win the election. As soon as Trump was elected, Flynn quit, but not before he wrote a column in *The Hill* calling on the United States to improve its relations with Turkey.

Nothing Flynn did was irregular or illegal. Rather, it was likely a clerical oversight. He disclosed to Congress that he was working for Alptekin's company but did not file an equivalent form under the Foreign Agents Registration Act because he didn't think he had to. Alptekin's sole connection with the Turkish government is that he sits on a Turkish economic relations board that is overseen by an appointee of the Turkish president. So how was Flynn an agent of a foreign government when he was working for Alptekin? But, under "political pressure" from the Justice Department, Flynn registered, albeit six months after he stopped working on the project.

Score: Spooks 1, Flynn 0.

But the spooks really cleaned up when their wiretapping of Russian ambassador to the United States Sergey Kislyak revealed that Flynn had a series of telephone calls with the ambassador on December 29, 2016.

That was the date on which President Obama imposed new sanctions against Russia to punish Moscow for its "interference" in the American election. Claiming that Russia was "responsible for hacks" into the Democratic National Committee and related servers, Obama ordered thirty-five Russian operatives expelled from the United States and listed as "persona non grata."[28]

Russia had not attacked the United States. It had only gone after the Democratic Party. It did not plant false news or propaganda, it simply may have used its technology to expose to the American people what was actually being said by leaders of the Democratic Party. For this sin, it was sanctioned.

Was Obama's purpose in imposing the sanctions twenty-three days before he left office to punish Russia or to embarrass Trump?

Or did he issue the sanctions to set up a trap for Flynn? Was it like an opening gambit in a chess champion's game?

Apparently—and predictably—as soon as the sanctions were imposed, Flynn was on the phone with Kislyak, assuring him that the Trump administration would review the policy on taking office and urging Russia not to retaliate with sanctions against the United States.

The NSA/FBI had been tapping Kislyak's phone because he was the Russian ambassador. They recorded his call with Flynn.

Of course, it was not only normal but necessary that Flynn and Kislyak communicate to avoid an escalation of the sanctions. Russian dictator Vladimir Putin put it into perspective when he asked, "What is the [Russian] ambassador there for? He's there to speak to people, to maintain contacts with the political elite, with businessmen, with members of the House and the Senate, with administration officials." Putin dismissed the scandal as "nonsense."[29]

But, technically, Flynn had not been sworn in yet—Obama was still president—so his communications with the Russians, as a private citizen, violated the centuries-old Logan Act, which bars private citizens from interfering with diplomatic relations between the United States and foreign governments.

This, of course, was a charade. Nobody has ever been prosecuted under the Logan Act, and the only indictment came in 1803 when a Kentucky farmer wrote an article urging the west to succeed from the union and ally with France. The indictment was dropped and never prosecuted. When the Logan Act was passed, in the eighteenth century, international contacts were rare. But now, with global communications so frequent, a total ban on contacts between private American citizens and foreign government officials is just plain silly and impossible to enforce.

Obama knew that Flynn had spoken to Kislyak since his national security team had the transcripts of the NSA wiretap of the conversation.

But the NSA intercepts were not permitted to identify that Michael Flynn was the American speaking with Kislyak. Because Flynn is an American citizen, FISA rules did not permit him to be identified in the phone intercepts. He is listed only as "Citizen One" or some such description, and his actual name is redacted.

So Susan Rice, Obama's national security advisor, asked the NSA to "unmask" Flynn's name so it could be proven that it was he who had the conversation with the Russians. Somehow, someone, whose identity has yet to be published, leaked the fact that it was Flynn who had spoken to the Russians.

Then Flynn fell into the trap the Intel/Media complex had set for him. Shortly after the inauguration, in a meeting with Vice President Mike Pence, Flynn did not tell him that he had discussed sanctions with the Russian ambassador. He should have.

The media, tipped off by anonymous sources about the contents of Flynn's phone call, was waiting in a well-planned ambush when Pence went on the Sunday morning shows. He was asked at every turn about whether or not Flynn had spoken with the Russians. The Obama administration, of course, knew that he had, since it had wiretapped the ambassador's talk with Flynn.

One after another, the media piled on. Asked by Chris Wallace of Fox News if there had been contact between Trump or his team with the Kremlin, Pence said "no" and called the question "a distraction."[30]

"Of course not," Pence answered. "Why would there be any contact between the campaign? This is all a distraction, and it's all part of a narrative to delegitimize the election and to question the legitimacy of [Trump's] presidency."[31]

On CBS, Pence repeated that "of course" there had been no contact between the Trump people and Russia.[32]

Caught in a lie on national talk shows, the vice president and the president had to make Flynn resign.

The liberals at the FBI took it from there. The *New York Times* reported, the morning after Flynn resigned, that anonymous intelligence officials said that Flynn was "grilled" by the FBI about the content of his call with the Russian ambassador and that "the Justice Department suspects that Flynn did not provide truthful, accurate information."[33]

(There was, of course, nothing wrong with the incoming national security advisor speaking with the Russian ambassador. In fact, in an effort to lessen tensions with the Russians, the call was commendable. But, in the framework of the phony scandal the Democrats were pushing—claiming Trump was Putin's man and that the Russian had "hacked" the U.S. election to stack it against Hillary—the meeting looked bad.)

The rogue spooks had their first victim.

They had played the Washington game with skill and cunning.

The perfect ambush.

And it cost Donald Trump the one man he knew and trusted above all others on national security and foreign affairs. Plucked out of Trump's orbit at the very beginning, Flynn's departure forced Trump to play with a depleted hand in the great poker game of foreign relations.

SEVEN

AND THE LEAKS KEPT COMING . . .

THE ROGUE SPOOKS WERE FAR FROM FINISHED. THEY HAD NOW PERFECTED A domestic American application of the techniques that had proven so effective abroad—anonymous leaks, rumors, disinformation, unconfirmed reports, fake news, phony scandals, ambushes, and then more leaks to show how everybody was turning on the president.

Now it was time for the major leagues: Try it out on the president himself. Their goal: To turn the honeymoon every president gets into a divorce—or at least a separation—for Trump.

Just as Trump was taking office, anonymous sources from within either the intelligence community or the Obama White House leaked a series of stories based on actual transcripts of personal conversations President Trump had with foreign leaders. The purpose of the leak was to further the image of a president who was out of control and out of his league.

After a phone call with the president of Mexico, the Associated Press reported that the president had told his Mexican counterpart: "You have a bunch of bad hombres down there. You aren't doing enough to stop them. I think your military is scared. Our military isn't, so I just might send them down to take care of it."[1]

Where did AP get the story? It reported that "a person with access to the official transcript of the phone call provided an excerpt to the AP.

The person gave it on condition of anonymity because the administration did not make the details of the call public."[2]

The media also obtained the transcript of another Trump phone call—this one with Australian prime minister Malcolm Turnbull.

Trump was annoyed by a deal the Obama administration had made to admit 2,500 people from Iran, Iraq, Sudan, and Somalia, nations whose refugees Trump was seeking to ban from entry into the United States. On the phone, Trump railed against Obama's concession, calling it "the worst deal ever" and accusing Australia of seeking to export "the 'next Boston bombers.'"[3]

How did the texts of these calls end up in the media? Again, through rogue spooks—Obama holdovers—who wanted to embarrass the president.

Bloomberg News explained how texts of presidential contacts with foreign leaders could provide important political information to Trump's critics: "The intelligence reports were summaries of monitored conversations—primarily between foreign officials discussing the Trump transition, but also in some cases direct contact between members of the Trump team and monitored foreign officials. One U.S. official familiar with the reports said they contained valuable political information on the Trump transition such as whom the Trump team was meeting, the views of Trump associates on foreign policy matters and plans for the incoming administration."[4]

The drip-drip-drip of negative stories about Trump, planted in the media by unidentified sources, took its toll. As Trump's inauguration approached, the *New York Times* gloated: "Mr. Trump will take office on Friday with less popular support than any new president in modern times, according to an array of surveys, a sign that he has failed to rally Americans behind him, beyond the base that helped him win in November. Rather than a unifying moment, his transition to power has seen a continuation of the polarization of the election last year."[5]

From every corner, Trump's presidency was assailed as being a failure. The *New York Times* said that "once again, Mr. Trump's agenda was subsumed by problems of his own making, his message undercut by a seemingly endless stream of controversy he cannot seem to stop himself from feeding."[6]

"Chaos" became the watchword the media used to describe and denigrate the Trump administration. Teddy Wayne, writing in the style section of the *New York Times*, went above and beyond, saying that his was "arguably the most turbulent presidency since Richard M. Nixon's, the nation is entering an era of volatility unseen for decades."[7]

Oh really? Teddy seems to have forgotten that Bill Clinton's presidency held the nation on edge for two years as the impeachment drama and his uncontrolled personal behavior played itself out. By contrast, Trump's tenure has been placid and uneventful.

The anti-Trump leaking during his transition and the early months of his presidency were so widespread that they dominated the national news. Almost every story about Trump was sourced anonymously, always to give the impression of disorder in the White House and, by implication, of Trump's inability to govern.

The leakers and the journalists conspired in an echo chamber to kill the president through death by a thousand cuts. No one slash was deep enough to be lethal, but the cumulative effect was quite sufficient for the purpose.

And, when their biased reporting had done its work, the media reveled in the resulting poor ratings Trump got in polls (the same polls that said he would never win).

James B. Stewart, a *New York Times* reporter, wrote an article headlined: "CASE STUDY IN CHAOS: HOW MANAGEMENT EXPERTS GRADE A TRUMP WHITE HOUSE." His premise was that "'Chaos' seems to be the word most often invoked" to describe the Trump White House. He continued: "In less than two weeks, Mr. Trump created upheaval at the nation's borders, alienated longtime allies, roiled markets with talk of a trade war and prompted some of the largest protests any president has faced."[8]

Is he kidding?

Did Trump "roil the markets" when the Dow gained 3,000 points after his inauguration? Were the demonstrators, ginned up by Obama's Organizing for Action (OFA), more numerous than those that bedeviled Johnson and Nixon? Was there "upheaval" on the border with Mexico when illegal immigration dropped by 71 percent in Trump's first three months?

Despite all this, believe it or not, the "management experts" Stewart interviewed dutifully told him that "the Trump administration is a textbook case of how not to run a complex organization like the executive branch."[9]

Reporter James Stewart might have benefited from emulating his namesake Jimmy Stewart by going to Washington like Mr. Smith to find out how things worked.

Every day, every story seemed to come from unidentified sources. It was as if the only people entitled to know what was going on were the journalists who covered the story, their sources cloaked in anonymity.

Here's a sample from just one day—April 6, 2017. Four major stories appeared in the *New York Times,* each heavily or entirely relying on anonymous sources:

- Three reporters—Matthew Rosenberg, Maggie Haberman, and Adam Goldman—wrote a story saying that Trump aides showed the House Intelligence Committee chairman, Congressman Devin Nunes (R-CA), proof that Obama's people had spied on Trump officials during his transition period. They named the Trump aides but cloaked their own sources in anonymity, describing them only as "four American officals."[10] Appointed by whom? Serving where? With what possible motivation for lying? None of these questions is even addressed in the story.
- That same day, reporters Peter Baker and Glenn Thrush— again joined by Maggie Haberman—wrote a long story about White House advisor Steve Bannon's ouster from the National

Security Council meetings. The source for this detailed story chronicling Bannon's ups and downs during Trump's months in office was simply given as "White House officials." Again, the answers to Who? Why? When? were hidden from the reader.[11]

- And again, that same day, Nicholas Fandos wrote a story about how expensive it was to protect the Trump family as the president shuttled from Washington to New York to Florida. The article implied that his travels were costing so much that they deterred the Secret Service from pursuing necessary criminal investigations. "To keep up [with security during Trump's travels], dozens of agents from New York and field offices across the country are being temporarily pulled off criminal investigations to serve two-week stints protecting members of the Trump family, including the first lady and the youngest son in Manhattan's Trump Tower."[12] What criminal investigations? Who said they were being cut back? It turns out that Fandos's source was anonymous—"a former agency official briefed on its staffing." The former official said that work on "protective intelligence, financial crime and cybercrime cases" was being given short shrift to accommodate Trump's travel and security needs.

- And, again that same day, the trio of Haberman, Rosenberg, and Thrush covered President Trump's accusation that former Obama national security advisor Susan Rice had broken the law by demanding the names of Trump transition aides inadvertently swept up in NSA wiretaps. Under a headline that said Trump was making the charge but was "Citing No Evidence" to back it up, the reporters quoted anonymous sources again to refute Trump's claim. "Mr. Trump gave no evidence to support his claim, and current and former intelligence officials from both Republican and Democratic administrations have said they do not believe Ms. Rice's actions were unusual or unlawful." Which officials? With what qualifications? When? With what caveats? No answers are provided. Just trust us. We are, after all the New York Times.[13]

Even the most important stories are routinely sourced anonymously in the mainstream media. The *Washington Post*, for example, in breaking the story of the Trump dossier and its author, Christopher Steele, assured us of Steele's reliability, noting, "U.S. officials, speaking on the condition of anonymity to discuss intelligence matters, have said that Steele's source network was viewed as credible."[14]

Even when the *Washington Post* reported that Steele had gone into hiding so as not to be interviewed in connection with his dossier (and its unreliable sources), it did so citing anonymous sources like "British reports" or "British media reports."[15]

And when CNN shattered the media boycott of the dossier story, finally taking the bait Obama's people were offering to peddle the unverified allegations, they also did so with anonymous sourcing. Headlining that the FBI had briefed Trump on the dossier's charges, CNN cited "multiple US officials with direct knowledge of the briefings."[16]

Given how false the charges were and how unverified the information was, the real story of the dossier was who compiled it, why, and with what funding. But, by sourcing the story anonymously, CNN made further investigation more difficult.

President Trump lashed back at the media for using anonymous sourcing for its stories. He charged that the media was dominated by "made up stories and made up sources." He said that the practice made it very hard for readers to judge the accuracy of the stories. He said the media "shouldn't be allowed to use sources unless they use somebody's name. Let their name be put out there."[17]

He particularly singled out the FBI for scathing criticism of its frequent leaking, saying, "the FBI is totally unable to stop the national security 'leakers' that have permeated our government for a long time.

They can't even find the leakers within the FBI itself. Classified information is being given to media that could have a devastating effect on U.S. FIND NOW."[18] Did Donald realize this admonition was like asking the mob to inform on itself?

In reporting on Trump's remarks, the Associated Press cheekily ran his comments under a headline that blared: "TRUMP BLASTS MEDIA, ANONYMOUS SOURCES—AFTER WH USES THEM."

The story noted that "just hours [after Trump's comments] members of his own staff insisted on briefing reporters only on condition their names be concealed."[19]

(Of course, there is all the difference in the world between a staffer asking for anonymity as he elaborates and contextualizes what his boss just said and a hostile critic using anonymity like a wall behind which to hide while lobbing grenades.)

Intelligence officials, eager to demolish Trump's candidacy during the election, constantly leaked stories about how unreliable he was—all based on anonymous sourcing.

Shortly after Trump won the Republican nomination, the *Washington Post* reported that there was "deep unease" about briefing Trump on national security. The story reported that "some intelligence officials have deep reservations about sharing sensitive information with Trump." It reported on "new signs of deep discomfort with Trump among the upper ranks of the intelligence community. In a measure of that growing animosity, one senior intelligence official said Wednesday that he would decline to participate in any session with Trump."[20]

Again, no names. Anonymous sources. No evidence. No specifics. Just innuendo.

On June 2, 2016, before the Republican Convention, Reuters ran a story citing eight unnamed "senior security officials" who had "concerns over briefing Trump" on foreign policy. The article noted that "most of the officials asked for anonymity to discuss a domestic political issue." But that didn't stop them from interfering from behind the protective shield of anonymity.

One of these unnamed officials said, "People are very nervous." He said intelligence officials were trying to determine "who on (Trump's) team are trustworthy." The unnamed official bemoaned, "We've never had a situation like this before. Ever."[21]

So, by indirection and implication, the media tried to raise voters' concerns about the stability of Trump as a possible president and about whether he could be trusted with classified material.

That this concern was about Trump and not about Hillary Clinton, who had put all of the nation's most important secrets out there for all to see on her private server, is ironic and indicative of the partisanship of those involved.

How do reporters make up what Trump calls "fake news"?

Anyone who has been in or around politics frequently gets calls from reporters asking about a certain story. Almost always, the reporter has already written the story in his mind and is now on the hunt for sources to prove that he's right.

When you give him what he wants—a quote agreeing with his premise—he includes you in the story. If you don't oblige, your dissent isn't covered. Only that sourcing that tends to confirm the journalist's preconceptions makes it into print.

Frequently, the reporter, in search of verification for the story he has already composed mentally, will offer to let sources go off the record in their verification. This procedure permits them to approve a story without leaving their fingerprints. But it also provides an easy way to let the reporter write what he wants without taking blame for it. That's how fake news is typically invented.

The *New York Times* overtly defends its practice of relying on anonymous sources. Liz Spayd, the public editor of the newspaper, lavishly praised the *Times*'s reporting of the early days of the Trump presidency but noted that "There was something else notable about these stories. All of them relied heavily—some entirely—on a reporting tactic many readers despise: the use of anonymous sources. Presumably for fear of losing a job, a security clearance, access or something else, the people interviewed did not want to be named, and so were assigned nebulous titles like 'government official' or 'congressional aide' or, even more vaguely, those 'familiar with' the thing they were talking about."

She observed that while "reporters and editors trust such information . . . Readers, on the other hand, couldn't be more suspicious—and with reason."[22]

Good reason, indeed. The *New York Times*' appetite for Spayd's criticism of its anonymous sourcing may, however, have reached its limits. She announced on June 2, 2017, that she was leaving her job and the office of public editor will be no more at the *Times*. As she said, "turn off the lights."[23]

But all the focus on the ethics of the journalists who ran stories based on leaks begs the question: Who were the leakers and why were they leaking?

Certainly, many of the leaks came from the intelligence community and, even with names omitted, were sourced that way by the reporters. Why did the intel operatives become rogue spooks leaking to destroy their president? Here we have to go back to the history of the CIA and the FBI right as Obama was taking office in 2009.

The bloodletting that followed at both agencies and in the broader Department of Justice replaced often docile, well-trained career employees with ideological firebrands who saw government service as an opportunity to help implement their worldview of what needed to be done. These folks brought long-standing personal political agendas to their new jobs and saw their work as the key to vindicating their views.

In fact, the evidence is that John Brennan at the CIA and Eric Holder at Justice and the FBI chose employees to fill these job slots for precisely that reason. Both officials developed policies to create as many payroll vacancies as possible and then implemented hiring practices, nominally designed to achieve "diversity," that put these ideologues in top jobs and seeded them throughout the bureaucracy.

By the time Obama left office in 2017, the FBI and the CIA had little in common with their own agency histories. Gone were the right-wing investigators at the FBI and prosecutors at Justice going after communists. And also gone were the CIA sleuths battling leftists abroad. Instead, their jobs were taken by men and women for whom public service was primarily a place from which to serve their liberal ideologies.

ALL HELL BREAKS LOOSE: TRUMP FIRES COMEY

Tired of FBI leaking, aggrieved over Comey's role in outing the dossier, and determined to purge his administration of its enemy within, President Trump fired FBI director James Comey on May 9, 2017.

Deputy Attorney General Rod Rosenstein laid the basis for firing Comey in a memo entitled "Restoring Public Confidence in the FBI." He cited Comey's "'handling of the conclusion of the investigation of Secretary [Hillary] Clinton's emails.' Rosenstein criticized Comey for holding a press conference on July 5, 2016, to publicly announce his recommendation not to charge Clinton, and for announcing on Oct. 28, 2016, that the FBI had reopened its investigation of Clinton."[24]

The Democrats seized on Trump's decision as evidence that he was fearful that an FBI investigation would reveal that he was in league with Putin all through the election. FactCheck.org noted that "Comey's firing came less than two months after the director confirmed at a congressional hearing on March 20 [2017] that the bureau is investigating 'whether there was any coordination between the [Trump] campaign and Russia's efforts' to influence the 2016 presidential election."[25]

Now Trump's opponents in the media auditioned to play the roles of Woodward and Bernstein in the Watergate saga of forty-three years earlier. The lure "Pulitzer Prize" flashed in the distance.

But it is an exercise in acting out the Hans Christian Andersen story about the emperor who had no clothes.[26] In all likelihood, there was and is nothing there. In modern lingo, it is probably just a nothing sandwich.

The intel community responded to the invasion of its home turf with the usual assortment of anonymous leaks. *The Hill* reported "for days [after Comey was fired], the FBI's J. Edgar Hoover building has been a sieve of leaks contradicting the president's account of his decision to fire Comey, painting Trump as paranoid and vindictive. In a *New York Times* story Thursday night, allies of Comey said the president had summoned him to the White House for dinner and demanded that he vow political loyalty—but was rebuffed."[27]

The leakers defended the chief leaker with leaks.

OBAMA: THE CATALYST

The tone for resistance to Trump by the intel community, even after he was elected to be their boss, was set by the former president himself. Nobody was more freaked than Obama by Hillary's defeat. As Politico reported, "never has there been such raw and clear mutual personal hatred and dismissal between two presidents. Trump was elected president on the back of the years he spent delegitimizing Obama. Obama has spent years denigrating Trump in return, and focused on proactively delegitimizing a Trump presidency he never thought was a real possibility."[28]

The *New York Post* reported that Obama is "working behind the scenes to set up what will effectively be a shadow government to not only protect his threatened legacy, but to sabotage the incoming administration and its popular 'America First' agenda."[29]

The newspaper explained that "he's doing it through a network of leftist nonprofits led by Organizing for Action (OFA)."[30]

OFA, created in 2013, is run by former Obama aides and campaign workers and has 32,000 activists at its disposal. With help from Obama's people, it has raised more than $40 million since it was created.

As Trump approached the White House once the votes were tallied, OFA put its anti-Trump efforts into high gear, working through a network of 250 offices around the country.

Street protests against Trump are a crucial part of their playbook (and were used by the CIA to destabilize governments after the wrong people won elections). Even at Trump's inauguration, OFA ginned up protesters to try to mar the event with catcalls and picket signs.

Obama cheered them on, saying, "It is fine for everybody to feel stressed, sad, discouraged," in a conference call from the White House. "'But get over it.' He demanded they 'move forward to protect what we've accomplished.'"[31]

"'Now is the time for some organizing,' he said. 'So don't mope.'"[32]

Eric Holder, too, has been busy. The former attorney general, working with the Obama Foundation, is dedicated to ending Republican control of Congress.

The "shadow" government of former president Obama even has a "shadow" White House, a mansion two miles from 1600 Pennsylvania Avenue, which the *New York Post* reported Obama is "fortifying with construction of a tall brick perimeter, and a nearby taxpayer-funded office with his own chief of staff and press secretary. Michelle Obama will also open an office there, along with the Obama Foundation."[33]

But, behind the scenes, away from the rallies and demonstrations, the real anti-Trump operation unfolded shortly after the election, when the sleeper cells—the rogue spooks with which Obama, Holder, Brennan, and the others had seeded the executive branch of government—came into action.

Their goal: destabilize Trump. Their method: leaking to friendly reporters. Reality Winner, who—as noted above—was arrested in June 2017 for leaking classified material, is a perfect example of these anti-Trump resisters left behind as Obama moved on. She hid in the relative safety of her position as an employee of an NSA contractor to leak classified material to embarrass Trump. She got caught. But so many others are going free.

Their efforts bore fruit. Despite record job growth, a successful Supreme Court appointment, a sharp drop in illegal border crossings, and hundreds of executive orders rolling back Obama programs and policies, the media sold Americans on the idea that Trump's transition and first hundred days were a failure.

The *Washington Post* headlined its wrap-up of the transition: "IT WENT OFF THE RAILS ALMOST IMMEDIATELY: HOW TRUMP'S MESSY TRANSITION LED TO A CHAOTIC PRESIDENCY."[34]

As the *Washington Post* described it, "Viewed through the lens of the first months of the new administration, Trump's transition provided the template for what has unfolded since Inauguration Day on personnel and other matters. No transition goes exactly as planned, but Trump's proved messier than most and that has carried over into the first months of his presidency."[35]

And what was the newspaper's source for its headline that Trump's presidency was "off the rails almost immediately"?

You guessed it. An anonymous source—"one knowledgeable person who spoke on the condition of anonymity to offer a candid assessment."[36]

Trump did not take to the leaking kindly. He tweeted: "The real scandal here is that classified information is illegally given out by 'intelligence' like candy. The spotlight has finally been put on the low-life leakers! They will be caught!"[37]

Why didn't Trump get rid of the leakers at the outset? He couldn't.

Any new appointments in the cabinet agencies have to be confirmed by the Senate. Under Republican control, this doesn't seem like it would have been a problem, but it was.

While Democrats in the Senate did not have enough votes to block Trump's nominees, they could use confirmation hearings, document requests, and other Senate procedures to delay their confirmations and, thus, keep Trump's players off the field in the game's early months.

A good example was Trump's nominee for secretary of the Army, Mark Green, who was not confirmed for four months. Eventually, on May 2, 2017, Green had to withdraw because of his views supporting the theory of biblical creationism. Would somebody please enlighten me as to what that has to do with being secretary of the Army? But the final piece of the confirmation of Trump's cabinet did not come until late April 2017.

Part of the fault lay with Trump himself. The *Washington Post* reported that of the "530 other vacant senior-level jobs requiring Senate confirmation, the president has advanced just 37 nominees." The paper reported that "Trump's Cabinet secretaries are growing exasperated at how slowly the White House is moving to fill hundreds of top-tier posts, warning that the vacancies are hobbling efforts to oversee agency operations and promote the president's agenda, according to administration officials, lawmakers and lobbyists."[38]

And, while the nominations and confirmations were slow in coming, the posts were still occupied by the liberals that Brennan, Holder, and Obama put there.

And, once a cabinet nominee is confirmed by the Senate and can start work, it is likely going to take weeks and even months for him to figure out what is going on. It takes quite a while to get to know the staff and to figure out who to trust and who to dismiss. That this process could not even begin in many agencies until the spring of 2017 explains why so many Obama appointees remained after their president left, free to take potshots at President Trump and protected by journalists offering anonymity.

Obama's people tried to increase the number of these embedded liberals and to keep them beyond Trump's reach.

Gary Berntsen, a former CIA officer, explains that "I think part of the problem that we've seen during the handover of power from President Obama to President Trump was that there was a number of holdovers that went from political appointee to career status that had been placed in the NatSec [national security] apparatus and certain parts of the intelligence organisations. It is clear that President Trump and his team are determined to remove those people to make sure that there's a continuity of purpose and people aren't leaking information that would put the Administration into a negative light."[39]

The Obama people knew that the Trump administration would clean house as soon as it could, so—the Washington Free Beacon reported—they carefully instructed their loyalists to "accrue substantial amounts of vacation time in its last year in office. As soon as team Trump entered the White House, it was obligated to pay out all of these hours. White House sources say the cost was in the millions of dollars."[40]

"The payout prevented the Trump White House from hiring key staff in its opening days due to insufficient funds," the Washington Free Beacon reported. Flynn, for instance, was able to hire only twenty-two people to work on the White House National Security Council, which topped around 420 staffers under Obama. "They put landmines everywhere."[41]

As the president ended his first three months in office, the media breathlessly reported on the failure of the Trump presidency. Having sown discontent with the Trump administration by all manner of exaggerated and even concocted news stories, the media now reaped its harvest by proclaiming Trump's presidency a disaster.

The *Washington Post* reported that presidential historian Douglas Brinkley said that Trump's first months on the job have been the worst of any president in U.S. history. "This is the most failed first 100 days of any president," Brinkley told the *Washington Post*. "I don't know how it can get much worse."[42]

Summing up, less than one month into his presidency, the *Washington Post* said that "Trump has had more scandals and screw-ups than many presidents have in their entire term."[43]

To read these articles, many anonymously sourced, one could believe that Trump had done nothing but stumble in his first months in office. But the facts are quite different. Trump's record of achievement in his first months rivals that of almost any other president.

Have a look:

Trump's Accomplishments in Office January 21–May 7

- A 27 percent increase in jobs created
- A 13 percent hike in houses sold
- A 71 percent cut in illegal border crossings
- A 10 percent cut in the trade deficit

- Confirmation of Neil Gorsuch for Supreme Court.
- Blocking refugees from terror nations (still in litigation)
- Partially funding construction of the Mexican border wall
- 5,000 new ICE agents
- A stop to federal money to sanctuary cities
- Elimination of two federal regulations for each one added
- A cut to Obamacare regulations on health insurance
- No lobbying for five years after leaving office
- No lobbying for foreign governments ever
- A federal hiring freeze
- The Keystone Pipeline
- A rule that prevents feds from telling local police what they can and can't do
- A reversal on Obama's regulations on power plants
- An agreement that only "shovel-ready" projects get stimulus money
- A retaliation bombing on Syria to stop poison gas attacks
- The support to al Sisi in Egypt—in order to stop the Muslim Brotherhood
- $3 billion in fines for illegal imports
- No U.S. aid for groups pushing abortion

In addition, he also

- Formed a task force on opioid abuse
- Let energy companies do what it takes to get foreign contracts
- Killed EPA regs on small rivers and streams
- Ordered NASA to study travel to Mars
- Rolled back car fuel-efficiency standards
- Audited all federal agencies
- Ordered investigation of Russian meddling in U.S. election
- Called for scholarships to promote school choice
- Planned an increase in defense spending

- Revoked Obama orders on federal contractors
- Ordered study on how to reduce attacks on police
- Rescinded Obama regulations on retirement advice
- Stopped visas to foreigners taking U.S. jobs
- Required Justice Department to publish info on how many illegal immigrants are in prison for other crimes
- Signed trade deals with China to open their markets to our products
- Increased power of states to drug test applicants for unemployment and welfare benefits
- Rescinded Obama regulation that set federal requirements for college teacher evaluations
- Rolled back Obama regulations on education

Pretty good, right?

The contrast between Trump's actual record and that described in the media could not be more dramatic.

EIGHT

THE MEDIA INVENTS A SCANDAL

RUSSIAN INTERVENTION IN THE U.S. ELECTION

HAVING JUST PREDICTED A VICTORY FOR HILLARY CLINTON LOUDLY AND FRE-
quently, Democrats, liberals, and the media shared a common predica-
ment: How to explain her defeat? And, even worse, how could they
account for the victory of the despised Donald Trump?

Rather than admit the reality—that America had not only rejected
Hillary, the Democrats, and Obama but had also turned its back on the
news media that propped them up and serviced their every need—the
media decided to start spinning a new story.

At first, they denied the Trump victory, clinging to the fact that
Hillary had polled three million more votes, despite losing the Electoral
College by 306–232. Claiming a moral victory, if not a legal one, the
Democrats minimized the Trump triumph.

It was as if the Cleveland Indians baseball team, having lost the
2016 World Series to the Chicago Cubs by four games to three, con-
tended that it was really a tie because each team had scored 27 runs in
the seven games combined.

Hillary and Bill Clinton were full of reasons why she had lost.

She blamed an anti-woman bias, saying, "Certainly misogyny played
a role. I mean, that has to be admitted."[1]

Beyond anti-female bias, Hillary blamed FBI director James Comey for her defeat for saying—eleven days before the election—that he had revived his inquiry into Hillary's private email server. She told her donors in a conference call one week after election day that "our analysis is that Comey's letter raising doubts that were groundless, baseless, proven to be, stopped our momentum."[2]

(Of course, she ignored the fact that the reason the investigation had to be reopened was that the FBI had just discovered the emails Hillary had deleted. They were found on the computer of former congressman Anthony Weiner, the husband of her aide Huma Abedin.)

Bill Clinton was even more definite in pinning the blame on Comey, declaring flatly that "James Comey cost her the election."[3]

Hillary also blasted WikiLeaks for its repeated publication of her and her campaign manager John Podesta's emails. She said, "WikiLeaks which played a much bigger role than I think many people understand yet, had the determinative effect."[4]

But there was a basic problem with those explanations: They left Hillary holding the blame. After all, there would have been nothing for the FBI to investigate if Hillary had conformed to the practices almost everyone else followed and used the government server for her emails. And, had she been forthcoming in releasing them once her use of the private server was discovered, the issue would have gone away. But the fact that she and her people deleted emails, even while they were sought by a congressional committee, cast her in a bad light.

The Clintons, Obama, and the Democratic Party desperately needed someone or something else to blame.

So they chose Russia. No blame could attach to Hillary or her allies if the election was actually hacked or stolen by Russia.

"A foreign power meddled with our election" in an "act of aggression,"[5] she told the media and her supporters.

And the rest of the Democratic Party and the Obama administration picked up the chant. And the CIA stepped up to affirm it—again anonymously.

To understand the political impact of the stories of Russian hacking, we need briefly to revisit the recent history of U.S.-Russian relations and to understand how and why they have deteriorated.

U.S.-RUSSIA RELATIONSHIP DETERIORATES

After the dissolution of the Soviet Union in 1989 and the defeat of the communist coup in 1991, relations between the United States and Russia warmed considerably. The Cold War was clearly over.

But when Russia invaded Crimea and then set its imperialist sights on Ukraine in 2015, it appeared that Russia, the imperial power of old, was gobbling up territory again.

(Henry Kissinger theorized that Russia, communist or not, could only be stable if it was expanding. If it tried to stand still on its borders, Kissinger explained, it would inevitably contract as ethnic groups pulled it apart in each of its border regions. It was only the momentum of imperialism that lent stability to the state.)

Ukraine and Crimea had always been particularly important to Russia. With only 143 million people, Russia needs Ukraine's 45 million, along with its food production and mineral wealth, to be a superpower again. Crimea, a peninsula jutting out into the Black Sea, was Russia's best shot at the warm water port it could not find anyplace else in its enormous landmass.

So Russia, from the czars through the commissars, made sure to control both nations. But it wasn't enough to conquer them. The Russian leaders—particularly Stalin—undertook to colonize them so they would be as Russian as English emigration had made the thirteen colonies British.

With Russians pouring over the border to settle in Ukraine, the eastern part of the country became Russified. Now about one-third of the population speaks Russian as its native tongue and their number dominates eastern Ukraine.

When Ukraine became independent of the Soviet Union in 1989, its new government began to reverse the pro-Russian cultural, political, and linguistic policies that had prevailed in the Soviet era. Its free elections revealed a split right down the middle of the country, with the western part—including its capital city of Kiev—wanting closer ties with the United States and Europe and, perhaps, membership in the European Union and NATO. But the eastern residents clung to their Russian past and rejected the westward moves of their nominal countrymen.

It was in this context that Putin fomented native Russians in Ukraine to rise against their government and demand autonomy. In Crimea, he had a ready majority at hand, but Ukraine settled down for a long, protracted civil war.

To the West, Putin was a latter-day Stalin grabbing land and suppressing people's freedom. To Russians, he was trying to protect the indigenous Russian population against domination by ethnic Ukrainians. As is always the case in Eastern Europe, history gave each side ample cause to hate the other. The Russians had suspected their Ukrainian countrymen ever since many of them collaborated with Hitler's invading forces. The Ukrainians, on the other hand, saw Putin as trying to continue the brutal military dictatorial rule of Stalin and his successors. (Stalin had starved the Ukrainian peasants to death by confiscating their crops at harvest time, killing more than ten million people.)

They were both right. And both wrong.

But the situation was not a simple one.

Putin's new aggressiveness scared Europe even as Ukraine's westward drift terrified Russia.

As Ukraine's internal tensions stoked the old Cold War back to life, Obama was getting alarmed at Russia's increasing imperial ambitions.

Putin originally sought to use the democratic process to gain influence in Ukraine. His proxy was Viktor Yanukovych, who was defeated for election by pro-Western forces in 2004. After years of economic pressure by Russia—which included cutting off gas deliveries to

Ukraine—the Ukrainians caved and voted for Yanukovych to resume power in the elections of 2010. His campaign was masterminded by American consultant Paul Manafort (later to be Trump's campaign manager).

But when Yanukovych began to move away from a close association with the European Union and toward a closer bond with Russia, Ukraine erupted.

Pro-democracy demonstrators occupied downtown Kiev in November 2013. When Yanukovych tried to crack down in January 2014, the protests turned violent. Ukraine's parliament ousted Yanukovych and called for new elections. Voting was strictly along ethnic lines, and Petro Poroshenko, the pro-Western candidate, won over 50 percent of the vote.

The next month, Putin invaded Crimea, adjacent to Ukraine, using Russian troops at the Sevastopol Navy Base to occupy the country. At the same time, pro-Russian separatists in Eastern Ukraine started a civil war. Armed and supported by Russia, the conflict has raged ever since.

No longer could Obama ignore the Russian threat, and, in the spring of 2014, he imposed sanctions on Russia, limiting travel to and from the United States and seizing the American bank accounts of several key Russians. The European nations lined up behind the United States and imposed sanctions of their own.

A second and third round of sanctions followed in April and July 2014, targeting Russia's vulnerable energy and banking sectors. As the sanctions bit and expanded, Russia began to feel the pain.

THE PUTIN-TRUMP BROMANCE

In this environment, the Obama administration was surprised to hear candidate Donald Trump say nicer things about Putin than Americans had been hearing from their politicians lately.

In September 2015, in a Republican presidential debate, Trump was asked if he would get along with Putin and Russia despite Putin's support for Syrian dictator Bashar al-Assad. "I would get along with him," Trump said. "I would get along with a lot of the world leaders that this country is not getting along with."[6]

A bromance between Trump and Putin seemed to blossom when they sent each other verbal Christmas gifts in separate TV appearances on December 17, 2015.

Putin went first, saying that Trump is "a really brilliant and talented person, without any doubt."[7]

Trump replied the same day during an interview on the TV show *Morning Joe*. Asked how he could get along with Putin after knowing that he had murdered political dissidents and journalists who opposed him, Trump replied, "he's running his country and at least he's a leader, unlike we have in this country."[8]

Pressed about Putin's tactics in crushing political dissent, Trump seemed to excuse it, saying, "Well, I think our country does plenty of killing also."[9]

Putin purred back: "[Trump's] saying he wants to go to another level of relations, closer, deeper relations with Russia. How can we not welcome that? Of course we welcome that."[10]

The warm comments between the two must have raised the eyebrows—and the antennae—of the Obama White House and State Department.

While the verbal bouquets were flowing between Trump and Moscow, Britain's Government Communications Headquarters (GCHQ), the British equivalent of the NSA (signal intelligence and wiretapping), alerted Washington that the bromance might not be just platonic. In autumn of that year, as Putin and Trump were exchanging warm messages, the British raised the "alarm that Moscow had hacked the computer servers of the Democratic National Committee." The *Guardian* explained that "the compromise of email exchanges among senior Democrats was spotted when voice intercepts, computer traffic or agents picked up content of the emails flowing towards Moscow."[11]

But when the FBI passed the British warning to officials at the Democratic Party, they brushed them off, refusing to take them seriously.

Seriously?

The *New York Times* reported the bungling, blaming a series of "missed signals, slow responses, and a continuing underestimation of the seriousness of the cyberattack" that allowed Russia to "roam freely through the committee's network for nearly seven months."[12]

When the FBI called the DNC, in September 2015, to pass on the British warning of a hack of the party's computers, their call was initially referred to the "Help Desk." From there it went to a DNC contract worker with limited computer skills.

Apparently the genius who took the call from the FBI thought it might be a "prank call" and, after a "cursory search of the D.N.C. computer system logs to look for hints of cyberintrusion," paid it no heed. The FBI called back several times but was still ignored. According to an internal memo, the staffer said he "had no way of differentiating the call I just received from a prank call."[13]

The Democratic National Committee even delayed the FBI investigation into the hacking by initially refusing to give the FBI direct access to servers and data.[14]

While we do not know for certain if Russia was responsible for the hacking, we have to suspect it was, based on the unanimous opinion of U.S. intelligence.

All we do know is that on July 22, 2016, just as the Democratic National Convention was being called to order, 19,253 emails and 8,034 attachments contained in the emails of seven key DNC staffers were made public by WikiLeaks. The emails dated from January 2015 to May 2016.

The emails showed overt bias by the chairman of the Democratic National Committee, Debbie Wasserman Schultz, in favor of Hillary Clinton's nomination.

With the Democratic Party locked in a close seesaw contest between Hillary and Vermont senator Bernie Sanders, the national party apparatus—and its chairman—was supposed to be neutral.

But the emails showed a very different story. The party machinery had been closely coordinating with the Clinton campaign and doing all it could to advance her candidacy.

For example, in May 2016 DNC chief financial officer Brad Marshall told the DNC chief executive officer, Amy Dacey, that they should get the media to ask Sanders if he was an atheist.

Donna Brazile, who succeeded Wasserman Schultz as party chairman, tipped off Hillary about what questions she would be asked at an upcoming town hall–style debate with Sanders.

WikiLeaks also released ten years of hacked emails from John Podesta, Hillary's campaign manager. Oddly, a typographical error may have been at fault in opening Podesta's door to the hackers.

The *New York Times* reported that in March 2016, the Democratic Committee got an email purportedly from Google saying hackers had tried to infiltrate Podesta's Gmail accounts. As *The Hill* summarized, "When an aide emailed the campaign's IT staff to ask if the notice was real, Clinton campaign aide Charles Delavan replied that it was 'a legitimate email' and that Podesta should 'change his password immediately.'"[15]

Oops! Delavan meant to type that it was "illegitimate." And, by telling Podesta to change his password, "he had inadvertently told the aide to click on the fraudulent email and give the attackers access to the [real] account."[16]

Meanwhile, the investigation into the hacking of the Democratic computers continued. The *Washington Post* reported, in December 2016, that "The CIA has concluded in a secret assessment that Russia intervened in the 2016 election to help Donald Trump win the presidency, rather than just to undermine confidence in the U.S. electoral system, according to officials briefed on the matter."[17]

The paper reported that "Intelligence agencies have identified individuals with connections to the Russian government who provided

WikiLeaks with thousands of hacked emails from the Democratic National Committee and others, including Hillary Clinton's campaign chairman, according to U.S. officials. Those officials described the individuals as actors known to the intelligence community and part of a wider Russian operation to boost Trump and hurt Clinton's chances."[18]

"It is the assessment of the intelligence community that Russia's goal here was to favor one candidate over the other, to help Trump get elected," said a senior U.S. official briefed on an intelligence presentation made to U.S. senators. "That's the consensus view."[19]

Again, no sources, just "a senior U.S. official."

But many had their doubts.

Donald Trump, for example, sneered that "These are the same people that said Saddam Hussein had weapons of mass destruction." He told *Time* magazine: "I don't believe they interfered" in the election. He said that the hacking "could be Russia. And it could be China. And it could be some guy in his home in New Jersey."[20]

Senate Majority Leader Mitch McConnell (R-KY) said in a September 2016 briefing for congressional leaders that he doubted the veracity of the intelligence.

For his part, Julian Assange, the founder of WikiLeaks, says flatly that the "Russian government is not the source" for his published leaks.[21]

On December 29, 2016, as noted, Obama imposed sanctions against Russia to retaliate for their meddling in the U.S. election. The president expelled thirty-five Russians living in the United States who were suspected spies. He seized two luxurious waterfront properties in Upper Brookville, New York, and on Maryland's Eastern Shore that, he said, were being used for intelligence.

Putin denied the charges, paraphrasing former president George H.W. Bush, who, in the 1988 campaign, famously denied that he would raise taxes, saying "read my lips." Putin replied, when he was asked if he had sought to influence the U.S. election, "read my lips—no."[22]

Putin blamed the accusations on U.S. politics and warned that it was dangerous to pit Washington against Moscow. "Do we want to completely destroy our diplomatic relations, to bring the situation to how it was in the 1960s, with the Cuban missile crisis?" Putin asked.[23]

And how did Russia supposedly "meddle" in the U.S. election? Actually, the verb "meddle" was a comedown from the earlier charge that Moscow "hacked" the election, implying that they may have monkeyed with the vote count itself. But, on January 5, 2017, Director of National Intelligence James Clapper testified before the Senate Armed Services Committee that Russia "did not change any vote tallies or anything of that sort."[24]

Even if Russia was behind the hacking, there was no way that the release of these emails was responsible for Hillary's defeat. While one can argue credibly that Hillary's entire handling of her emails, her deletion of tens of thousands of work-related correspondence, and her secrecy all contributed significantly to her defeat, the actual hacking of the DNC and Podesta's emails did little to destroy her candidacy. While they embarrassed the Democratic Party in general and Podesta in particular, there was no way the hacked emails contained information that crippled Hillary's campaign.

In making the accusation of meddling, the Democratic/media establishment invoked the idea of "fake news," suggesting that Russians had used online and social media news sources to plant phony stories that were widely read and even more broadly believed. Some speculated that Russia generated these stories and that their propagation was a major example of the Kremlin meddling in the U.S. election.

In an effort to pin the blame for Hillary's defeat on fake news, Hunt Allcott of NYU and Matthew Gentzkow of Stanford published a study in March 2017, "Social Media and Fake News in the 2016 Election."[25]

Their research found that "fake news was both widely shared and heavily tilted in favor of Donald Trump" during the 2016 election cycle. They said they found 115 pro-Trump fake stories that were shared on Facebook a total of 30 million times, and 41 pro-Clinton fake stories shared a total of 7.6 million times.[26]

But the bottom line, they said, was that 15 percent of respondents recalled seeing at least one of the fourteen fake news headlines tested in the study. The authors cited this fact to show how widely fake news was spread—to one in seven American voters![27]

But their finding was totally debunked because, when they read to the same voters in their study fourteen bogus headlines they had just made up for the survey and which had not been in circulation during the election, 14 percent also recalled reading at least one of them during the election! So the study's finding—that fake news permeated deeply—was disproven by its own data.[28]

But whether or not Russia's supposed intervention in the election was decisive, the question remained: Did Donald Trump or his people try to solicit and aid Russian meddling in the election?

Ever since Hillary's defeat, the entire apparatus of the intelligence community—with its echoes in the media and in Congress—has sought to create a phony scandal with the implication that the new American president was treasonously involved with Russia and Putin.

The scandal was the key element in the campaign to destabilize Trump and to cast doubt on the legitimacy of his presidency. The campaign of anonymous stories and leaks has led to formal investigations of Trump and his campaign by the FBI and the congressional intelligence committees.

Could the intelligence community create enough disinformation to lead to impeachment proceedings? The question hangs over the Trump presidency. Exactly as the CIA, the FBI, and the intelligence community planned. And as they have done in so many countries around the globe.

During the Senate debate on the nomination of Justice Neil Gorsuch to the Supreme Court, Senator Jeff Merkley (D-OR) characterized the investigation of Russian meddling as "a huge shadow over the incoming administration. The more we know the darker the cloud becomes."[29]

Suspicion and pseudo-scandal have always been the destabilizing hallmarks of the intelligence community. The phony scandal of Russian meddling served this purpose admirably as it grew in intensity as the election campaign proceeded.

At first, Obama refused to take the hacking story seriously. The *New York Times* reported that Obama did not publicly name the Russians, so the Russians escalated again—"breaking into systems not just for espionage, but to publish or broadcast what they found."[30]

And the bromance between Trump and Putin continued to blossom. Questioned by Matt Lauer during a candidate forum in September 2016, Trump again praised Putin as a "leader" and said he was "highly respected within his country and beyond." Trump noted that Putin "does have an 82 percent approval rating."[31] When Lauer asked Trump about Putin's praise of him, the candidate replied, "If he says great things about me, I'm going to say great things about him." Trump said, "The man has very strong control over a country. Now, it's a very different system and I don't happen to like the system. But certainly, in that system, he's been a leader, far more than our president has been a leader."[32]

Lauer persisted, naming Putin's bad deeds—invading Ukraine, annexing Crimea, supporting Iran, and backing Assad. He even told Trump that, "according to our intelligence community, [Putin] probably is the main suspect for the hacking of the DNC computers."[33]

Trump responded, saying Obama was just as bad: "Do you want me to start naming some of the things that President Obama does at the same time?" Trump asked.[34]

Earlier, on March 28, 2016, Trump had called attention to Russia when he hired longtime Republican political consultant Paul Manafort to run the show. Manafort had many business ties with pro-Russian Ukrainians, and served without pay in the Trump campaign. He had received millions in fees from his Ukrainian clients, much of it allegedly in cash.[35]

Was it a coincidence that Trump, who had warmly praised Putin, now hired a consultant who had represented the Russian's favorite candidate in the Ukraine?

Suspicions of a Trump quid pro quo with Putin were heightened when the Republicans avoided a sharp condemnation of Russia's Ukraine policy. Diana Denman, a platform committee member from Texas and former Ted Cruz supporter, proposed an amendment during a national security platform meeting to support arming Ukraine to fight Russia.

Josh Rogin, writing in the *Washington Post*, said that "The Trump campaign worked behind the scenes . . . to make sure the new Republican platform won't call for giving weapons to Ukraine to fight Russian and rebel forces, contradicting the view of almost all Republican foreign policy leaders in Washington."[36]

The climax came on July 22, 2016, when the hackers—Russian or not—released the Democratic Party's emails. The resulting storm forced the resignation of the party chairman and blighted the opening day of the Democratic National Convention.

Trump laughed it off, inviting Russia to hack and release Hillary's State Department emails, too. He said, five days after the Democratic Party's emails were published, "I will tell you this, Russia: If you're listening, I hope you're able to find the 30,000 emails that are missing, I think you will probably be rewarded mightily by our press."[37]

Trump said he was only kidding, but was he?

The question seemed to hang in the air.

Now that Trump was the official Republican nominee and Democratic fantasies that someone else might overtake him were dashed, the nominee's relationship with Putin seemed to offer new fodder as a campaign issue.

Hillary's allies in the media pounced.

The *Washington Post* headlined its story: "INTELLIGENCE COMMUNITY INVESTIGATING COVERT RUSSIAN INFLUENCE OPERATIONS IN THE UNITED STATES." In the story, *Post* reporters confirmed that U.S. intelligence believed there is a "broad covert Russian operation in the United States to sow public distrust in the upcoming presidential election and in U.S. political institutions."[38]

NBC joined in with the story "Could Russian Hackers Spoil Election Day?"[39]

Politico ran "How to Hack an Election in 7 Minutes," in which a Russian hack was reported as being all but imminent.[40]

Shortly after the release of the DNC documents, U.S. intelligence agencies launched a full-scale investigation. As it proceeded, their confidence grew that Russia was behind the hacking.

Days after the hack, the *New York Times* reported that "American intelligence agencies have told the White House they now have 'high confidence' that the Russian government was behind the theft of emails and documents from the Democratic National Committee."[41]

One month after the convention, the intel agencies were more convinced of Russia's role. One official told NBC News that the attacks had been attributed to Russian intelligence agencies. "This is the closest we've come to tying a recent hack to the Russian government," the official said.[42]

On September 26—six weeks before the election—Hillary blasted Russia for intervening in the election. She said, "increasingly, we are seeing cyber attacks coming from states, organs of states. The most recent and troubling of these has been Russia. There's no doubt now that Russia has used cyber attacks against all kinds of organizations in our country, and I am deeply concerned about this. I know Donald's very praiseworthy of Vladimir Putin, but Putin is playing a really . . . tough, long game here. And one of the things he's done is to let loose cyber attackers to hack into government files, to hack into personal files, hack into the Democratic National Committee."[43]

With one month before the election, the intel agencies said they were "confident that the Russian Government directed the recent compromises of e-mails from U.S. persons and institutions, including from U.S. political organizations. . . . These thefts and disclosures are intended to interfere with the U.S. election process."[44]

But, now, the intelligence agencies were going further. No longer did they say these hacks were for the purpose of undermining confidence and stability in the United States. They now flatly believed that the Russians were trying to help Trump win.

As noted, Hillary pounded the issue in her debates with Trump.

The situation escalated one week before the election, when President Obama called Putin personally on the special hotline connecting the White House and the Kremlin that had been installed during the Cold War. According to NBC, Obama emphasized the gravity of the situation by using the "Red Phone" to tell Putin: "International law, including the law for armed conflict, applies to actions in cyberspace. . . . We will hold Russia to those standards."[45]

Then, after her defeat, Hillary and the Democrats piled on, attributing the loss to Russian hacking. Both houses of Congress ordered investigations and the intelligence agencies delved deeply into what had happened.

The entire incident has loomed large in Democratic efforts to cast aspersions on Trump's victory and to question its legitimacy.

But what actually went on and what impact did it have?

If we assume it was Russia and Putin who hacked U.S. computers and that they did so with the goal of electing Donald Trump, what was the real impact of their efforts?

It's a big deal when a country like Russia tries to influence elections in the United States. Of course, during the Cold War, both Russia and the United States worked overtime to influence elections in other countries. Russia controlled elections in Eastern Europe with an iron fist and subsidized communist parties all over the world. The United States, through the CIA, as noted, worked hard to defeat communist and leftist politicians running in supposedly free elections.

But Russian hacking of the Democratic Party—if true—was clearly a new kind of tactic. What was particularly worrisome was the implication that the Kremlin wanted Trump to beat Hillary. This fact gave rise to speculation that there had been a deal between Trump and Putin or even that Russia felt it could control Trump through use of the blackmail material Steele had amassed in his dossier.

But the very unreliability of the information contained in the dossier undermined the likelihood that it could be used as blackmail. Nor did it seem that there had been any deal in which Putin helped Trump in return for an expectation that he would go easy in opposing Russia's geopolitical ambitions.

Pardon the cliché, but the proof was in the pudding.

Two months after taking office, Trump ordered U.S. cruise missiles to attack the base in Syria from which dictator Bashar al-Assad launched chemical weapons attacks on civilians.

On April 6, 2017, fifty-nine U.S. Tomahawk cruise missiles crashed into the Syrian military base at Shayrat, destroying 20 percent of Syria's operational aircraft. The attack, ordered by President Trump, was in retaliation for Syrian dictator Assad's sarin gas attack on his own people the week before.[46]

The air strikes were clearly against Russia's interests. Russia, a longtime sponsor of Assad and his most dependable ally, was angry at the missile strike and vowed to retaliate. The bromance between Trump and Putin seemed to be either over or, at least, on the rocks.

Putin called the air strikes "aggression against a sovereign state in violation of the norms of international law." He said that the United States was using a "trumped-up pretext" to justify the attacks. Putin said that "this move by Washington has dealt a serious blow to Russian-US relations, which are already in a poor state."[47]

If Putin thought he had Trump in his pocket, it looks like he miscalculated.

The larger question, however, is whether Putin was a decisive factor in Trump's victory.

He wasn't.

Donald Trump won the election of 2016 because he appealed to angry, white, high school–educated voters—largely men—and brought them out to vote in record numbers.

Fox News polls leading up to election day told the tale. With three weeks to go until the voting, Trump's lead over Clinton among white, male, high school graduates was 15 points. With two weeks left, they went for him by 30 points. One week out, he led among them by 40 points. And exit polls show that on election day, Trump defeated Hillary among white men who had not been to college 67 to 20—by 47 points!

To appreciate the impact of this swing among white, high school–educated voters, we need to compare the results in the elections of 2012 and 2016 in the industrial north with those in the south.

While voters in both places have their share of pain and angst about the direction of the country, the higher unemployment and resulting social anger are much more prevalent in northern states like Ohio, Michigan, Wisconsin, and Pennsylvania than in Florida or North Carolina. While all six of these states went for Trump in 2016 and all but North Carolina voted for Obama in 2012, Trump closed a huge gap in the northern states and much less of a gap in the southern ones.

In Florida, for example, where the recession was shorter and less drastic, Trump ran better than Romney had, but only by 2 points. And, in North Carolina, which has had a vast increase in population and income over the past few decades, Trump ran only 1.7 points ahead of Romney.

But in Ohio, where the recession dragged on for years and joblessness rose to new heights, Trump outperformed Romney by 11.1 points, much more than he did in Florida or North Carolina. And in Michigan, where the devastation that hit the auto industry was especially bad, Trump ran 9.2 points ahead of Romney's 2012 pace.

There are lots of explanations for the results of the 2016 election.

Democrats blame Russian meddling, FBI Director Comey's various statements, and anti-women bias for their defeat.

Republicans attribute their victory to Hillary's many scandals. But the mega-trends that delivered the election to Trump were much more manifest in the north, suggesting a swing related to the particular economic facts of life in those regions and among the white, high school–educated demographic.

The point is: Russian interference had nothing to do with it.

But that didn't stop the Democrats and their allies in the intelligence community from using this phony scandal to fill the news media during Trump's transition and his first months in office.

The intel community reported every detail of every contact between any Trump staffer and anyone in Russia.

The *Washington Post*, commenting on the contacts, said that each new revelation was "adding to a cloud of suspicion that hangs over the White House as critics demand an independent investigation."[48]

The goal of this pantomime of a scandal was to force Trump and Attorney General Jeff Sessions to appoint a special prosecutor to investigate it. Special prosecutors have huge budgets, broad latitude, and the ability to convene grand juries and issue subpoenas. Because trying to get the president is the full-time job of the prosecutor, the prosecutor tends to be relentless and usually succeeds in at least crippling and perhaps bringing down the president.

And, like a game of tag, the media races to follow up any report of contact between anyone connected with Trump, no matter how loosely, and any Russian official, no matter how lowly placed.

There has never been any evidence that any of the meetings that did actually take place between Trump's people and the Russians were, in any way, part of a conspiracy to meddle in the election.

And the charge that Trump was vulnerable to blackmail because he had asked the Russians to hack the Democrats was also absurd. Indeed, Trump had publicly called on Russia to release any hacked emails from Hillary's stack of deleted communications to which it might have access. So, what more could have been said in private to warrant this paranoia?

But what of the charge that the Russians had compromising material on Trump, a bomb that could drop any day? The short answer is: Why hasn't it? If Russia has this kind of material, where is it? Why haven't they used their leverage to exact cooperation from Trump in Syria, for example?

But the McCarthyite witch hunt continues through the media. Every encounter between Trump's aides and the Russians is reported with the excitement and urgency of the discovery of a smoking gun.

- Attorney General Jeff Sessions met twice with Russian ambassador Sergey Kislyak while he served in the U.S. Senate. In a classic game of DC "gotcha," Democratic senator Al Franken (D-MN) asked Sessions, during his confirmation hearing, whether he was aware if campaign associates had any contact with Russian government officials. Sessions said he had no such knowledge nor did he communicate with Russian officials. Then the other shoe dropped and unnamed Justice Department officials leaked that he had "met with the Russian ambassador."[49]

- Sessions explained that Senator Franken's question related to contacts between the Trump campaign and the Russian ambassador. His meetings had been in his capacity as a senator and a member of the Senate Armed Services Committee. He had not met with the Russians in connection with his unofficial role as an advisor to the Trump campaign. But no matter, his answer and the facts diverged sufficiently for him to recuse himself from any investigation of Russian meddling in the election. Coming on the heels of National Security Advisor Mike Flynn's resignation, it seemed as if the administration was falling apart before it had begun.

- After Trump's election, in December, 2016, the president-elect's son-in-law Jared Kushner met with Sergey Gorkov, chief of Russia's state-owned bank VEB and reputedly a "crony" of Vladimir Putin. VEB had helped start the Trump International Hotel and Tower project in Toronto in 2010. VEB was and still is under U.S. sanctions imposed by Obama to retaliate against Russia for its actions in Ukraine and

Crimea. Kushner was looking for $1 billion from investors to refinance his company's debt on 666 Fifth Avenue, a building Kushner owns that is in serious financial trouble (and in which his office is located). Was the meeting to discuss Kushner's financial troubles or sanctions on the bank? Nobody knows . . . but it bears watching.[50]

- Russian deputy foreign minister Sergei Ryabkov told Interfax news agency in November, after the U.S. election, that "there were contacts" between Russia and Trump's aides. "Obviously," Ryabkov said, "we know most of the people from his entourage."[51] Russia, however, has been quick to point out that any meetings were "normal practice" and offered to "Democratic presidential nominee Hillary Clinton's campaign" as well.[52]

- In April 2016, the *Washington Post* reported that "Kislyak popped up at the Mayflower Hotel, where he was seated in the front row at one of Trump's first major foreign policy addresses." Later they met on the receiving line, where the Russian also met Sessions and Kushner. The organizer of the event put the "meeting" in context: "Let me put it more bluntly: They [the Russian diplomats] would be derelict in their duty if they didn't try to get to know him."[53]

- Kislyak also showed up at the Republican Convention in July and met Sessions briefly at a Heritage Foundation event there.

- Two days later, Kislyak met with Trump advisors Carter Page and J. D. Gordon after a convention-related Global Partners in Diplomacy event at Case Western Reserve University. Gordon says it was a "brief, informal conversation" during which he repeated public Trump statements about improving relations with Russia.[54] Page, who had no formal role in the Trump campaign, spoke out critically of the U.S. handling of Russian relations in a speech in Moscow on July 8, 2016.

That's it. There has never been any implication that Donald Trump met or spoke with any Russians regarding the campaign. And, if there were, it is unlikely that he could have gone farther in private than he did in public when he called on Moscow to release Hillary's deleted emails.

Yet, the Democrats and their allies in the intel community and the media have focused on the issue of Trump-Russia contacts as if it were the modern equivalent of the Russian espionage operation that stole the U.S. atomic secrets in the forties.

One of the crazier reactions came from former acting CIA director Michael Morell, who called Russian meddling the "political equivalent of 9/11." He said, "A foreign government messing around in our elections is, I think, an existential threat to our way of life. To me, and this is to me not an overstatement, this is the political equivalent of 9/11."[55]

Day after day, the coverage of the new Trump administration was almost drowned out by a journalistic focus on Russian meddling. Here's a sample of the headlines:

SENATE INTEL DEMS PRESS OBAMA TO DECLASSIFY
MORE OF RUSSIAN HACKING PROBE

RUSSIAN HACKING CRISIS TESTS OBAMA'S NERVE

TRUMP DISMISSES INTEL ON RUSSIAN HACKING

PUTIN ON TRUMP: "NOBODY BELIEVED HE
WOULD WIN EXCEPT FOR US"

DEMS WANT CRUZ TO INVESTIGATE
TRUMP'S RUSSIAN HACKING PLEA

MCCAIN AND SCHUMER PRESENT UNIFIED
FRONT AGAINST RUSSIAN HACKING

FORMER TRUMP ADVISER CARTER PAGE
ALSO MET WITH RUSSIAN ENVOY

RUSSIAN GOVERNMENT HACKERS BROKE INTO
DNC SERVERS, STOLE TRUMP OPPO

Trump set to get the full Russian hack briefing

Obama White House rebuffed plan
to combat Russian influence

Lindsey Graham gets passed over
for Russian hacking panel

Albright: Trump fits the mold of Russia's "useful idiot"

Heritage Foundation: Obama
"emboldened" Russia to meddle

Trump sides with Assange, Russia over U.S. intelligence

Obama administration accuses Russian
government of election-year hacking

U.S. shares election-hacking intel with Europe

Sorting out how to probe alleged
Russian election hacking

McConnell: We won't ignore Russia's election meddling

How weak cybersecurity could disrupt the U.S. election

Trump team rejects intel agencies'
claims of Russian meddling

How the Senate's Russian meddling probe almost blew up

On Russian hacking connection, the U.S.
isn't as sure as Clinton says it is

Corker downplays Russian hacking into U.S.

McCain and Graham: U.S. needs to hit
Russia hard for election hacking

The damage to the incoming Trump administration has been extreme. Even though there is no proof of a deal between Trump and Putin, the headlines continue to scream that there might be.

But with his attack on Putin's close ally Syria, Trump did more to debunk the charges that he was in bed with Putin than a year's worth of denials had done. As noted, Putin, outraged by the attack, called it a violation of international law, and even raised the prospect of a conflict with the United States. Saying the attack crossed "red lines," Putin said that Russia and Iran would "respond with force" if Trump attacked Syria again.[56]

Despite the implausibility of Russia interfering in the elections, the fact is that a similar intervention has happened before. In 1996, the Chinese did all they could to elect an American running for president. But back then, the Clintons were the beneficiaries.

NINE

IT WASN'T THE FIRST TIME

IN THE PRESIDENTIAL DEBATES BETWEEN HILLARY AND TRUMP, THE DEMOCRAT
went out of her way to describe the supposed hacking of the U.S. election process as unprecedented.

She said: "We have never in the history of our country been in a situation where an adversary, a foreign power, is working so hard to influence the outcome of the election."[1]

Really? Mrs. Clinton has a short memory. It has happened before, and not so long ago.

CHINA'S EFFORTS TO MEDDLE IN THE 1996 U.S. ELECTION

In 1996, when President Bill Clinton faced an uphill battle for re-election, after the Republicans had captured both houses of Congress two years before, China was heavily implicated in a series of illegal campaign contributions to the president's campaign.

U.S. law is explicit that it is unlawful for a person who is not a U.S. citizen or a permanent resident to give money to a political campaign. But here, the evidence not only implicated several foreign individuals but the Chinese government as well.

The scandal was unearthed by Bob Woodward (of Watergate fame) and Brian Duffy of the *Washington Post,* who broke a story that a Department of Justice investigation into President Clinton's and the Democratic Party's fund-raising activities in the 1996 election cycle had shown that the Chinese embassy in Washington was used to coordinate contributions to the Democratic National Committee. China, of course, denied it.

Beijing's bête noire has always been Taiwan, which China regards as a breakaway province that it is determined to bring back under its rule. When President Clinton responded to congressional resolutions and granted a visa to Taiwan president Lee Teng-hui—after Secretary of State Warren Christopher had assured China that Teng-hui would not get one—Beijing concluded that it needed to increase its political clout in Washington. So it launched a determined effort to pass campaign cash to top American politicians, from the president on down.

The donations from Chinese sources flowed rapidly.

Yah-Lin "Charlie" Trie, the owner of a Chinese restaurant in Little Rock, Arkansas, frequented by the Clinton family over the years, donated $450,000 to Clinton's legal defense fund in various checks and money orders. When it turned out that some of the money orders' signatures were in the same handwriting (and were sequentially numbered) but had different names, the fund had to return the money. Trie also donated $220,000 to the Democratic Party, but that had to be returned as the scandal grew.[2]

Johnny Chung, a native of Taiwan who raised funds for Clinton, admitted to Congress—under oath—that Chinese general Ji Shengde, then the head of Chinese military intelligence, told him, "We really like your president very much. We hope he will be reelected. I will give you $300,000 U.S. dollars. You can give it to . . . your president and the Democrat Party."[3]

John Huang and James Riady, both of the Indonesian company Lippo Group, raised $3.4 million for the Democrats in 1995. A frequent White House visitor, Huang worked in the Commerce Department as deputy assistant secretary for international economic affairs, responsible for Asian-U.S. trade. With the job came access to classified material about U.S.-China trade.

Unlike the current Putin-Trump scandal, Huang's activities may have involved espionage as well as an attempt to buy influence. While in his Commerce Department job, Huang met nine times with Chinese embassy officials.

Huang and Riady funneled money to the Clinton campaign and the Democratic Party from employees at Lippo and then reimbursed those employees who had contributed. According to a report by the Senate Governmental Affairs Committee, Riady also "had a long-term relationship with a Chinese intelligence agency."[4]

So when the media and Democrats called the Russian efforts to elect Trump unprecedented, they had failed to review their own history.

But there was also a direct precedent for the United States and Russia to get mixed up in each other's elections. In 1996, it was the other way around: The United States tried to influence the outcome of a Russian election.

CLINTON MEDDLES IN 1996 RUSSIAN ELECTION; TRIES TO RE-ELECT BORIS YELTSIN

It is stunning how short memories are in politics, current affairs, and the news business. When, on January 6, 2017, the *Washington Post* reported that the U.S. intelligence agencies depicted Russian interference in the U.S. election as "unprecedented in scale,"[5] they obviously forgot or overlooked what Bill Clinton did to influence the Russian elections of 1996.

This saga begins just after Clinton was elected president in 1992. One of his first acts was to receive a phone call from former president Richard Nixon offering advice on foreign policy. Nixon's message was clear: Don't lose Russia. The warning came one year after the aborted communist coup sought to oust Russian president Boris Yeltsin and bring back the communists. Nixon, who had made his political career in the fifties bemoaning the loss of China to the communists in 1949, had kept asking of the Truman administration, "Who lost China?"[6]

His advice did not fall on deaf ears. When President Clinton returned from his October 23, 1995, summit meeting with Russian president Boris Yeltsin, he laughingly told Dick Morris over the phone that "Yeltsin has only an 8 percent vote share and he thinks he can get re-elected."[7]

After Dick replied, "You have a 36 percent rating and you think you can get elected," the president turned serious and said, "it's very important that Yeltsin win."[8]

Taking the hint, Dick suggested a way to influence the election in Yeltsin's direction. Dick's former business partner, Dick Dresner, had been meeting with Yeltsin's daughter—his de facto campaign manager—to try to get hired by the Russian's campaign. Dick suggested that Clinton contact Yeltsin and urge him to hire Dresner to provide a conduit for advice and assistance in the campaign.

President Clinton took Dick up on the idea and Yeltsin hired Dresner, commissioning him to take weekly polls on his behalf.

Each week, Dresner would send Dick the polling data and he would bring it to the White House to share with the president in secret one-on-one meetings late at night in the White House residence. Then, the president would pick up the hotline connecting the White House with the Kremlin and advise the Russian president on where to campaign and what to say.

Once, when Dresner was having difficulty persuading Yeltsin to produce a television commercial, Clinton, tipped off by Dick, spoke to Yeltsin and got him to do the ad.

Clinton was also instrumental in persuading Yeltsin to get out and campaign extensively in person, something new to Russians, who were accustomed to rarely seeing their leaders in person.

In April and May 1996, as the June election approached, Yeltsin started to heed the U.S. president's advice. *Foreign Affairs* magazine recounts that "after visiting a couple of regions in February and staying home in March, Yeltsin visited five more in April, ten in May, and six in the first half of June. These visits were almost always combined with offers of largess, which Yeltsin delivered with relish."[9]

If there was one thing Yeltsin gleaned from Bill Clinton, it was his understanding of electoral politics, a relatively strange topic to any Russian reared in a totalitarian society where elections were just for show.

Sandy Berger, Clinton's national security advisor, once intercepted Dick and asked if he was sharing "Dresner's polls" with Yeltsin. Berger said he knew Dick was doing it because "the president was citing numbers the other day in the Security Council that were different from our [the CIA's] data." Dick asked the president what he should tell Berger and Clinton replied: "tell him you've stopped [giving me his polls] but keep doing it anyway."[10]

Yeltsin's re-election—with 54 percent of the vote—was a surprise to the international community, and most observers found it hard to account for his recovery from political oblivion. *Foreign Affairs* wrote that "Boris Yeltsin's rise from the depths of unpopularity to win Russia's presidential election in July [1996] is one of the most surprising feats of recent political history."[11]

What role did Bill Clinton's meddling play in Yeltsin's triumph? Did it encourage Putin to return the favor by interfering in the U.S. elections in 2016? Were the two connected?

TEN

HOW THE INTEL COMMUNITY CAME TO POSE A THREAT TO DEMOCRACY

AS THE INTELLIGENCE COMMUNITY BEGAN ITS EFFORTS FIRST TO DEFEAT, THEN to besmirch, and, ultimately, to destroy Donald Trump, it drew on the lessons and precedents of its previous century of operation.

How could the intelligence community mount an operation against first a candidate for president, then the president-elect, and finally a sitting president? The answer lies in the evolution of the ethos and roots of its two key agencies: the FBI and the CIA.

Gradually, step by step, these two agencies have crept closer to allocating to themselves the power and the moral justification to act independently of—and antagonistically toward—a popularly elected president. And, at the same time, their very vulnerability in a democracy has fueled an introversion in which the needs of their own bureaucracy seem to supersede those of the country as a whole.

This institutional paranoia could not handle the idea of Donald Trump as president, someone who might reverse policies the bureaucratic organizations had cherished for years. And, as his election approached, they moved against him.

Bill Clinton's national security advisor—and, in the past, Henry Kissinger's right-hand man—Tony Lake put it best when he said, "To the CIA, everyone is an outsider."[1]

Before there was a CIA or any intelligence agency in our government, there was the FBI. Originally founded by President Theodore Roosevelt in 1908, the Bureau was charged with handling the chores of domestic surveillance. Roosevelt had been motivated, in part, by the national alarm generated by the assassination of his predecessor, President William McKinley, in 1901.

But the FBI really acquired stature and power under its legendary director, J. Edgar Hoover, who led it from 1935 until 1972. Under Hoover, the FBI became the premier investigative agency in the free world, building its reputation by laying low the likes of Al Capone and John Dillinger.

In the twenties and thirties, as Hoover was taking power, our national consensus was firmly rooted in the famous quote by President Herbert Hoover's secretary of state and Franklin Delano Roosevelt's secretary of war, Henry Stimson: "Gentlemen do not read each others' mail."[2]

J. Edgar Hoover, more than anyone else, was responsible for moving decisively away from this ideal into an era fraught with government-sponsored espionage and surveillance. In his thirty-seven-year reign atop the FBI, Hoover perfected the justification for surveillance—to protect national security. And, at the same time, he protected the FBI bureaucracy as it spied and surveilled by maintaining a political empire based on blackmail and coercion.

Hoover had files on everybody. His surveillance reached into every bedroom, boardroom, and bank account in or around the DC beltway.

Like a bureaucrat on steroids, he used the vast investigative machinery of his Bureau to dig up dirt on powerful figures, even—or especially—on his boss, attorney general of the United States (and future Supreme Court justice) Frank Murphy.

Murphy, who took office vowing to rein in Hoover, was a vulnerable target: "a lifelong bachelor . . ." and "'notorious womanizer' . . . with apparently little regard for the marital status of his conquests."[3] Hoover diligently chronicled Murphy's romantic conquests. And, after Murphy saw the file Hoover had amassed on him, he suddenly reversed field and announced that the Bureau was in such "capable hands"[4] that he would leave it alone.

First appointed by FDR, Hoover used the president's appetite for gossip and his obsession with having dirt on his political opponents—and on his own appointees—to keep the FBI funded and relevant.

Initially, Roosevelt used Hoover primarily to keep his own people in line, tapping their phones to be sure that they were loyal and toeing the party line. It was one way of preventing leaking.

So Hoover's spying was less than popular with Roosevelt's own people, but the fact is that the president, while listening sympathetically to their complaints, and attacking surveillance as immoral, was quite satisfied that Hoover was keeping tabs on his appointees.

Even as FDR postured that he was opposed to wiretapping and surveillance, he quietly let it happen. *New Republic* columnist John T. Flynn put it very well when he said, "J. Edgar Hoover could not continue these [surveillance] activities for ten minutes in the administration of a man who did not approve them."[5]

But soon, Roosevelt saw the potential to use Hoover's skills to hobble his political opponents. Anxious to accommodate his new buddy, the president, Hoover began spying on Roosevelt's critics. As far back as the 1930s, it was the team of FDR and J. Edgar Hoover that established the precedent of covert intervention in American politics by government intelligence agencies.

Hoover's most famous wiretap victim was Charles A. Lindbergh, the national hero who, in 1927, was the first person to fly solo across the Atlantic Ocean. Widely celebrated at home and abroad, Lindbergh became world famous. The "Lindy Hop" became the most popular dance in the twenties. The wave of adulation was followed a few years later by widespread national sympathy when his infant son was kidnapped and murdered in 1932. The whole world hung on every step of the investigation until the killer was captured.

Ten years later, Lindbergh had moved into politics, vigorously attacking Roosevelt for leading us into the war that raged in Europe.

Lindbergh helped to found the America First movement, opposing aid to Britain, intervention in Europe, and even the institution of a military draft.

Lindbergh was highly critical of Roosevelt, but much less so of Hitler. He expressed fervent admiration for the "New Europe" of Fascism and Nazism that the German dictator was trying to impose on the continent. He also capitalized on his fame as an aviator to tell Americans that Germany was far ahead of everybody else in developing its air force. He warned that the United States would face massive slaughter from the air if we fought with the Germans.

Addressing the nation frequently by radio, Lindbergh whipped up sentiment against FDR's efforts to gradually acclimate Americans to the need to defeat Hitler. His pitch fed off a widespread skepticism about U.S. intervention in World War I and anger that the death of over one hundred thousand Americans had seemed to have accomplished so little. Americans felt that the British had manipulated the United States into the First World War and suspected that they were now leading Roosevelt down the same road.

FDR advisor Rex Tugwell said that "Lindbergh's radio addresses were just next to treasonable but they had an unmistakably receptive audience."[6]

FDR had to bring the aviator down a notch. Taking a huge political risk, he turned to Hoover to hunt for dirt. And Hoover struck gold.

Curt Gentry reports, in his biography of Hoover, *The Man and the Secrets,* how the director's "investigations dug up the fact that Lindbergh had been feted by the Nazi high command. He had accepted a decoration from Hermann Göring, the head of the German air force [the vaunted Luftwaffe] and said that Germany was invincible. He worked to persuade Americans that Britain was doomed to defeat, and that America had no business involving itself, particularly on the losing side."[7]

Hoover also found that Lindbergh had a German mistress. Hoover implied that she may have served as a conduit to the Nazi high command.

The precedent of using the FBI as a political weapon was thus firmly built into the fabric of the Bureau during Hoover's days. FDR came to use Hoover as a weapon of political convenience. When his own postmaster general and former political mentor, James A. Farley, tried to run for president to block FDR's third term, Hoover reported that the cabinet member was having trouble with his income taxes. After a few whispers here and there, Farley was a problem no longer.

FDR even had Hoover investigate his presidential predecessor and Edgar's namesake—Herbert Hoover (no relation). On July 2, 1940, right after the French surrendered to Hitler, FDR heard, from journalist Marquis Childs, that former president Hoover had "sent telegrams to the former French premier Pierre Laval, hoping to persuade him to reveal that Roosevelt had secretly promised to send American troops to aid the French."[8] FDR asked the head of the FBI to investigate the claims. The FBI's New York field office looked into it, but couldn't confirm the report.

Continuing his surveillance of the former president, the FBI director gave FDR the details of a February 4, 1941, private lunch meeting between Lord Halifax, the British ambassador to Washington, and the former president. The meeting was important because Halifax had been an advocate of appeasement of Germany before the war and urged British surrender after the fall of France. President Hoover, who opposed Roosevelt in general and U.S. intervention in particular, was a major opponent of FDR's policies. The president wanted to know what went on at the meeting and J. Edgar obliged.

It was one thing to move against high-level political adversaries like Lindbergh and former president Hoover, but quite another to amass files and negative material on ordinary Americans who expressed opposition to FDR's programs. But throughout the lead-up to war, Roosevelt and Hoover crossed that line.

Before America entered the war, as Roosevelt battled the isolationists and steered measures through Congress that made American involvement inevitable, he used the FBI to gather information about people who disagreed with his policies.

On May 16, 1940, FDR sent a message to Congress on national defense, urging rearmament, a hot topic because it was seen as moving the United States closer to war. Opposition from around the country was immediate and intense. Telegrams flooded the White House. FDR asked his aide Steve Early to forward the negative ones to Hoover. While Roosevelt didn't spell out what he wanted Hoover to do with them, the director took the hint and soon reported to Roosevelt that he had opened files on the citizens who dared criticize the president. In doing so, Gentry notes that Hoover went "beyond what FDR had requested," but speculates that Hoover was "probably [doing for] Roosevelt exactly what he wanted."[9]

This project marked the first time the FBI had been used to spy on ordinary citizens exercising their First Amendment right of free speech.

Within a few weeks, Hoover had conducted background checks on 1,311 critics of the president, among them senators Burton K. Wheeler and Gerald Nye as well as Lindbergh and many other leaders of the America First Committee—the group opposing intervention in World War II. And, of course, on a number of ordinary Americans.

His efforts earned Hoover a letter of commendation from Roosevelt.

The precedent of using wiretaps and electronic snooping to keep tabs on the president's political opponents had been set.

Until the end of World War II, the FBI and Hoover functioned as a conduit to the president, satisfying his curiosity about the motives of his opponents and helping him survive in the Washington minefield. In all, FDR tapped the phones of more than two hundred political opponents in the 1940 election cycle. Roosevelt's part of the bargain was that he would keep Hoover in his post and augment his budget and his power.

The record reflects that Hoover drew the line and refused FDR's requests only once—when Roosevelt asked Hoover to tap the phones of Wendell Willkie, his Republican opponent in the election of 1940.

Roosevelt, who had already been elected twice, had chosen to defy the tradition initiated by none other than George Washington in 1796 that barred a president from seeking a third term. (This was before the ratification of the Twenty-second Amendment that codified this tradition.)

Winning a third term was a hard sell despite Roosevelt's popularity. And, when the Republicans nominated Willkie—an attractive, moderate, young, and charismatic candidate—it became harder still.

So Roosevelt reached out to Hoover to dig up dirt he could use. On July 2, 1940 (four months before the election), Interior Secretary Harold Ickes—FDR's favorite messenger boy for partisan shots—asked Hoover to investigate Willkie. Gentry notes that "there was a rumor that Willkie had changed his name from Wulkje; if true, this could be used to alienate not only Polish-American voters but all those Americans still reacting to the fall of Poland."[10]

For once, Hoover turned Roosevelt down after his chief aide Ed Tamm told the director that it would be "a serious mistake" for the Justice Department to conduct political investigations.[11]

In the years to come, Hoover's scruples would melt away.

But before Roosevelt's third election, and before the United States even entered the war, Hoover's increasingly close collaboration with Roosevelt had helped him to win the right to wiretap.

At first, Hoover and Roosevelt both expressed their abhorrence of wiretapping. Hoover called it "unethical" and a "thing of the past."[12]

The FBI said it only placed wiretaps in cases involving kidnapping, "white slavery,"[13] and national security. Even in the face of such limited use, in 1934 Congress passed the Federal Communications Act, which banned wiretapping entirely.

Gentry reports that while the Bureau did not use wiretapping extensively, it still "simply ignored the ban,"[14] maintaining that, while the act prohibited the disclosure of material gained through a wiretap, the actual tapping itself could proceed.

But, in 1939, the Supreme Court slammed the door on such slicing and dicing of the statute's intent and ruled that nothing obtained in or through a wiretap could be used by investigative agencies. Even leads generated by the information gleaned from taps were "the fruits of the poisonous tree," in the words of Justice Felix Frankfurter in *Nardone v. United States*.[15]

His wrist slapped by the Court, Hoover announced that the FBI would no longer wiretap, declaring piously—and publicly—"I do not wish to be the head of an organization of potential blackmailers."[16]

But privately, Hoover worked feverishly to undermine the Court ruling. He complained to Secretary of the Treasury Henry Morgenthau, FDR's close friend and Duchess County neighbor, saying that the wiretap restriction was stopping him from catching Nazi spies. Morgenthau, the most prominent Jewish supporter of the president, was particularly hawkish when it came to the Nazis. He got Roosevelt to direct his attorney general to ignore the poisonous tree ruling. FDR said that while he personally agreed with the Court, he felt it could never have intended to deny the use of wiretaps in national security cases.

Hoover walked through the door FDR had opened and the use of wiretaps became ubiquitous. In fact, Hoover's new boss, Attorney General Robert Jackson, who took over in 1940, after his predecessor Frank Murphy joined the Supreme Court, didn't even want to know whose phones Hoover was tapping, or when or why. Hoover, in a memorandum to his files, wrote: "The Attorney General decided that he would have no detailed record kept concerning the cases in which wiretapping was utilized. It was agreeable to him that I maintain a memorandum book in my immediate office, listing the time, places and cases in which this procedure is to be utilized."[17]

Bullied by Roosevelt, Jackson now wrote the House Judiciary Committee to say that he interpreted the 1934 Federal Communications Act to read that it was only illegal to divulge a tapped conversation to the public, but that the tap itself was permitted.

From then on, wiretapping was rampant.

And then, suddenly, in the first month of his fourth term as president, Franklin D. Roosevelt died. His successor, Harry S. Truman, had a long-standing bias against J. Edgar Hoover.

Truman felt that Hoover had gotten "too big for his britches" and did not like the idea of "building up a Gestapo."[18] But what really turned Truman off was that Hoover would spy on the sex lives of congressmen and senators.

Hoover's easy relationship with FDR had clearly spoiled him. He became accustomed to hearing the president inveigh in public about the right to privacy and hold out his hand—under the table and in private—for the latest gossip from his FBI director.

But Truman was not the soft touch that FDR had been. From his first days in office, Truman tried to rein in the FBI and its director, banning them from overseas operations and closely limiting their ability to snoop on Americans.

Hoover didn't like his new boss and, as the election of 1948 came around, was determined to do his bit to defeat Truman.

In 1940, Hoover had refused FDR's request to dig up dirt on Willkie, then the Republican nominee, but by 1948 Hoover had had a change of heart. Now that it was not a request from the president but a matter of self-preservation in the bureaucratic wars of Washington, Hoover was willing to do what it took to keep power.

He began a secret liaison with the 1948 GOP nominee, Governor Thomas E. Dewey of New York.

Gentry writes that Hoover negotiated a deal with Dewey under which, if Dewey won, Hoover would be appointed attorney general and, when a vacancy occurred, go on the Supreme Court, he hoped, as chief justice.

But before Dewey could grapple with Truman in the general election, he faced Minnesota's "boy governor" Harold E. Stassen in the Republican primaries.

As their contest got into high gear, the pair faced a crucial national radio debate (in the pre-television era) on May 17, 1948. Hoover scoured the landscape for any derogatory material he could find on Stassen. One

FBI agent recalled: "many agents—I was one—worked for days culling FBI files for any fact which could be of use to Dewey. I remember that there was such a rush to get the material to him once it was collected that it was sent in a private plane to Albany [where Governor Dewey lived]. . . . Armed with everything the Bureau gave him [Governor Dewey] demolished Stassen when they met. . . . Dewey got the nomination and Hoover started planning his move to the attorney general's office."[19]

In the general election, Hoover ratcheted up his political activity, sending Dewey reams of negative material on Hoover's boss, President Truman. The negatives focused particularly on the president's personal aide, Brigadier General Harry Vaughan, revealing that Vaughan had taken gifts from people seeking favor at the White House. The *Washington Post* explained in Vaughan's obituary that he "had accepted a deep freezer costing $520 from persons interested in expediting the freeing of some European oil from war-time regulations."[20] The resulting scandal was one of the most important in the Truman presidency. With Vaughan refusing to resign and denying any wrongdoing and Truman too loyal to the former general to fire him, the affair bedeviled the president for years. (In 1952, corruption loomed large in the Republican attack on Truman, much of the fodder coming from Hoover's investigation of Vaughan in 1948.)

Truman ultimately beat Dewey, despite the best efforts of the FBI. However, under Hoover, in 1948, the FBI had an active, if covert, part in the presidential elections, though it was but a pale precursor of the role it was to play in the election of 2016.

THE BIRTH OF THE CIA

While Hoover was expanding the FBI's reach within American borders, a new intelligence network aimed at America's overseas enemies was growing in the nurturing heat of World War II.

Back then, America's thinking was still dominated by the dictum of its newly appointed secretary of war, Henry Stimson, against gentlemen opening one another's mail.

But, facing the wartime emergency, FDR realized that without an intelligence service, America was vulnerable. When the United States failed to anticipate the Japanese attack on Pearl Harbor—despite having broken Japan's code—the danger was even more obvious.

So FDR set up the Office of Strategic Services (OSS) under General William J. Donovan to handle wartime spying operations. Donovan, a romantic figure, became a legend as he parachuted agents behind enemy lines and kept the resistance in Nazi-occupied territories supplied with weapons and necessities.

But as the war came to an end in August 1945 and the OSS began to dissolve, Donovan saw the need to continue a U.S. intelligence operation abroad, writing to President Harry Truman that "all major powers except the United States have had for a long time past permanent worldwide intelligence services, reporting directly to the highest echelons of their Government." But, Donovan noted, "prior to the present war, the United States had no foreign secret intelligence service. It never has had and does not now have a coordinated intelligence system."[21]

During the war, most Americans saw the Soviet Union, as well as its dictator Joseph Stalin, as an ally, teaming up with the United States to defeat Hitler. With the huge casualties on the Russian front, most Americans held their breath, hoping that Russia would prevail.

But, after the war, there was a sudden and harsh denouement as America came to realize that Stalin, whom FDR had affectionately called "Uncle Joe," was no avuncular figure but a rabid dictator intent on the conquest of all of Europe.

And, when Winston S. Churchill declared in his famous 1946 speech in Fulton, Missouri, that "an iron curtain" had descended across the middle of Europe, Americans woke up to the need to battle in what came to be known as the Cold War.[22]

Everyone agreed that we needed a new intelligence service that would operate overseas—the FBI was limited to domestic activity. But the question loomed: Who would head it?

The obvious candidate was General Donovan, based on his successes in World War II. But Hoover saw the general as a mortal threat and set about to bring him down.

He planted news stories extolling the FBI's efforts to win the war and belittling those of the OSS. Hoover:

- peddled the fiction that war heroes Matthew Nimitz and Douglas MacArthur didn't trust the OSS;
- charged that the OSS was filled with communists; and
- got the FBI's budget increased to $43 million, and slashed the OSS outlay to only $24 million.

Hoover's final triumph was in persuading Truman to fire Donovan—which Truman did—saying that the OSS would "not be needed in time of peace."[23]

But it clearly was. As the Cold War replaced the hot one, the need for a global intelligence service became obvious to all of Capitol Hill.

But Harry Truman was determined to head off Hoover's efforts to expand his role to foreign espionage. On September 5, 1945—a month after Japan's surrender, Truman said that he intended to limit the FBI's activities to the United States. Six months later, the president moved to fill the void left by the end of the OSS. On January 22, 1946, Truman signed an executive order establishing the National Intelligence Authority (forerunner of the National Security Council) and the Central Intelligence Group (precursor of the Central Intelligence Agency).

Hoover and his FBI were cut out of both new agencies. As far as international intelligence gathering, J. Edgar was out in the cold.

The formal birth of the Central Intelligence Agency came on July 26, 1947, when Truman signed the National Security Act of 1947. In addition to creating the Defense Department under a cabinet secretary (replacing the old War and Navy departments), establishing the Air Force as a separate service, and creating the National Security Council, it gave birth to the CIA. The six paragraphs that established the Agency authorized it, as expected, to "evaluate, correlate, and disseminate departmental intelligence."[24]

But it also said the Agency could perform "other functions and duties related to intelligence affecting the national security."[25]

An eleven-word loophole through which skillful bureaucrats and their lawyers could drive a truck!

At the start, the CIA was, simply enough, a vehicle to keep the president informed of developments throughout the world. But it became so much more—virtually a state within a nation—referred to by many as the "deep state."[26]

The pains of bureaucratic childbirth that attended the CIA's creation were both acute and chronic. The Pentagon and the State Department did not like the new kid on the block and tried to cut it down at every juncture whenever an opportunity presented itself.

The infant CIA had no formal charter and received no congressional appropriations. In fact, at the beginning this orphan agency had to depend on small appropriations put together by its supporters in Congress.

Dean Acheson, about to be appointed secretary of state, said he "had the gravest forebodings about this organization [the CIA]." He "warned the President that as set up neither he, the National Security Council, nor anyone else would be in a position to know what it was doing or to control it."[27]

But, as the Cold War escalated, the need for the CIA increased, and its funding, staffing, and operations expanded exponentially.

In the process, it acquired all the abilities and each of the techniques that it would later use to try to sabotage Donald J. Trump when the time came. The first of these black op skills was covert action.

THE CIA MOVES INTO COVERT ACTION

The military was not enthusiastic about the emergence of an intelligence establishment. Their vision of what intel should entail was sharply limited. In 1945, the Joint Chiefs of Staff had called for a new intelligence agency. But it was designed to serve their needs, not those of the White House. They wanted to save themselves time and effort by having an intelligence organization that could boil down information gathered by military attachés and ambassadors. They pictured an agency made up of mid-level officers.

For his part, Truman didn't really know what he wanted from an intelligence service either. He, too, wanted only a summary of foreign developments so he wouldn't have to go through the cables himself.

How quaint!

But it became clear that neither the military nor the president understood either the ferocity or the secrecy with which the Cold War was about to be waged. Those that did had a far more expansive view of intelligence gathering and believed in taking the offensive through secretive, quasi-military action.

Despite Truman's reticence about the Agency's activities, the CIA did manage to conduct eighty-one covert operations during his presidency.

But it was during the regime of Truman's successor, Dwight D. Eisenhower, that the CIA mushroomed into the power it became.

Two events just prior to Eisenhower's inauguration in 1953 shaped his opinion that the CIA had a major place in American foreign policy.

One was the advent of the atomic bomb. As a general, Eisenhower appreciated the difficulty in containing a conventional war once it had started and considered the risk of it escalating into a nuclear war to be very grave. When the Soviets acquired the bomb in 1949, it became clear that a new global conflict could never again happen. There could be no World War III. Churchill, as always, said it best, warning that "If you go on with this nuclear arms race, all you are going to do is make the rubble bounce."[28]

The other event was the Korean War. Begun in 1950 when North Korea—and later China—invaded South Korea, the war's casualties were horrific: 36,574 Americans were killed and 7,800 more unaccounted for.

Particularly galling to domestic American morale was the casualty creep after the battlefront had stabilized in July 1951, one year into the war. The fighting dragged on for two more years with little shift in the demarcation line separating the two forces. In those bloody years, almost half of the ultimate total of American dead lost their lives. The drip-drip-drip of deaths frustrated and enraged Americans.

A country that had accepted massive casualties in World War II seemed now to grow restive as the death toll mounted. We were not the same people who absorbed 20,000 deaths in the three-month battle for Okinawa and 7,000 dead in the seven-week battle on Iwo Jima, both in 1945, without a murmur of dissent.

The Korean War deaths brought a storm of protest, which, while it fell short of the massive anger against the Vietnam War, still indicated that Americans would not accept huge casualties.

Czechoslovakia had gone communist through a coup d'etat in 1948 and China had fallen in 1949; a red tide seemed to be engulfing the world. Yet, knowing that conventional war was politically risky if it meant big casualties, and concerned that it might escalate into a nuclear conflict, Eisenhower cast about for a way to stem the global tide of communist expansion.

To fight this expansion and, if possible, to roll it back, Eisenhower chose to use covert action through the CIA.

The implementation of this foreign policy was left to two brothers—John Foster Dulles and Allen Dulles. The former became secretary of state and the latter took over the CIA. During the fifties, this tandem orchestrated regime change in Iran, Guatemala, and Guyana and tried to do so in seven other countries, including Albania, East Germany, Costa Rica, Syria, Egypt, Indonesia, and, of course, Cuba.

While the coup in Iran, in particular, may have stopped communist encroachment in a vital country, the CIA's intervention in toppling a popularly elected regime certainly laid the basis for the overt hostility between the United States and Iran that prevails today.

Perhaps more perniciously, the CIA, under the Dulles brothers, came to function as a virtual international political party, intervening routinely in foreign elections, particularly those in Western Europe, where communists threatened to achieve power democratically.

The Agency supported and funded German chancellor Willy Brandt, French prime minister Guy Mollet, and the entire Christian Democratic Party in Italy, spending tens of millions of dollars to influence politics throughout those countries.

Thomas Fina, the U.S. consul general in Milan in the seventies, described the process of subsidizing Italian politics. He said the CIA worked daily to move money around as it suited their policy goals. Cooperating parties got money. Those who showed a streak of independence found their bank accounts depleted.

The Agency also helped friendly book publishers, newspapers, and even individual journalists with money and political help. And behind it all remained the capacity to use the information the CIA was amassing to blackmail politicians and force them into line.

Former CIA director Richard Helms explained that, "There have been numerous instances when, facing the threat of a Communist Party or popular front election victory in the Free World, we have met the threat and turned it successfully." Helms said that "Guyana in 1963 and Chile in 1964 are good examples of what can be accomplished under difficult circumstances." The CIA chief warned that "similar situations may soon face us in various parts of the world, and we are prepared for action with carefully planned covert election programs."[29]

This blurring of the line between fighting communist tyranny and trying to stop red victories in democratic elections reared its head again and again as the sixties and seventies unfolded.

In the late 1960s and the first half of the seventies, the tag team of the Dulles brothers was replaced by a new duo—President Richard

M. Nixon and his national security advisor and then secretary of state Henry Kissinger.

While both men were secretive and manipulative, their personalities could not have been more different. Kissinger was an affable extrovert who charmed his victims while Nixon was a sullen, private man who saw the rest of the world with thinly veiled hostility.

Together, they agreed that they would run covert operations for their own political purposes. Nixon made the White House an impenetrable political redoubt. Kissinger, who was nominally initially only the national security advisor, used intelligence to become the de facto secretary of state, shunting aside the hapless William Rogers, who formally held the office (until Kissinger replaced him officially in 1973, serving until 1977).

Kissinger ran the CIA with an iron hand, just as Allen Dulles had. Three-quarters of the covert operations it conducted were the product of his sole decision, as he ignored the more formal committee-based decision-making process. Under Nixon and then under President Gerald R. Ford, the CIA was Kissinger's private fiefdom.

Implicit in the CIA operating doctrine was the assumption that the U.S. government knew better than regular civilians, both foreign and American, about who should be in positions of power.

This core institutional arrogance was on full display in 2016 when Donald Trump beat Hillary Clinton. The results were contrary to the will of the intelligence community. The electorate had erred, and the intelligence people needed to make it right.

Similarly, the CIA does not scruple to reverse the democratic verdict of foreign electorates. Historian and critic of U.S. foreign policy William Blum estimates that the American government has tried to topple governments in over sixty countries since World War II.[30]

The CIA was at its worst when it sought to reverse the will of the voters and topple a democratically elected government. The poster child for this kind of action was Chile.

This South American country had a long democratic tradition. Since 1932, elections had determined who led the nation without military intervention. But, in 1970, leftist Salvador Allende was moving ahead in the polls as election day in September approached.

The United States had blocked Allende in the previous elections of 1964 when he seemed likely to win. Back then, Presidents Kennedy and then Johnson approved a covert plan to defeat Allende. "Declassified documents show that from 1962 through 1964, the CIA spent a total of $2.6 million to finance the campaign of Eduardo Frei and spent $3 million in anti-Allende propaganda 'to scare voters away' from Allende's FRAP coalition."[31]

The money subsidized efforts to turn out Frei's vote and involved a massive distribution of cash. The Agency also put up the money for efforts by the Vatican to defeat Allende, working through churches and unions. The CIA also began a long-term effort to turn the military, normally above politics, and the national police against a possible Allende regime.

It worked. Allende lost the election of 1964. Now President Nixon and Kissinger had to figure out how to stop Allende again in 1970.

The option of letting the country plot its own destiny seems not to have occurred to them. The specter of Cuba lurked before Nixon and Kissinger and their fear of another communist dictatorship in South America was palpable.

But it was nonsense. Chile had a long democratic heritage and an army that was protective of it. There was not the massive discontent that forty years of dictatorial rule had spawned in Cuba, and it was unlikely that Allende would have become another Castro.

In Chile, President Frei could not run again. Allende's two main opponents were Christian Democrat Radomiro Tomic and pro-American right-winger Jorge Alessandri.

Facing the "loss" of Chile to the communists, Kissinger approved almost $2 million to stop it from happening. The CIA spoon-fed reports with anti-Allende propaganda. An in-house Agency report commented:

"Particularly noteworthy in this connection was the *Time* cover story which owed a great deal to written materials provided by CIA."[32]

Richard Helms recalls that in Chile, "posters were printed, news stories planted, editorial comment encouraged, rumors whispered, leaflets strewn, and pamphlets distributed . . . to show that an Allende victory risked the destruction of Chilean democracy."[33]

But, this time, the CIA's covert operations didn't work, and, on September 4, 1970, Allende won the three-way election by a 1.5 percent margin.

After losing at the ballot box, the CIA tried to oust Allende by force through a coup d'etat. The coup failed and the leftist seemed firmly ensconced in office.

Nixon and Kissinger were furious with the CIA's failure. General Alexander Haig, Kissinger's deputy, said that CIA officers undermined the coup because of an attack of conscience. Haig wrote that these political misgivings "flavor[ed] their final assessments and their proposals for remedial action in the covert area." Haig called for a purge of "the key left-wing dominated slots under [CIA Director] Helms."[34] He also called for "a major overhauling of the means, the attitude, and the conceptual basis on which CIA's covert programs should be carried out."[35]

Nixon told his budget director George P. Shultz to slice the CIA budget in half.

But Nixon and Kissinger were determined to mount a coup and were not to be deterred either by the voters of Chile or by their own failure to topple Allende after his election.

With Nixon's budgetary axe hanging over its head, the CIA came to feel that its very existence depended on success in Chile.

To stage the coup, the CIA "built a web of military men and political saboteurs who sought to shift the Chilean military off its constitutional foundation" to get it to oust Allende.[36]

Reacting to the incessant efforts of the CIA to topple him, President Allende created his own military force, Grupo de Amigos del Presidente (Friends of the President). With support from Cuba's communist leader Fidel Castro, Allende intended to stake his fortunes not on the institutional integrity of his military, but on his own paramilitary force.

Finally, the military felt threatened and resolved to oust Allende.

Three years after Allende's election, the CIA case officer in Chile alerted Kissinger that a coup was in the works. His request for immediate aid was answered and funds were sent.

Allende met his end on September 11, 1973. Trapped in the presidential palace and his fate sealed, Allende reportedly killed himself.

General Augusto Pinochet seized power that very day. "Pinochet reigned with cruelty, murdering more than 3,200 people, jailing and torturing tens of thousands in the repression called the Caravan of Death."[37]

But the CIA wasn't through yet.

Pinochet's intelligence chief, Colonel Manuel Contreras, joined the CIA as an agent. And, operating on American soil, he assassinated Orlando Letelier, Allende's ambassador to the United States, and his aide Ronni Moffitt, killed by a car bomb fourteen blocks from the White House.

The end product of the CIA intervention in Chile was a decade of military rule throughout South America.

In Argentina, 22,000 people were killed or disappeared as the military regime sought to perpetuate itself in power.

In Brazil, a dictatorship replaced a democracy throughout the seventies.

The ripple effect of the CIA intervention was widespread. It was not until the eighties that the momentum for self-government and democracy was rekindled.

While Americans, as a whole, are inclined to see the judgment of the electorate as final—and perhaps even sacred—the men and women of the CIA came to have a totally different worldview. Elections, in their emerging dogma, conferred no more legitimacy than coups or monarchic birth. They were snapshots of public opinion that could be reversed or even totally disregarded.

And, increasingly, this was how they came to elections in their home country—the United States of America.

THE CIA TURNS ITS MALICIOUS SKILLS ON AMERICANS

The single most important restraint imposed on the CIA from its inception was the prohibition against operating within U.S. borders. The FBI was charged with stopping domestic espionage and sabotage and Hoover did not welcome another agency horning in on his turf.

But the niceties of limiting the CIA to foreign activity ended in the maelstrom of domestic dissent ushered in by the war in Vietnam. Protests spread around the country and focused increasingly on opposition not only to President Lyndon B. Johnson's policies, but also to the man himself.

As casualties mounted and anti-war sentiment raged, crowds surrounded the White House, taunting the vain and embattled president by singing, "Hey, hey, LBJ, how many kids did you kill today?"

And, when the paranoid Richard Nixon succeeded Johnson, the White House grew even more prickly amid the mounting tide of criticism.

Soon the cry went out to the FBI and the CIA to work on quelling domestic dissent.

The FBI had worked for decades in monitoring leftist activity in the United States. But now, at the height of the Cold War, the CIA joined in, violating the most fundamental restriction in its charter.

In 1967 the leftist magazine *Ramparts* broke the story that the National Student Association, a worldwide organization of college students, had been on the CIA dole for years. As the scandal spread, evidence emerged that the CIA had infiltrated an entire range of domestic voluntary organizations. The CIA headquarters warned the White House, as the storm was about to break, that a scandal was imminent over "CIA involvement with . . . private voluntary organizations . . . The CIA will probably be accused of improperly interfering in domestic affairs, and of manipulating and endangering innocent young people. The Administration will probably come under attack."[38]

And the prediction proved prescient. A massive outpouring of condemnation showered the Agency. Much of the CIA's secret work, going back to the fifties, was now open for public viewing.

The fact that the CIA had been funding such nominally independent organizations as Radio Free Europe, Radio Liberty, and the Congress for Cultural Freedom came as a shock to a nation that had long been told that the CIA did not operate domestically. Even the venerable Ford Foundation turned out to be a conduit for CIA money.

The magazine that exposed the CIA—*Ramparts*—had itself been under investigation by the Agency for years, as the CIA monitored the personal lives of its staff. In fact, nobody really was able to keep track of the domestic operations of the CIA. More than three hundred major covert operations had been authorized by the Agency since 1961. It was out of control.

The escalation of the Vietnam War and the rising student opposition, however, created ever more demand from the political powers for greater covert spying on Americans, even as the CIA's past activities were being exposed.

On October 21, 1967, the National Mobilization Committee to End the War in Vietnam sponsored a march on Washington that drew 100,000 people.

His suspicions fanned by sycophantic aides, President Johnson came to believe that the peace movement was a creature of Russia and China, funded and controlled from Moscow and Beijing. The president ordered Richard Helms, the CIA director, to prove his supposition.

When Helms objected that the CIA was barred from spying on Americans, the president responded, "I'm quite aware of that. What I want for you is to pursue this matter, and to do what is necessary to track down the foreign Communists who are behind this intolerable interference in our domestic affairs."[39] But it was Lyndon Johnson, not the communists, who was intolerably interfering in American domestic affairs by ordering the CIA to spy on Americans in a clear violation of its founding charter. The CIA found no evidence that the student movement was being directed or funded from abroad.

The code name for this illegal domestic surveillance operation was, quite simply, "Chaos." For seven years, agency personnel "grew their hair long, learned the jargon of the New Left, and went off to infiltrate peace groups in the United States and Europe."[40]

Ultimately, the CIA compiled a list of 300,000 people who participated in these supposedly subversive groups; 7,200 American citizens came in for special investigation.

Sometimes the results of this clandestine surveillance bordered on the ridiculous. The CIA claimed that "the students (agents) were [being] infiltrated into the United States" to conduct "subversive activities against the United States" including "sabotage in connection with race riots." One contingent was to be "infiltrated into the U.S. from Canada through Calais, Maine."[41]

Johnson had a fit. "I'm not going to let the Communists take this government and they're doing it right now," he screamed at Helms and secretaries of state and defense Dean Rusk and Robert McNamara. "I've got my belly full of seeing these people put on a Communist plane and shipped all over this country. I want someone to carefully look at who leaves this country, where they go, why they are going."[42]

Ultimately, Helms had to report to the president, on November 15, 1967, two weeks later, that there was no evidence that anti-war leaders were acting under any outside direction. Not Russia. Not Cuba. No foreign involvement.

All the president's paranoia had done was to virtually eliminate the line between foreign and domestic spying at the CIA, a precursor of the seamless integration of its efforts with those of other intelligence agencies to influence the 2016 elections and destabilize the eventual winner.

When Nixon and Kissinger took over in early 1969, the surveillance of Americans increased.

This time, Kissinger was not just seeking out foreign sources of support for the anti-war movement, but was also directing the CIA to begin amassing files on ordinary American citizens. The Rubicon had been crossed.

Under Nixon, the CIA became part of the president's defense against domestic political opponents, an unprecedented corruption of the Agency's mandate and charter.

Abbot Smith, head of the CIA's Office of National Estimates under Nixon, said this "was really the first one [presidency] in which intelligence was just another form of politics. And that was bound to be disastrous, and I think it was disastrous."[43]

That quote by Smith has proven to be prescient—that intelligence can be "just another form of politics." That is exactly what the CIA has come to represent over the decades and that ethic has spread throughout the intelligence community.

Initially, the "politics" was in other countries, where the CIA's role in supplying funds, equipment, and propaganda in support of favored candidates and parties became our modus operandi in fighting the Cold War.

Then it spread to domestic politics, where, in combination with the FBI, the CIA targeted domestic dissenters, undermining their credibility, tapping their phones, and smearing their leaders.

Finally, this expansion of the concept of intelligence jumped the final chasm and made it a tool to win domestic elections in the United States. The CIA began digging up dirt on opposing candidates or tipping the scales in the media and then moved to manipulating intelligence and selectively leaking to try to determine the next president.

It was a straight-line progression involving both the CIA and the FBI and culminating in their ultimate effort: to remove and discredit a sitting U.S. president—Donald Trump.

MEANWHILE, THE FBI INCREASES ITS DOMESTIC SURVEILLANCE

While its Washington, DC, rival, the CIA, was turning its electronic and espionage skills on its fellow Americans, Hoover's FBI was coming to use its investigations as a way to gain the upper hand in Washington's internal bureaucratic wars.

Throughout the sixties the FBI went on a rampage of wiretapping with special focus on using wiretaps and the dirt they collected to influence politicians and protect the FBI's budget and Hoover personally. William Sullivan, former head of intelligence for the FBI, described how the process worked: "The moment [Hoover] would get something on a senator . . . he'd send one of the errand boys up and advise the senator that 'we're in the course of an investigation and we by chance happened to come up with this data on your daughter. But we wanted you to know this; we realize you'd want to know it.' Well, Jesus, what does that tell the senator? From that time on, the senator's right in his pocket."[44]

Hoover and his successors amassed approximately 135 files on individuals, mainly politicians. Among those having the honor of inclusion in Hoover's net were seventeen current or former members of Congress, including John F. Kennedy, Harry S Truman, Edward M. Kennedy, George S. McGovern, Richard M. Nixon, Majority Leader Mike Mansfield, Speaker Carl Albert, and Congressman Hale Boggs.

And the files were not only amassed but distributed, illegally, to others in the government and leaked to the media. FBI materials on at least eleven members of Congress have been proven to have been distributed outside the FBI. The files "contained considerable derogatory information furnished by [the FBI] Washington Field Office on a variety of matters and individuals including members of Congress," an investigation found.[45]

Hoover used his files to keep John F. Kennedy under control throughout the man's entire political life. The process began when JFK was a young man in the early days of World War II.

JFK, always the most susceptible of bachelors, became involved with Inga Arvad, the "Beauty Queen of Denmark." At age 28, she was quite a catch, but it was JFK who bit—hook, line, and sinker.

Hoover had had Inga in his sights for some time. She had attended the wedding of a German friend and socialized with Adolf Hitler and Hermann Göring. Then she had interviewed the German dictator twice for a Danish magazine.

Tipped off, Hoover put her under surveillance, tapping her phone and bugging her room. The taps confirmed that she was a spy and was having a torrid affair with JFK, whose father, Joseph P. Kennedy, was the U.S. ambassador to Britain. It turned out that Hitler wanted to learn all he could about FDR's instructions to his ambassador.

Hoover, a close friend and political ally of Joe Kennedy, briefed the ambassador on the situation. The tapes confirmed that JFK had no idea of Arvad's secret life; Joe told Jack to cut the affair off and he did so. To be sure there was no backsliding, Joe had Navy under secretary James V. Forrestal assign Lieutenant Kennedy to the South Pacific.

That's where JFK became a war hero.

After Kennedy became president, Hoover continued to keep watch over him, even though he was now the director's boss. And, more to the point, John Kennedy appointed his brother Robert to be the attorney general, to whom Hoover had to report.

Hoover kept JFK and many of his appointees under surveillance. At one point, he reported to the president that one of his ambassadors was seen fleeing from a bedroom at a motel in Maryland. Asked what he was going to do about it, Kennedy said, "From now on, I'm going to appoint faster ambassadors."[46]

But more important, Hoover again found evidence that the president was embroiled in a romance that could compromise him. Kennedy, married by now, was seeing Judith Campbell Exner, a twenty-five-year-old who was also seeing mob boss Sam Giancana. Not only did the liaison threaten the integrity of the Department of Justice's investigation of the mobster, but it also threatened to uncover the administration's efforts to kill Cuban dictator Fidel Castro. Giancana had enlisted with the CIA to try to assassinate Castro.

The FBI's most outrageous wiretap during that turbulent decade was aimed at civil rights leader Rev. Dr. Martin Luther King, Jr.

Hoover, raised in the South, was deeply racist. In 1965, he told an audience of newspaper editors, supposedly off the record, that colored people are "quite ignorant, mostly uneducated, and I doubt if they would seek an education if they had an opportunity." "Many who have the right to register [to vote] very seldom do register." Only in "due time" can they "gain the acceptance which is necessary and rights equal to those of the white citizens of their community."[47]

As the civil rights movement gripped America and King's prestige soared, Hoover conceived an abiding personal hatred of the black leader. When King won the Nobel Peace Prize in 1964, Hoover went nuts.

He pestered Bobby Kennedy, still attorney general even after his brother's death the year before, to authorize surveillance of King. Known to be sexually promiscuous, King was a luscious target for Hoover.

The FBI had been sniffing around King for years. In 1961, it discovered that attorney Stanley Levison and Jack O'Dell, two close associates of the reverend, were members of the U.S. Communist Party even as they served on his staff at the Southern Christian Leadership Conference.

Hoover warned the president, who was at that point strongly supporting landmark civil rights legislation. Exposure of King's communist staffers could have had a very detrimental effect. On June 22, 1963, prompted by Hoover's information, JFK warned King to drop the two staffers, but the civil rights leader refused, which prompted the attorney general—Robert Kennedy—to suggest that King should be wiretapped. But, when warned by his staff to consider the political backlash that would follow any disclosure that King was being tapped, Kennedy wavered on authorizing the taps. Finally, after much debate, the wiretaps were installed on October 21, 1964. Kennedy agreed to the taps on King for a trial period of thirty days. But nobody moved to end the taps when the thirty days expired, and they remained in place until 1965.

They found nothing compromising about King except the confirmation of his adultery. Consumed by hatred for King, Hoover ordered the tapes of a King orgy to be sent to his home in the mail, to arrive when the reverend would not be home but his wife would be. Hoover hoped she would open the mail.

And, to twist the knife, the FBI enclosed a letter that in effect urged him to commit suicide. "King, look into your heart," the letter said. "You know you are a complete fraud and a great liability to all of us Negroes. . . . King, there is only one thing left for you to do. You know what it is. You have just 34 days in which to do it. . . . There is but one way out for you. You better take it before your filthy, abnormal fraudulent self is bared to the nation."[48]

In between venting his personal vendettas, Hoover found time to be useful politically in helping to elect yet another American president.

When Lyndon B. Johnson succeeded to the presidency after JFK's murder, many civil rights advocates were concerned that the former senator from Texas would have little empathy for the civil rights of black people. In retrospect, considering Johnson's extraordinary accomplishments in ending legal racial discrimination, this fear appears far-fetched, but, at the time, it seemed quite rational and loomed as a real obstacle to Johnson's election to a full term in 1964.

As the Democratic National Convention approached in the summer of 1964, Mississippi civil rights groups formed a slate of alternate delegates to replace the all-white "Dixiecrats."

The issue festered and became a flash point as the convention convened, forcing Johnson to choose between the black civil rights groups and the white southern Democratic Party establishment that still controlled the politics of all eleven states of the old Confederacy. (Blacks were largely denied the vote in those states.) This was a big problem, and he looked to Hoover to solve it.

The director, always happy to do dirty work for a president, happily agreed. Kessler describes how Cartha DeLoach, number three at the FBI, "sent a team of thirty agents to the convention and sent back forty-four pages of reports to Johnson informing him of any plans to try to deny him the nomination for president." On August 29, 1964, DeLoach reported that he had successfully completed the assignment, using informants, wiretaps, bugs, and FBI agents posing as reporters. "Through our counterintelligence efforts," DeLoach wrote, "the FBI was able to advise the president in advance regarding major plans of the MFDP delegates,"[49] information that was vital to the president in handling the crisis.

In the end, the civil rights delegates did not get seated, adding to the momentum that led to the passage of the Voting Rights Act of 1965.

While the tales of Hoover's wiretaps make lurid reading, their permanent importance was that they established the tradition and precedent of the FBI meddling in domestic American politics. Whether used for digging up dirt on Truman in 1948, saving Kennedy from himself in the sixties, or keeping files on anti-war protesters in the late sixties and early seventies, FBI surveillance came to be an essential part of any president's political survival.

As Richard Nixon succeeded Johnson in 1969, it was becoming evident that Hoover was getting older and more risk averse. When secret American bombing raids in Cambodia—an escalation of the war in Vietnam—were uncovered by the media, Nixon, as usual, ordered the FBI to investigate the leak. And again, in 1971, when the Pentagon Papers—a secret history of the war in Vietnam that the Defense Department had commissioned—were leaked to the news media, Nixon was on the phone to Hoover demanding an investigation.

But, both times, Hoover proved unwilling to do the president's bidding. His obstinacy enraged Nixon and led directly to the formation of the Plumbers Unit, a White House–directed squad designed to find who was leaking to the media. Nixon turned to the Plumbers Unit—not the FBI—to come up with dirt on Daniel Ellsberg, one of the authors of the Pentagon Papers, who had leaked it to the press.

The Plumbers broke into the offices of Ellsberg's psychiatrist and rifled through his files for compromising material.

As more and more skullduggery, once farmed out to Hoover, came to be planned and executed in the White House itself, the presidency became more vulnerable.

When Hoover finally passed away in his sleep on May 2, 1972, Nixon appointed L. Patrick Gray to succeed him. But Gray, who was derided by the Bureau staff for his fabled three-day Tuesday to Thursday workweek, was not the hard charger that Hoover was. And, when the Nixon White House needed someone to carry out its ultimate black box operation—the bugging of the Democratic National Committee Headquarters in the Watergate building complex—it could not turn to the FBI and had to rely on retired CIA agents instead.

Eventually, the White House destroyed itself when its surveillance and obsession with secrecy led to the Watergate scandal. And, in the process, dragged down the CIA as well.

WATERGATE: HOW THE FBI DESTROYED THE CIA

The history of the Watergate scandal has been told and retold, but most of the stories are from before a crucial element became known: the identity of the secretive Deep Throat. It was he who guided *Washington Post* reporters Bob Woodward and Carl Bernstein on their search for the true story that lay behind the apparent facts. Deep Throat was like the lovable lion Aslan in the Narnia chronicles, shepherding the reporters through the wilderness of Watergate, correcting them when they took wrong turns, and counseling them, famously, to "follow the money" to arrive at the truth. But for three decades his identity was hidden from history.

For over thirty years, Deep Throat was known only as a part of the FBI bureaucracy, a man stricken by his conscience who felt disgusted by the tactics of the Nixon White House. In 2005, it was revealed who Deep Throat really was.

His name was Mark Felt. He had worked at the FBI for decades, retiring as the Bureau's deputy director in 1973. Felt's power was second only to that of Hoover himself and, after Hoover's death, to that of the new director, L. Patrick Gray.

But Felt was much more than that. As Hoover became more dysfunctional at the end of his life and Gray proved to be weak and incompetent, it was Felt who really came to run the Bureau. The Bureau had been forced to recognize its limits and had even begun refusing Nixon's requests to investigate leaks, tap reporters' phones, and burglarize the offices of Daniel Ellsberg's psychiatrist. In contrast, it seemed that the CIA was a bunch of lawless cowboys capable of anything. Determined not to be typed with the CIA, the FBI leaders grew increasingly determined to draw a contrast between the two agencies.

So Deep Throat was no lucky find for the intrepid *Post* reporters. He was part of a deliberate effort by the FBI to distance itself from its crosstown rival, the CIA.

In private conversations with Bob Woodward, Mark Felt revealed that he never liked Nixon, calling his White House "corrupt." The journalist writes that "there is little doubt Felt thought the Nixon team were Nazis. During this period [the late sixties and early seventies], he had to stop efforts by others in the bureau to 'identify every member of every hippie commune' in the Los Angeles area, for example, or to open a file on every member of Students for a Democratic Society."[50]

About a year before Hoover's death, Hoover promoted Felt to be the number three official at the Bureau. But with Hoover on his last legs and the director's number two man (and lover) Clyde Tolson ill, it was increasingly Felt's show to run.

The Watergate saga began on Saturday, June 17, 1972, when it was reported that five men in business suits, carrying $100 bills and eavesdropping equipment, had been arrested at the Democratic National Committee headquarters at the Watergate office building complex in DC.

As Woodward dug further, he learned that two of the burglars had the phone number of E. Howard Hunt in their personal address books. From there, Woodward was able to learn that Hunt worked for the CIA.

Meanwhile, at the Agency, there was a hurried meeting of CIA brass two days after the Watergate break-in. Bill Colby, number three at the Agency, recalled that Director Richard Helms was concerned that since some of the burglars were former CIA employees, the Agency would be blamed. "The next morning, the *Washington Post* placed the responsibility for Watergate at the door of the Oval Office."[51]

Distrusting the FBI, Nixon told his chief of staff, H. R. Haldeman, to shut down any investigation by the Bureau and to get Vernon Walters, deputy director at the CIA, to come up with hush money to keep the burglars quiet.

The CIA refused and resisted Nixon's efforts to pin the blame for Watergate on the Agency. Director Helms later said that had he agreed to deliver the cash—$1 million—the CIA would have been destroyed. He predicted that not only would he have gone to jail, but that his beloved Agency's credibility would have been destroyed. He could not and would not do what Nixon wanted.

So, the CIA became the object of Nixon's wrath after Helms refused to take the rap for the Watergate break-in. Retaliating, Nixon fired Helms in November 1972, right after his re-election. Furious at Helms's refusal to play ball over Watergate, the president followed the recommendation of Henry Kissinger and replaced Helms with the more pliant James Schlesinger.

Nixon's orders to Schlesinger as he took over the CIA were blunt: "Get rid of the clowns. What use are they? They've got 40,000 people over there reading newspapers."[52]

It turned out that Helms's dismissal was the beginning of the end of the CIA. When Schlesinger took over, all hell broke loose. In office for only seventeen weeks, Schlesinger purged more than five hundred analysts and more than one thousand people from the clandestine service. Officers serving overseas received unsigned coded cables informing them that they were fired. In response, Schlesinger received anonymous death threats, and he added armed guards to his security detail.

But Schlesinger could not stem the Watergate tide. Its irresistible course led to not only the conviction of the burglars themselves, but also the indictment of forty government officials, including Attorney General John N. Mitchell, presidential counsel John W. Dean III, White House chief of staff H. R. Haldeman, and domestic policy advisor John Ehrlichman. Nixon himself was named as an unindicted coconspirator and eventually was pardoned by his successor, Gerald R. Ford.

The FBI covered itself with glory by leading the investigation of Nixon—and by guiding Woodward and Bernstein to make the resulting information public. Watergate was one of the FBI's finest hours.

When Nixon tried to suppress the FBI Watergate probe, the Bureau responded angrily and magnificently. Kessler writes how FBI assistant directors Bucky Walters and William Soyars both decided, on April 23, 1973, that they would resign if Director L. Patrick Gray implemented Nixon's requests to destroy files and evidence.

Unaware that their boss Mark Felt was supplying the *Washington Post* with detailed information on the progress of the investigation, Walters recounts that "I told Felt that I would not work for a director who had destroyed evidence in a case the FBI was investigating. I told him I would retire by the end of the day. I also told him I would ask the other assistant directors to do the same."[53]

When Walters rallied the other assistant directors, all of whom threatened to resign, Gray realized the jig was up and announced his own resignation.

Unnoticed, however, in the Watergate flap was the setting of a key new precedent. Until this scandal, the media had always played the role of exposer of off-the-shelf intelligence operations. The leadership of the intelligence community did its best to keep the fact of these operations from reporters and to mislead them when they happened upon the trail.

But this was a new situation. In Watergate, the FBI wanted the media to find out what it was discovering. As the media made progress in unraveling the administration's false leads, explanations, rationales, and outright lies, FBI Deputy Director Felt kept Woodward and Bernstein closely informed. No sooner did the FBI discover a key fact than it was relayed to the *Post* reporters for publication.

In Watergate, the media was an integral part of the intelligence community's operations. Indeed, one of the goals of Deputy Director Felt's work was to alert the public, through the news media, to what was going on.

This had never happened before. An agency of the government was in covert revolt against the president of the United States and worked through the media to bring him down. The cooperation between the *Washington Post* and the FBI on Watergate was seamless, and similar to the intelligence community's attempted takedown of Donald Trump in 2016. The playbook was written in Watergate.

During the tumultuous Watergate period, America was fortunate that at least one government agency—ironically the FBI—stood up for legality and the rule of law. Yet, as America survived its worst constitutional crisis since the Civil War, another dangerous precedent was being set. Nobody ever elected the FBI or the CIA. Yet each agency took it upon itself to decide if it would obey the orders of the man who was elected by the American people: Richard M. Nixon.

Forty-three years later, the successors to the leadership of the Agency and the Bureau would make a similar decision—to rebel against the leadership of Donald Trump.

CONGRESS STRIKES DOWN THE CIA

By 1975, the CIA had ventured so far from its original mandate to work only overseas—and had acted with such arrogance and ruthlessness there—that Congress had to step in and curb its activities.

The catalyst was the reporting of Pulitzer Prize–winner Seymour Hersh, who revealed that the CIA was indeed spying on American citizens—a no-no under its charter—simply because of their political views. The day after the Hersh story ran, Representative Robert W. Kastenmeier, a Wisconsin Democrat who was chairman of the House Judiciary Committee's Administration of Justice Subcommittee, said that the CIA practice was as "insidious as Watergate" and that he would conduct hearings on the subject.[54]

At the CIA, where James Schlesinger had succeeded Richard Helms, the new director was astonished at what he found on taking over. The Agency had totally overstepped its charter, conducting robust operations on American soil against U.S. citizens.

On May 9, 1973, Schlesinger ordered "all senior operating officials of this Agency to report to me immediately on any activities now going on, or that have gone on in the past, which might be construed to be outside the legislative charter of this Agency. I hereby direct every person presently employed by CIA to report to me on any such activities of which he has knowledge. I invite all ex-employees to do the same. Anyone who has such information should call . . . and say that he wishes to tell me about 'activities outside CIA's charter.'"[55]

Congress spent 1975 rooting out the facts of the CIA's transgressions. The new president, Gerald R. Ford—who had succeeded after Nixon's resignation—was shocked when he learned that the Agency had spied domestically, tapped journalists, and broken into homes and offices to conduct illegal searches.

As Henry Kissinger—held over to the new administration as secretary of state—looked over the evidence, he called it "the horrors book."[56] Kissinger did not write down half of what was happening under his watch at the CIA. He told President Ford that much of what the Agency was doing was illegal outright and that other parts caused serious moral questions.

Though he had served a decade on the small CIA subcommittee in the House of Representatives, President Ford knew nothing about the domestic spying, assassination attempts, and other nefarious activities of the Agency. He was shocked and realized that the trail of guilt went all the way back to the days of Dwight D. Eisenhower.

On January 3, 1975, President Ford told the top leaders of his government that the CIA could not survive the publication of its secrets.

It wasn't until early in 1976 that the Senate committee investigating the Agency—called the Church Committee after its chairman, Senator Frank Church (D-Idaho)—rendered its final report. Famously, the committee called the CIA a "rogue elephant."[57]

CIA: PICKING UP THE PIECES

Watergate shattered the CIA. Under Gerald Ford's successor, President Jimmy Carter, the Agency hobbled along, its operations—overt and covert—largely structured to support the president's focus on human rights.

It was Carter—now seen as a liberal—who laid the basis for Ronald Reagan's success in bringing down the Soviet Empire. By calling attention to Moscow's human rights abuses, Carter embarrassed the Soviets and lent comfort—and material aid—to the dissidents who were protesting its authoritarian bent.

Everybody recognized that the Agency had been disabled as a result of the investigations of the seventies. The estimates of Soviet military capabilities and intentions that the CIA had made in the early 1970s had come to form the basis for America's foreign policy. But now that it was laid bare that the Agency manipulated its findings and its reports to suit its own political agenda, presidents and their advisors could no longer trust it. Experts traced the birth of this political interference to 1969, when Nixon made the CIA change its opinion to increase fears of Russia's first-strike nuclear capability. It continued to get worse from then on.

The CIA's abominably bad judgment was on display in 1979, when it failed to warn Carter of the two most significant foreign events of his tenure as president: the Soviet invasion of Afghanistan and Ayatollah Khomeini's revolution, which overthrew the Shah in Iran.

The CIA missed them both.

Even as Soviet troop transports and military equipment approached the Afghan border, the CIA insisted that no Russian invasion was imminent. When the invasion actually did take place, the CIA insisted that it was not an invasion, but a limited action. President Carter had no opportunity to warn Russia off the invasion or counter it with U.S. forces. The best he could do was to cancel U.S. participation in the 1980 Olympics held in Moscow.

Similarly, the CIA failed to predict, much less stop, the Ayatollah Khomeini from removing America's key ally in the Middle East—the Shah of Iran—from power. One CIA leader admitted that "we were just plain asleep."[58]

The Shah, who had been put in power by British intelligence in 1941, was kept in office through the crucial interventions of the CIA. In 1951, Mohammad Mosaddegh, a populist/nationalist, was elected premier in a free election. As he began to drift leftward, the CIA—led by President Theodore Roosevelt's grandson, Kermit Roosevelt—ousted him from office in 1953 and gave the Shah full control of the government.

For more than twenty-five years, the Shah was America's principal client in the Middle East. He maintained power through torture and imprisonment under the guidance of the CIA.

When a revolution exploded, led by Islamic fundamentalist Ayatollah Khomeini, the CIA failed to see it coming. It had put the Shah in power and it could not bring itself to believe that he was in trouble. The CIA confidently reported that he was doing fine, even when he was on the verge of ouster, saying that Iran was not nearing a revolution—a revolt others could see quite plainly.

On January 16, 1979, the Shah fled Tehran. But the question remained: Where would he go? An international hot potato, nobody wanted him. Everyone was afraid of alienating the new Islamists in power in Iran. He tried Egypt, Morocco, and the Bahamas before settling in Mexico. All the while, the Shah was eagerly seeking asylum in the United States. Suffering from advanced cancer, he pleaded that he could only get good medical treatment in the United States.

Over the years, the Shah had made many friends and collected a large stack of IOUs. One was from Henry Kissinger. While out of office, the former secretary of state still had enough political heft to reach out to President Carter.

The president wrestled with whether or not to admit the former ally to the United States. "Blank the Shah!" he reportedly said. "He's just as well off playing tennis in Acapulco as he is in California. What are we going to do if they take twenty of our Marines and kill one of them every morning at sunrise? Are we going to go to war with Iran?"[59]

But Carter relented and granted the Shah asylum in the United States. A few days later, militant followers of the Ayatollah seized the American embassy in Tehran and held fifty-three Americans hostage. The crisis lasted 444 days and led to Carter's defeat for re-election. His nightmare had come true.

The seventies, a decade of near-death for the CIA following Watergate, gave the Agency a real sense of its own mortality. Watergate had demonstrated that an intelligence agency could bring down a president. But the Ford administration and the Church Committee showed that Congress and the president could bring down an intelligence agency.

The CIA came to think defensively. It shied away from controversy, and individual agents began to worry about their own careers and the risk of scandal before they authorized operations.

This self-concern led to a key conclusion by the agents of the CIA: Presidents were a threat to their jobs and their power. The Oval Office had to be in friendly hands or all bets were off.

THE "ROGUE ELEPHANT" GETS A TRAINER: BOB CASEY TAKES OVER THE CIA

Ronald Reagan, an enthusiastic Cold Warrior, took office in 1981. Determined to roll back the Soviet Empire, he and his new CIA director, William Casey, hit upon the strategy that won the Cold War: bleed the USSR to death.

Woodrow Wilson had won World War I for the Allies by adding America's huge population and rapidly increasing army to the allied side in the war of attrition with Germany. The attrition was in human bodies as the death toll climbed.

Franklin Roosevelt had helped to win World War II by bringing America's vast industrial might to bear on a conflict dominated by planes and tanks. The attrition was in materiel and weapons.

Ronald Reagan brought victory in the Cold War by competing with the Soviet Union in armament spending. With America's huge economy—at least three times as large as the USSR's (and even larger when you counted NATO), Reagan and Casey realized that the Soviets could not compete in an all-out arms race.

So they set out to bleed the Soviet Union, fighting it in Afghanistan and raising the costs of that war. They also took aim at two key mainstays of the Soviet economy: oil and diamonds, reducing the price of the former by persuading Saudi Arabia to increase its production and doing likewise on the diamond market with South Africa. They blocked plans for a Russian oil pipeline into Europe and staked Russia to an expensive competition to develop space-based missile interceptors (the U.S. program was called "Star Wars").

Back in the Western Hemisphere, the Reagan-Casey duo was determined to counter leftist regimes that had sprung up in Central America. The leftist Sandinistas, having overthrown the forty-year dictatorship of the Samosa family, had taken over Nicaragua and were threatening nearby El Salvador and Honduras. Casey told Reagan, "I'll take care of Central America. Just leave it to me,"[60] and prepared to use the CIA to stop the leftists from creating a second Cuba in the region.

Congressional liberals looked askance at Casey's plans. There were no worse dictators on Earth than the Central American ones, all ruthless, vicious war criminals who had pledged undying loyalty to the United States. In our infamous School of the Americas, we trained their security forces in the black arts of interrogation, espionage, and torture. It was our nation's darkest hour.

The liberal bloc in the Senate was determined to stop the United States from starting a war to save these regimes and their death squads, which roamed their countries doing the government's grisly business. So they passed the Boland Amendment in various forms from 1982 through 1984, restricting American activity on behalf of the right-wing regimes and movements in Central America.

Specifically, it forbade American tax money to be used to support the Contras, a right-wing army the CIA had set up, equipped, and trained to fight the Marxist Sandinistas in Nicaragua.

Reluctantly signed by President Reagan—it was included in the defense appropriations so he couldn't veto it—the amendment brought all the operations to overthrow the Nicaraguan government to a halt.

His hands tied, Casey chafed under the Boland Amendment and cast about for a way around it. He found a kindred spirit in Colonel Ollie North, a military aide to the National Security Council. North, working with the national security advisors Robert McFarlane and, on his retirement, Admiral John Poindexter, conceived a plan to sell weapons to Iran—then the subject of an arms embargo—and to funnel the money to the Contras to sustain their rebellion. The arms sales to Iran were allegedly to convince the regime there to free seven Americans held hostage (although the United States denied it was an arms-for-hostages deal).

As Reagan started his first term, the CIA and the intelligence community was placed under the control of two select intelligence committees—one in each house of Congress. These committees were supposed to review and approve the covert operations of the intel agencies. They meant little to Casey, who, Robert Gates, future head of the CIA, said, "was guilty of contempt of Congress from the day he was sworn in." Gates explained that when Casey was called before the intelligence committees, he would say what he had to say to get by—truthful or not—and, Gates remembers, he'd add, "I hope that will hold the bastards!"[61]

The CIA staff took its cue from Director Casey and refined their skills at concealment and misdirection.

The Iran-Contra plan was totally illegal. We were not allowed to sell weapons to Iran in violation of the arms embargo and could not intervene on behalf of the Contras, which would violate the Boland Amendment. And U.S. policy was to never pay ransom for hostages or negotiate with terrorists for their release. But the Iran-Contra plan did all three.

By the time the program had been exposed and run its course, the scandal led to the indictment of top officials, including Defense Secretary Caspar Weinberger, National Security Advisors Robert C. McFarlane and John Poindexter, Assistant Secretary of State Elliott Abrams, Ollie North, and a dozen others. Some were pardoned by President Bush (41), and other convictions were reversed on appeal. Nobody served time in prison.

The scandal sapped President Reagan's approval ratings and cast a shadow over Bush's 1988 race for president.

But the real victim of the scandal was the concept of the rule of law in the United States. The White House had actually defied an act of Congress to sell arms to Iran and give funds to the Contras.

In the past, the CIA had violated its charter and spied on Americans in the United States. The FBI had gone way beyond its legal authority in wiretapping. But neither of these activities rose to the level of Iran-Contra.

This was not an instance of the intelligence agencies running afoul of the regulations that governed them in the course of conducting an operation. In the case of Iran-Contra, the operation itself was illegal, specifically barred by a contemporaneous act of Congress.

It was not some old law or regulation gathering dust in an archive that the CIA and the White House were violating. It was an amendment specifically passed precisely to stop them from doing exactly what they attempted.

With the ink still wet on the president's signature, the White House willfully and knowingly violated the law. Indeed, the entire purpose of the circuitous route they chose was to make it unlikely that they would be caught.

The intelligence community and the operatives at the White House had become a law unto themselves. Congress be damned.

On the heels of Watergate, a decade earlier, the stage was set for the events of our day. In Watergate, intelligence officials learned to use the media to accomplish their political objectives, making leaking an integral part of their MO. In Iran-Contra, they learned that they could get away with overt defiance of the most serious laws and suffer no consequences.

It remained a small leap to use their powers and independence to try to destroy an incumbent president of the United States.

THE BONFIRE OF INTELLIGENCE:
NEAR-DEATH EXPERIENCES AT THE CIA AND FBI

It wasn't just the CIA. The FBI found itself on the defensive during the seventies and eighties as its more extreme conduct finally caught up with it.

It was not a good time to be in intelligence and working for the U.S. government. This period of prosecution and persecution of the FBI left lasting scars in the institutional memory of the Bureau, much as it had on that of the CIA across town.

After Nixon resigned on August 8, 1974, three months before the midterm congressional elections, the stage was set for the total massacre of the Republican Party. Its congressional delegation shrank to less than one-third in the House (after a loss of forty-nine seats) and only forty seats in the Senate.

With the wind at their back, the Democrat-controlled committees in both houses closed in on the FBI like wolves on an injured moose. As they threatened to expose the inner secrets of the Bureau's operations over the years, President Ford became concerned about the impact on national security. He felt that the revelation of the FBI's secrets would tarnish every recent president from Eisenhower on.

As the then director of the FBI, Clarence Kelley, began to realize that the Bureau had constantly broken the law in conducting its surveillance and wiretapping.

So, knowing his agents had not obeyed the law, Kelley tried to persuade President Ford to expand the national security powers of the FBI.

Kelley said that the Court's ban on warrantless wiretapping of Americans had forced the Justice Department to drop its indictments of the leaders of the Weather Underground because they were the fruits of the poisonous tree of illegal surveillance.

But, in the poisoned atmosphere of the mid-seventies, no request to expand the FBI's powers was going to go anywhere.

As information about the FBI wiretaps of Martin Luther King, Jr., leaked out, the Bureau's public reputation plummeted. Ford appointed Edward Levi to serve as the fifth attorney general in three years, and the new AG issued the first-ever guidelines to govern the FBI's intelligence operations. He said that domestic terrorism was a job for law enforcement and that "government monitoring of individuals and groups because they hold unpopular or controversial political views is intolerable in our society."[62]

Levi ordered Kelley to make every agent report any black-bag job (surreptitious and warrantless breaking and entering) he knew about.

The FBI was, at last, investigating itself.

But the Bureau's new director, Clarence Kelley, didn't know what was going on underneath him in the FBI. He believed his aides when they told him—and Congress under oath—that the FBI was no longer doing the breaking-and-entering operations to gather intelligence.

Wrong.

On August 8, 1976, Kelley admitted that he had been fooled by the best in the business—that is, he was "knowledgeably, knowingly, and intentionally deceived"[63] by his top people. He attacked "an arrogant belief at high levels [in the Bureau] in the infallibility and appropriateness of *all* FBI activities and policies."[64]

Then, heads started to roll.

- Fifty-three agents were targeted in a criminal investigation.
- Kelley set up a new task force to handle internal investigations, in concert with Justice Department prosecutors.
- He said that there would be no more secret intelligence investigations against subversive Americans.

On August 19, 1976, the FBI raided itself as investigators from the Civil Rights Division of the Justice Department searched FBI offices in Washington and New York, where they found twenty-five volumes of evidence of secret break-ins in 1972 and 1973.

Morale at the FBI fell apart. FBI agents recoiled from terror investigations, fearing that if they crossed any lines nobody would back them up. As FBI Special Agent William E. Dyson put it: "Nobody wants to work terrorism. Everybody is trying to run away." He said agents thought: "nobody will support me. The Bureau won't support me. The Justice Department won't support me. The citizens won't support me."[65]

The next decade wasn't any better for the beleaguered FBI. Ronald Reagan brought a sense of purpose to the CIA with his militant anti-communism. But while the CIA was playing offense against the Soviet bloc—and helping to win the Cold War in the process—the FBI was mired in its own counterintelligence scandals. Infiltrated, exposed, and compromised, the Bureau stumbled through the Reagan era.

The spy scandals of the eighties shook the FBI to its foundation and stripped the Bureau of the reputation for competence it had painstakingly amassed in the previous decades. They revealed the gravest penetration of the American intelligence establishment in thirty years.

It began in July 1981, when French president François Mitterrand handed the newly elected Ronald Reagan the "Farewell Dossier," compiled from thousands of KGB documents that a defector had pirated out of the Soviet Union in the 1970s.

The documents revealed how skillfully the KGB and the intelligence services of its Eastern European satellites—working through

Line X, a division of the Soviet intelligence directorate for science and technology—had penetrated the FBI and the CIA.

They depicted how the Soviets used the spy services of Eastern Europe—especially the Poles' and the Czechs'—to steal weapons technology from the United States.

FBI Director William H. Webster, who served from 1978 to 1987, explained that the Eastern Europeans "were skillful collectors of intelligence on behalf of the Soviet Union. . . . due to some very interesting and helpful activity by the French intelligence service dealing with high-ranking KGB officials, we became aware of their program to steal our technology in the United States."[66]

The FBI had to start playing defense, bringing cases against Polish spies and the weapons contractors who were providing them with their information.

The cases piled up.

- John Anthony Walker, Jr., passed secrets for seventeen years. "Walker provided top cryptographic secrets to the Soviets, compromising at least one million classified messages." He recruited three people with security clearances into his espionage ring: his brother Arthur, his son Michael, and his good friend Jerry Whitworth. "The information passed by Walker and his confederates would have been devastating to the U.S. had the nation gone to war with the Soviets."[67]
- Sharon Marie Scranage, a CIA clerk stationed in Ghana, revealed the identity of CIA affiliates and intelligence on communications, radio, and military equipment.
- Larry Wu-tai Chin passed on CIA reports on Far East operations.
- Ronald William Pelton, an NSA analyst, was also caught. "Because of money problems, Pelton went to the Soviet Embassy in Washington, DC shortly after resigning from the National Security Agency and offered to sell secrets. Provided

classified information for five years, including details on U.S. collection programs targeting the Soviets."[68]

- A Hughes Aircraft executive was paid $110,000 and passed information on American air defense systems.[69]

- Karl F. Koecher, a Czech spy, became the only intelligence officer known to have penetrated the CIA. For ten years he and his wife passed along "classified CIA documents, lists and photographs of CIA employees in the United States and overseas and names of U.S. government officials who might be blackmailed into cooperating with the Soviets."[70] He also compromised our top agent in Moscow, Aleksandr D. Ogorodnik, who then committed suicide.

- Clyde Conrad sold top-secret files to Eastern Bloc intelligence services, revealing the locations of NATO's nuclear weapons and the order of battle for troops, tanks, and aircraft, for more than $1 million.[71]

- Edward Lee Howard defected to Russia in 1986 after selling out dozens of American agents in the Soviet Union, forcing them to leave Moscow.

- Robert Hanssen was described by the FBI as "the most damaging spy in [its] history." He "compromised numerous human sources of the U.S. Intelligence Community, dozens of classified U.S. Government documents, including 'Top Secret' and 'codeword' documents, and technical operations of extraordinary importance and value."[72] It took the FBI fifteen years to expose Hanssen.

There were scores of spy scandals that ripped the FBI in the eighties, twelve in 1985 alone, earning it the reputation for being "the year of the spy."

The effect on the Bureau was enormous. Once seen as almost omnipotent, the FBI came to be seen—and to see itself—as the gang that couldn't shoot straight.

The FBI wasn't any ordinary federal agency. It was iconic. Genera-
tions of children had grown up watching FBI TV shows, knowing that
the Bureau always got its man. Men and women dedicated their lives
and careers to what they considered noble service in one of Washington's most honored offices.

Now, it was in shambles. And it got worse.

William S. Sessions took over the Bureau in 1987, having had no
relevant experience. He came to see his role as reining in, not ruling, the
FBI and never really had control of the Bureau. Assistant Director Buck
Revell felt that Sessions had "effectively neutralized" the Bureau's ability
to carry out its counterterrorism responsibilities, grinding them "down
to ground zero."[73]

Sessions reassigned more than a third of the agents working on terrorism to street crime.

The institutional damage was extreme. And it left the FBI with a
sense of its own vulnerability. Savaged in the seventies by Nixon's esca-
pades and ripped by Soviet spies in the eighties, the Bureau had lost its
mojo.

This sense of institutional vulnerability remained with the FBI
through the next decades. Its agents remembered when the house of
cards came crashing down, and this may have influenced their fears of
what might happen under a Trump presidency.

THE CIA, TOO, WITHERS AND ALMOST DIES

After Watergate . . . after the Church Committee investigation . . . and
after the Iran-Contra scandal was exposed, the CIA also was staggering
on its last legs. Its aggressive anti-communism and blind allegiance to
the president's most extreme policies had left it depleted, discouraged,
and disorganized.

Robert Gates put the decline in Agency morale into perspective. He
wrote that risk aversion at the battered Agency "is slowly turning [it]
into the Department of Agriculture." He said that the Agency had "an

advanced case of bureaucratic arteriosclerosis." Gates said the CIA staff had become mediocre and was filled with men and women just waiting until they could draw their pensions. This, he said, was the reason for "the decline in the quality of our intelligence collection and analysis over the last fifteen years."[74]

Although sympathetic to the agency he once headed—the CIA—President Bush (41) took a meat axe to the Agency's staff, part of the so-called "peace dividend" that was to have accompanied the end of the Cold War in 1991. Its staff size dropped that year and for the next six. Many CIA outposts were closed, and others, in big cities, had their staffs cut by more than half. The number of spies overseas dropped dramatically. The quality of the analysts also plummeted. Doug MacEachin, now their chief, complained that he had to work with "a bunch of 19-year-olds on two year rotations."[75]

The élan, the spirit, had gone out of the Agency.

But both the CIA and the entire intelligence community were in for their most profound shock when Bill Clinton became president.

Used by FDR and Eisenhower, misused by Johnson and Nixon, and led into scandal by Reagan, the CIA was used to some rough treatment. But it experienced its most degrading moments under Clinton, when it was totally ignored.

IGNORED BY CLINTON

At least Bush-41 cared about the intel community. Having run the CIA—and loving it as he did—he gave the Agency leaders excellent access and listened to them carefully.

But when Bill Clinton took office in January 1993, everything changed. Foreign policy was not Clinton's thing. He knew little about it and felt that undue focus on it was a Cold War obsession to which he was determined not to fall prey.

Rather, Clinton saw his post–Cold War presidency in largely economic terms. His secretary of state, Warren Christopher, said that it was "a moment of immense democratic and entrepreneurial opportunity."[76] National Security Advisor Tony Lake said that the new foreign policy goal of the United States was to increase the number of the world's free markets, a more likely goal for a treasury secretary than for a national security advisor.

To babysit the CIA while he turned his attention elsewhere, President Clinton tapped R. James Woolsey to head the Agency. Woolsey had come to the president's attention through a well-noticed speech, saying the United States had fought a dragon for forty-five years and had slain it, only to find itself in a jungle filled with poisonous snakes.[77] On the strength of this metaphor, Clinton gave Woolsey the CIA.

And then Clinton abandoned him. Woolsey said that over the two years of his tenure, he met with the president only twice. "I didn't have a bad relationship with the president," Woolsey lamented. "I just didn't have one at all."[78]

Tom Twetten, chief of the clandestine service from 1991 to 1993, also said that he and his staff went from having a great relationship with the White House under Bush to no relationship under Clinton. He said that, after a few months, he realized that nobody had seen the president in quite a while.

If the CIA felt ignored, it was even worse at the FBI.

Louis Freeh, appointed by Bill Clinton to head the FBI, was at loggerheads with the man who had given him his job. He literally refused to go to the Oval Office to see the president! Literally.

Freeh returned his White House pass and would not enter the Oval Office. In his memoir, Freeh tells why: "My role and my obligation was to conduct criminal investigations. [Bill Clinton], unfortunately for the country and unfortunately for him, happened to be the subject of that investigation." He goes on to say that "Whatever moral compass the president was consulting was leading him in the wrong direction. His closets were full of skeletons just waiting to burst out."[79]

Freeh felt Clinton's hostility. The president, the FBI director wrote later, "came to believe that I was trying to undo his presidency."[80]

Clinton couldn't fire Freeh because he was under investigation by him. Investigation of the Whitewater scandal. Investigation of Chinese money to finance his 1996 campaign. Investigation of the firing of the Travel Office staff. Investigation of Hillary's work at the Rose Law Firm. No, Freeh could not be fired, however much Clinton wanted to.

Soon their estrangement became a threat to national security. The lack of communication left the FBI to "twist slowly in the wind."[81]

The chief counterterrorism aides at the National Security Council, Steven Simon and Daniel Benjamin, found Freeh extraordinarily unresponsive to their growing fears of a terrorist attack. "His mistrust of the White House grew so strong that it seems to have blinded him."[82]

So Bill Clinton governed with an FBI director who would barely speak with him and a CIA chief he never saw.

And the CIA had its own problem. His name was Aldrich Hazen Ames. Arrested on February 21, 1994, the fifty-three-year-old Ames had been spying for the Soviet Union—and then for Russia—for nine years. A drunk and a malcontent, he had risen in the depopulated CIA to the rank of chief of counterintelligence for the Soviet Union and Eastern Europe.

In exchange for $2 million in cash bribes, he gave Moscow the names of every American agent he knew about. They were all arrested and executed. Ames himself describes how "bells and whistles" went off throughout the intelligence community. "It was as if neon lights and searchlights lit up all over the Kremlin, . . . shone all the way across the Atlantic Ocean, saying, 'There is a penetration.'"[83]

It took more than a year to add up the damage. It was catastrophic.

Not only had almost all of our intelligence agents blown, but for ten years American presidents—from Reagan to Clinton—had been misled about Soviet and Russian capabilities and intentions.

The CIA's main task in the Cold War was to produce reports with a blue stripe on their sides (called blue border reports) to assess Russia's military strategy and capability.

From 1986 until 1994, those writing these reports knew that some of their sources were controlled by Russian intelligence. The report's CIA authors trusted themselves to sift out the phony info from the real deal. Why did they knowingly pass on data that was compromised? Because revealing the real truth—that the CIA had been compromised—would do too much damage to its reputation. Eleven reports went directly to Presidents Reagan, Bush, and Clinton.

How could they do this? Frederick Hitz, former inspector general of the CIA, explains: "The most senior CIA official responsible for these reports insisted . . . that he knew best. He knew what was real and what was not. The fact that the reporting had come from agents of deception meant nothing. 'He made that decision himself.'"[84]

The damage to the CIA's credibility was lethal. Hitz said, "What came out of this whole episode was a feeling that the Agency couldn't be trusted. . . . In short, it was a violation of Commandment Number One. And that's why it had such a destructive impact."[85]

Now the Agency was under fire from all sides. Lieutenant General Bill Odom, NSA director in the eighties, said, "I would disembowel the CIA. . . . It's contaminated. And if you take half-hearted measures, it will remain contaminated."[86]

The Ames scandal provides a distressing window into the attitudes that predominated in the CIA's culture. They knew best. They knew better than the politicians what was right or wrong. Elected presidents come and go. Sometimes they are misguided like Nixon, unconcerned with details like Reagan, or incompetent like Clinton, but the veteran analysts at the Agency were forever.

But there was more to come out.

It turned out that from 1994 to 1996, the head instructor at the CIA's training school had been selling Russians files on dozens of CIA officers stationed abroad. Three years' worth of potential new recruits had been blown. Now that they were exposed, they, obviously, could not be used overseas.

★ ★ ★

The wreckage of the CIA and the FBI as 9/11 struck America made it necessary for Bush to create new agencies on top of the old ashes. But it also made it possible for Obama to shape those agencies in his own image, moving them leftward so they could be useful tools for reshaping American politics.

We have seen with what devastating impact Obama refashioned both the purpose and the personnel of the American intelligence community.

But rogue spooks were not made in a day. Intel folks were only able to disrupt the presidency of Donald Trump because of everything they had learned over the years at their agencies. Over the decades, they had learned how to overthrow foreign governments and had acquired skills at media manipulation. They felt free to overthrow a president of the United States (and had Nixon's scalp in their bags), and felt no twinge of regret in lying to Congress and ignoring its statutes, just as they had in Iran-Contra.

America thought it was building an intelligence superstructure that would protect us. But we had also built one that could destroy us.

CONCLUSION

WHAT'S HAPPENING IN WASHINGTON BECOMES MORE OBVIOUS BY THE DAY. Sickeningly so.

A well-planned coup d'etat by the Intel/Media complex is underway. Will Trump survive? He can, but only if we realize what is going on and move to resist and to stop it.

First, let's review the stages we've been through:

1. A dossier is released that calls attention to the phony narrative of a Trump-Putin deal to steal the election.

2. The U.S. intelligence community leaks often-inaccurate stories to feed the fantasy that such an intervention was planned in meetings between Trump's people and Putin's operatives.

3. The media blows these disinformation leaks out of all proportion and makes enough noise to drown out the real workings and accomplishments of the Trump presidency.

4. Told he is not under investigation and knowing he did not plot with the Russians, Trump impatiently urges his intel community officials to move on and to reaffirm his own innocence.

5. Trump fires FBI director James Comey.

6. Comey leaks a memo of a private meeting with Trump, which leads to the suggestion that Trump's request to move on was obstruction of justice.

7. Pressure in the media builds and forces the Justice Department to name a special prosecutor. Because Trump's choice as attorney general, Jeff Sessions, has been sidelined by an ambush before a Senate sommittee, the designation of the prosecutor is made by the deputy attorney general. Robert Mueller III, Comey's friend, gets the nomination and becomes the prosecutor.

8. Mueller staffs his office with top criminal lawyers and it becomes evident that he is now investigating Trump personally on charges that he obstructed justice in his conversations with Comey.

What happens next is up to us!

Mueller will undoubtedly snoop around in all of Donald Trump's business affairs, examine his tax returns, review his company's bankruptcies, examine his sources of financing, and possibly probe such issues as the Trump University suit, the Miss Universe contest, and Trump's alleged and rumored mob connections.

He will troll for dirt. He'll find plenty.

Sol Wächtler, a judge in New York State, famously said that a grand jury could "indict a ham sandwich."[1]

He meant that even a simple, ordinary person living an honest life has probably violated one law or another and could be brought to account by a sufficiently motivated prosecutor.

Donald Trump is far from an ordinary person. With his controversial personal past and his far-flung business empire, he is an easy mark for a prosecutor with his own grand jury, a limitless budget, and plenty of motivation.

Fortunately, Robert Mueller and James Comey do not have the power to oust Trump.

That power resides in the Congress—the House to vote impeachment and the Senate to acquit or convict by a two-thirds vote.

With Republicans in charge of both houses, impeachment would seem to be a non-starter. But don't bet on it. The Republican establishment has no use for Donald Trump. Only a handful of Senate Republicans endorsed him before the convention and seven refused to do so even after he became the nominee.

Vice President Mike Pence, himself a creature of Congress, enjoys broad popularity. One cannot doubt that more GOP senators would have voted for Pence than for Trump had they opposed one another for the nomination. To the likes of Republican senators like John McCain (himself implicated in the release of the dossier) and Lindsay Graham (R-SC), a President Pence might come as a relief.

But if we, the people who defied the polls and the pundits and came out to elect Donald Trump stand up and say no to impeachment, we can likely intimidate enough of the timid souls who comprise the Republican majority to get them to vote no to impeachment or to acquit in the Senate.

We need the same kind of popular revolution that nominated and elected Trump if we are to keep him in office.

Donald Trump has delivered on his campaign promises to us. The economy is gaining real momentum. Illegal border crossings are way down and arrests of undocumented immigrants are way up. The United States has pulled out of the Paris climate accord and the Pacific Rim trade deal. The Keystone pipeline has been approved. Another Republican conservative now sits on the Supreme Court. Even if his order banning immigration from six terror nations is stalled by court judges, the Supreme Court will likely uphold it and, anyway, denials of visas from the named countries are up by 70 percent.

He is a very good president. Let's fight to keep him in the White House.

ACKNOWLEDGMENTS

WE WANT TO THANK ST. MARTIN'S PRESS FOR THE INCREDIBLE EXPERIENCE OF working with them on this book.

Our editor, Adam Bellow, was very generous with his insights and helped us to see our path ahead even as we felt we were drowning in data. His clarity as an editor, combined with his good political antenna, made him a perfect fit for us.

But that was just the beginning of the story. Alan Bradshaw, Jennifer Simington, and the entire production team were incredibly tolerant and flexible, even as we made changes and additions in our manuscript right up though the last minute. Or second.

Laura Clark, Tracey Guest, and Leah Johanson helped guide our post-publication publicity with skill and dedication.

We also want to thank Kevin Reilly, Jim Dugan, Maureen Maxwell. God bless St. Martin's.

And thanks also to Chuck Brooks and David Steinmann for all their help.

NOTES

PROLOGUE

1. https://www.documentcloud.org/documents/3259984-Trump-Intelligence
   -Allegations.html
2. Ibid., p. 11.
3. Ibid.
4. http://www.motherjones.com/politics/2017/01/spy-who-wrote-trump
   -russia-memos-it-was-hair-raising-stuff
5. Ibid.
6. https://www.washingtonpost.com/world/national-security/fbi-director-to
   -testify-on-russian-interference-in-the-presidential-election/2017/03/20/cd
   ea86ca-0ce2-11e7-9d5a-a83e627dc120_story.html?utm_term=.6ee32e745868
7. https://www.nytimes.com/2017/04/22/us/politics/james-comey-election
   .html?mtrref=t.co&_r=0
8. Ibid.
9. https://www.washingtonpost.com/politics/fbi-once-planned-to-pay-former
   -british-spy-who-authored-controversial-trump-dossier/2017/02/28/896ab
   470-facc-11e6-9845-576c69081518_story.html?hpid=hp_no-name_no-name
   %3Apage%2Fbreaking-news-bar&tid=a_breakingnews&utm_term=.e2fd2
   c5da9e5
10. http://www.cnn.com/2017/02/28/politics/christopher-steele-fbi-expenses
    /index.html
11. http://www.reuters.com/article/us-usa-trump-steele-idUSKBN14W0HN.
    On October 31, 2016, *Mother Jones* did publish an interview by David Corn
    with a "former senior intelligence officer for a Western country who specialized
    in Russian counterintelligence" who claimed to have provided the FBI with
    reports showing "an established exchange of information between the Trump
    campaign and the Kremlin of mutual benefit" and suggesting that Trump had
    been compromised by the Kremlin. http://www.motherjones.com/politics
    /2016/10/veteran-spy-gave-fbi-info-alleging-russian-operation-cultivate
    -donald-trump
12. http://www.independent.co.uk/news/world/americas/donald-trump-russia
    -dossier-leak-sir-andrew-wood-john-mccain-british-ambassador-spy-a7524
    931.html
13. http://abcnews.go.com/Politics/clapper-denies-trump-wiretap-claim-calling
    -distraction/story?id=45944926

INTRODUCTION

1. https://www.nytimes.com/2017/01/06/us/politics/russia-hack-report.html
?smprod=nytcore-iphone&smid=nytcore-iphone-share&_r=1
2. https://www.theguardian.com/uk-news/2017/apr/13/british-spies-first-to
-spot-trump-team-links-russia
3. https://townhall.com/tipsheet/katiepavlich/2017/05/30/clapper-we-still
-have-zero-evidence-wrongdoing-on-russia-n2333267
4. http://www.breitbart.com/big-government/2017/05/25/ex-cia-director
-john-brennan-ive-seen-no-evidence-collusion-russia/
5. http://www.theepochtimes.com/n3/2252532-despite-allegations-no-evi
dence-of-trump-russia-collusion-found/
6. https://www.washingtonpost.com/world/national-security/russian-gov
ernment-hackers-penetrated-dnc-stole-opposition-research-on-trump
/2016/06/14/cf006cb4-316e-11e6-8ff7-7b6c1998b7a0_story.html?utm
_term=.7b8f875a2553
7. Ibid.
8. https://www.nytimes.com/2017/05/24/us/politics/russia-trump-manafort
-flynn.html?_r=0
9. https://www.theguardian.com/uk-news/2017/apr/13/british-spies-first
-to-spot-trump-team-links-russia
10. https://www.nytimes.com/2016/12/13/us/politics/russia-hack-election-dnc
.html
11. https://www.nytimes.com/2016/12/13/us/politics/russia-hack-election-dnc
.html
12. http://thehill.com/policy/national-security/312767-fbi-never-examined
-hacked-dnc-servers-report
13. https://www.nytimes.com/2016/06/15/us/politics/russian-hackers-dnc
-trump.html
14. Ibid.
15. http://abcnews.go.com/US/fbi-investigating-unconfirmed-claims-trump
-compromised-election/story?id=44693343
16. https://www.nytimes.com/2016/07/22/us/ . . . /donald-trump-foreign-policy
-interview.html
17. https://www.nytimes.com/2016/08/02/world/europe/donald-trump-finds-a
-russian-policy-he-wont-defend.html
18. https://www.washingtonpost.com/blogs/right-turn/wp/2016/08/18
/russian-cheerleader-gets-classified-briefing/?utm_term=.5e7416ae475d
19. http://abcnews.go.com/US/fbi-investigating-unconfirmed-claims-trump
-compromised-election/story?id=44693343
20. https://www.nytimes.com/2016/07/26/us/politics/democrats-allege-dnc
-hack-is-part-of-russian-effort-to-elect-donald-trump.html
21. https://www.washingtonpost.com/politics/trump-invites-russia-to-meddle
-in-the-us-presidential-race-with-clintons-emails/2016/07/27/a85d799e
-5414-11e6-b7de-dfe509430c39_story.html?utm_term=.88410a298f85
22. http://www.latimes.com/politics/la-na-pol-trump-russia-emails-2016
0727-snap-story.html
23. http://www.latimes.com/nation/politics/trailguide/la-na-democratic-con
vention-2016-live-hillary-clinton-campaign-sounds-alarm-1469637426-html
story.html
24. https://www.nytimes.com/2016/07/28/us/politics/trump-conference-high
lights.html

25. http://www.politico.com/story/2016/07/robby-mook-russians-emails-trump -226084

26. https://www.nytimes.com/2016/07/25/us/politics/donald-trump-russia -emails.html?_r=0

27. https://www.nytimes.com/2016/07/26/us/politics/democrats-allege-dnc -hack-is-part-of-russian-effort-to-elect-donald-trump.html

28. https://www.washingtonpost.com/politics/after-dnc-leaks-obama-hints-at -possible-motive-for-russia-to-help-trump/2016/07/26/cfd33692-538a-11e6 -bbf5-957ad17b4385_story.html?utm_term=.13873bce5397

29. https://www.washingtonpost.com/news/wonk/wp/2016/08/07/what -is-hillary-clinton-trying-to-say-with-this-ad-about-donald-trump-and -putin/?utm_term=.a1ff7e193ebe

30. Ibid.

31. https://www.youtube.com/watch?v=sAKmtfTe2rc&list=PLXlk_TEo7Llx i5LqDR8q7DyaLt7AtQGGi

32. https://www.washingtonpost.com/world/national-security/fbi-obtained-fisa -warrant-to-monitor-former-trump-adviser-carter-page/2017/04/11/620192 ea-1e0e-11e7-ad74-3a742a6e93a7_story.html?utm_term=.4765e8e5a515

33. http://www.motherjones.com/politics/2016/10/veteran-spy-gave-fbi-info -alleging-russian-operation-cultivate-donald-trump

34. http://dailycaller.com/2017/04/22/heres-how-much-the-fbi-planned-to-pay -trump-dossier-author/

35. http://www.foxnews.com/politics/2017/05/05/comey-pressed-for-anti-trump -dossier-in-classified-russia-report-sources-say.html

36. http://www.kgw.com/news/politics/sen-merkley-vows-to-honor-the-peace ful-transfer-of-power/387358158

ONE

1. https://www.nytimes.com/2017/02/14/us/politics/russia-intelligence-com munications-trump.html; http://time.com/4682791/fbi-russia-reince-priebus -andrew-mccabe-justice-rules/

2. http://www.foxnews.com/politics/2017/05/05/comey-pressed-for-anti-trump -dossier-in-classified-russia-report-sources-say.html

3. https://www.washingtonpost.com/world/national-security/comey-testimony -trump-senate-hearing/2017/06/07/afadf87c-4bd0-11e7-bc1b-fddbd8359dee _story.html?utm_term=.af6ad1e76971

4. http://www.cnn.com/2017/06/08/politics/james-comey-testimony-donald -trump/index.html

5. https://www.washingtonpost.com/world/national-security/comey-testimony -trump-senate-hearing/2017/06/07/afadf87c-4bd0-11e7-bc1b-fddbd8359dee _story.html?utm_term=.af6ad1e76971 and https://www.washingtonpost.com /news/the-fix/wp/2013/05/30/james-comey-and-the-most-watchable-20 -minutes-of-congressional-testimony-maybe-ever/?tid=a_inl&utm_term=.8a 49ab217823

6. https://www.washingtonpost.com/news/the-fix/wp/2013/05/30/james -comey-and-the-most-watchable-20-minutes-of-congressional-testimony -maybe-ever/?utm_term=.af55b167996e

7. Ibid.

8. https://www.washingtonpost.com/opinions/a-tale-of-two-comeys/2017/06 /12/4ffa9d8e-4fb5-11e7-b064-828ba60fbb98_story.html?utm_term=.9487b 60418b1

9. https://www.nytimes.com/2017/02/14/us/politics/russia-intelligence-com munications-trump.html
10. Ibid.
11. Ibid.
12. http://www.foxnews.com/politics/2017/06/13/comey-admitted-single-trump -leak-but-were-there-others.html
13. https://www.youtube.com/watch?v=rg12DQhwTgg; https://www.realclearpo litics.com/video/2017/06/08/lynch_told_me_to_call_clinton_email_scandal _a_matter_and_not_an_investigation.html
14. http://thehill.com/blogs/blog-briefing-room/news/337152-former-attorney -general-lynch-made-justice-department-an-arm-o
15. http://www.foxnews.com/politics/2017/06/08/comey-says-lynch-tarmac -meeting-directive-to-downplay-probe-prompted-him-to-go-rogue-on-clin ton-case.html
16. ibid.
17. ibid.
18. https://www.cato.org/publications/commentary/lessons-martha-stewart-case
19. Ibid.
20. https://thefederalist.com/2017/06/12/james-comey-long-history-question able-obstruction-cases/
21. Ibid.
22. http://www.washingtonexaminer.com/byron-york-is-robert-mueller-con flicted-in-trump-probe/article/2625638. See also https://www.usatoday.com /story/opinion/2017/06/14/mueller-should-recuse-himself-from-investigat ing-russia—comey-william-otis-column/102827924/
23. http://www.cnn.com/2017/06/14/politics/robert-mueller-donald-trump /index.html
24. http://www.washingtonexaminer.com/gingrich-robert-mueller-is-the-tip-of -the-deep-state-spear-trying-to-bring-down-trump/article/2626057
25. http://www.cnn.com/2017/06/12/politics/robert-mueller-donations-demo crats-fec/index.html
26. Ibid.
27. Ibid.
28. http://dailysignal.com/2016/08/03/how-obamas-influence-could-continue -after-his-term-through-his-political-appointees/
29. http://www.dailymail.co.uk/news/article-4117040/I-introduced-wife-James -Bond-Former-spy-Chris-Steele-s-friends-shadowy-007-figure-MI6-bosses -brand-idiot-appalling-lack-judgement-Trump-dirty-dossier.html
30. http://www.washingtonpost.com/wp-srv/inatl/longterm/russiagov/putin .htm
31. https://www.forbes.com/sites/richardbehar/2017/01/11/could-this-be-the -british-mi6-agent-behind-the-trump-fbi-memos/#6c210cf94393   And Steele was in contact with Alex Younger, head of MI6, who included material allegedly uncovered by Steele about Russian cyberattacks in his first pubic speech.   http://www.independent.co.uk/news/world/americas/donald-trump -dossier-mi6-christopher-steele-russia-documents-alex-younger-a7528681 .html
32. https://www.washingtonpost.com/news/worldviews/wp/2017/01/12/this -former-british-spy-was-identified-as-the-trump-dossier-source-now-he-is-in -hiding/?utm_term=.1fd87054470a
33. http://www.bbc.com/news/world-us-canada-39435786
34. https://www.nytimes.com/2017/02/14/us/politics/russia-intelligence-com munications-trump.html?_r=0

35. http://www.cnn.com/2017/01/10/politics/donald-trump-intelligence-report
    -russia/
36. https://www.theguardian.com/us-news/2017/jan/12/intelligence-sources
    -vouch-credibility-donald-trump-russia-dossier-author
37. https://www.nytimes.com/2017/01/12/world/europe/christopher-steele
    -trump-russia-dossier.html
38. http://www.businessinsider.com/trump-dossier-looking-increasingly-credible
    -2017-1
39. http://www.cbsnews.com/news/ex-u-k-ambassador-to-russia-says-fsbs-use
    -of-sexual-entrapment-widespread/
40. http://www.aljazeera.com/indepth/opinion/2017/01/steele-trump-report
    -mi6-170115081202438.html
41. http://www.dailymail.co.uk/news/article-4117040/I-introduced-wife-James
    -Bond-Former-spy-Chris-Steele-s-friends-shadowy-007-figure-MI6-bosses
    -brand-idiot-appalling-lack-judgement-Trump-dirty-dossier.html
42. http://www.bbc.com/news/magazine-33678717
43. http://www.telegraph.co.uk/news/uknews/law-and-order/11381789/The
    -assassination-of-Alexander-Litvinenko-20-things-about-his-death-we-have
    -learned-this-week.html
44. http://www.telegraph.co.uk/news/2017/01/12/lurid-donald-trump-dossier
    -casts-shadow-mi6-christopher-steele/
45. http://www.aljazeera.com/indepth/opinion/2017/01/steele-trump-report
    -mi6-170115081202438.html
46. Ibid.
47. http://www.telegraph.co.uk/opinion/2017/01/12/christopher-steele-felt
    -kremlin-broke-rules-murdered-litvinenko/
48. Ibid.
49. Ibid.
50. https://www.chathamhouse.org/expert/sir-andrew-wood
51. https://www.chu.cam.ac.uk/media/uploads/files/Wood.pdf
52. http://www.businessinsider.com/sir-andrew-wood-russia-meddle-scottish
    -independence-referendum-2017-3
53. Ibid.
54. http://www.motherjones.com/kevin-drum/2017/01/us-intelligence-evidence
    -trump-russia-ties-might-be-credible
55. Dana Priest and William M. Arkin, "Top Secret America," *Washington Post,*
    July 19, 2010.

TWO

1. http://www.motherjones.com/politics/2017/01/spy-who-wrote-trump-rus
   sia-memos-it-was-hair-raising-stuff
2. http://www.independent.co.uk/news/world/americas/us-politics/donald
   -trump-russia-christopher-steele-dossier-us-senate-intelligence-hotel-british
   -spy-mi6-evidence-a7608456.html
3. http://www.bbc.com/news/world-us-canada-39435786
4. http://www.motherjones.com/politics/2017/01/spy-who-wrote-trump
   -russia-memos-it-was-hair-raising-stuff
5. Ibid.
6. https://www.documentcloud.org/documents/3259984-Trump-Intelligence
   -Allegations.html
7. http://www.motherjones.com/politics/2017/01/spy-who-wrote-trump
   -russia-memos-it-was-hair-raising-stuff

8. http://halifaxtheforum.org/participants
9. http://www.dailymail.co.uk/news/article-4119148/Theresa-told-dirty -dossier-Donald-Trump-MONTH-ago-Boris-Johnson-amid-fears-sex-alle gations-cause-diplomatic-crisis.htm
10. http://thehill.com/homenews/administration/314432-trump-nato-is-obsolete
11. http://atlantic.ctvnews.ca/halifax-conference-ends-on-uncertain-note-as -world-awaits-trump-white-house-1.3169186
12. http://www.metronews.ca/news/halifax/2016/11/16/trump-top-of-mind-at -halifax-international-security-forum.html
13. http://www.politico.com/story/2015/07/trump-attacks-mccain-i-like-people -who-werent-captured-120317
14. http://www.vanityfair.com/news/2007/02/mccain200702
15. Ibid.
16. http://thehill.com/blogs/ballot-box/306901-mccain-we-will-not-waterboard
17. http://thehill.com/business-a-lobbying/lobbying-hires/313041-ukraine-hires -lobby-firm-ahead-of-trump-inauguration
18. https://www.washingtonpost.com/world/europe/ukraines-yanukovych-missing -as-protesters-take-control-of-presidential-residence-in-kiev/2014/02/22/802f 7c6c-9bd2-11e3-ad71-e03637a299c0_story.html?utm_term=.8f8215e812e9
19. https://www.mccaininstitute.org/events/2016-tbilisi-international-conference/
20. http://www.motherjones.com/politics/2017/01/spy-who-wrote-trump-russia -memos-it-was-hair-raising-stuff/
21. https://www.theguardian.com/us-news/2017/apr/28/trump-russia-intelli gence-uk-government-m16-kremlin; see Scribd document appended.
22. https://www.theguardian.com/us-news/2017/jan/11/trump-russia-report -opposition-research-john-mccain
23. http://www.vanityfair.com/news/2017/03/how-the-explosive-russian-dossier -was-compiled-christopher-steele.
24. http://www.independent.co.uk/news/world/americas/donald-trump-russia -dossier-leak-sir-andrew-wood-john-mccain-british-ambassador-spy-a7524 931.html
25. https://www.theguardian.com/us-news/2017/jan/10/fbi-chief-given-dossier -by-john-mccain-alleging-secret-trump-russia-contacts
26. http://www.azcentral.com/story/news/politics/arizona/2017/01/12/john -mccain-intrigue-grows-donald-trump-dossier-affair/96498178/
27. http://transcripts.cnn.com/TRANSCRIPTS/1701/11/cnr.05.html
28. Ibid. When asked why he thought that he had been given the dossier, he replied, "I don't know."
29. https://www.washingtonpost.com/world/national-security/decision-to-brief -trump-on-allegations-brought-a-secret-and-unsubstantiated-dossier-into -the-public-domain/2017/01/11/275a3a6c-d830-11e6-b8b2-cb5164beba6b _story.html?utm_term=.35728a3ca5b
30. Ibid.
31. http://www.cnn.com/2017/01/11/politics/james-clapper-donald-trump
32. http://www.nbcnews.com/news/us-news/fbi-s-comey-told-trump-about -russia-dossier-after-intel-n706416
33. http://www.cnn.com/2017/01/10/politics/donald-trump-intelligence-report -russia/

THREE

1. http://m.washingtontimes.com/news/2017/apr/24/chuck-grassley-studies -dossier-money-source/

2. http://www.cnn.com/2017/01/10/politics/donald-trump-intelligence-report -russia/
3. Ibid.
4. https://www.infowars.com/trump-twitter-smackdown-hillary-guilty-as-hell -phony-allegations-from-failed-spy/
5. https://www.theatlantic.com/politics/archive/2017/03/its-official-the-fbi -is-investigating-trumps-links-to-russia/520134/
6. https://www.theguardian.com/us-news/2017/apr/28/trump-russia-intel ligence-uk-government-m16-kremlin
7. Ibid.
8. http://www.nbcnews.com/meet-the-press/video/full-clapper-no-evidence -of-collusion-between-trump-and-russia-890509379597
9. http://dailycaller.com/2017/03/10/obamas-intelligence-director-identifies -one-part-of-trump-dossier-that-is-accurate-video/
10. http://www.npr.org/2017/01/10/509222337/seriously-what-a-day-7-things -that-actually-happened-on-tuesday; https://www.theguardian.com/media /2017/jan/12/buzzfeed-editor-ben-smith-defends-decision-to-publish-trump -dossier
11. http://nypost.com/2017/01/10/buzzfeeds-trump-report-takes-fake-news-to -a-new-level/
12. https://www.merriam-webster.com/dictionary/disinformation
13. http://www.vanityfair.com/news/2017/03/how-the-explosive-russian-dossier -was-compiled-christopher-steele
14. https://www.theguardian.com/us-news/2017/apr/28/trump-russia-intelli gence-uk-government-m16-kremlin
15. https://www.documentcloud.org/documents/3259984-Trump-Intelligence -Allegations.html
16. Ibid.
17. Ibid.
18. https://www.theatlantic.com/politics/archive/2017/01/michael-cohen-it -is-fake-news-meant-to-malign-mr-trump/512762/
19. https://www.mediamatters.org/video/2017/05/09/cnns-jake-tapper-trump -administrations-handling-flynn-was-stunning-and-petty-partisan-politics /216357
20. Interview with authors, May 7, 2017.
21. Ibid.
22. https://www.documentcloud.org/documents/3259984-Trump-Intelligence -Allegations.html
23. https://www.documentcloud.org/documents/3259984-Trump-Intelligence -Allegations.html, dossier at 18
24. Ibid.
25. Ibid.
26. https://www.documentcloud.org/documents/3259984-Trump-Intelligence -Allegations.html, dossier at 34
27. https://www.documentcloud.org/documents/3259984-Trump-Intelligence -Allegations.html
28. Ibid.
29. Ibid.
30. https://www.rferl.org/a/czech-intelligence-trump-lawyer-prague-meeting /28226228.html
31. https://www.documentcloud.org/documents/3259984-Trump-Intelligence -Allegations.html, dossier at 30

32. https://www.documentcloud.org/documents/3259984-Trump-Intelligence -Allegations.html, dossier at 34-35

33. http://www.politico.com/blogs/on-media/2017/02/buzzfeed-sued-over -publishing-trump-dossier-sparking-apology-234638

34. https://www.theguardian.com/media/2017/jan/12/buzzfeed-editor-ben -smith-defends-decision-to-publish-trump-dossier

35. https://www.documentcloud.org/documents/3259984-Trump-Intelligence -Allegations.html, dossier at 35

36. http://dailycaller.com/2017/02/17/this-lawsuit-could-answer-lingering-ques tions-about-the-trump-dossier/

37. http://www.mcclatchydc.com/news/politics-government/article145755049 .html

38. Ibid.

39. Ibid.

40. https://www.documentcloud.org/documents/3259984-Trump-Intelligence -Allegations.html

41. Ibid.

42. https://www.washingtonpost.com/politics/who-is-source-d-the-man-said-to -be-behind-the-trump-russia-dossiers-most-salacious-claim/2017/03/29/379 846a8-0f53-11e7-9d5a-a83e627dc120_story.html?utm_term=.235104f16f4b

43. http://www.bbc.com/news/av/uk-politics-38607833/ex-mi6-officer -trump-dossier-hard-to-believe

44. http://freebeacon.com/politics/david-brock-offers-money-new-dirt-donald -trump/

45. http://www.businessinsider.com/david-brock-trump-tapes-the-appentice -2016-10

46. http://www.bbc.com/news/world-us-canada-38589427

47. http://www.oregonlive.com/books/index.ssf/2015/11/how_john_le_carre _reinvented_t.html. According to the Oxford English Dictionary (OED), it was John le Carré who coined the phrase "honeypot," which means "using sex to gain information."

48. http://www.cnn.com/2017/04/18/politics/fbi-dossier-carter-page-donald -trump-russia-investigation/

49. http://www.politico.com/story/2017/03/carter-page-russia-trip-trump-corey -lewandowski-235784

50. http://www.cnn.com/2017/04/18/politics/fbi-dossier-carter-page-donald -trump-russia-investigation/

51. https://www.washingtonpost.com/world/national-security/fbi-obtained -fisa-warrant-to-monitor-former-trump-adviser-carter-page/2017/04/11 /620192ea-1e0e-11e7-ad74-3a742a6e93a7_story.html?utm_term=.bfc08b4 d5075

52. https://www.documentcloud.org/documents/3259984-Trump-Intelligence -Allegations.html, dossier at 30

53. https://www.documentcloud.org/documents/3259984-Trump-Intelligence -Allegations.html, dossier at 31

54. http://dailycaller.com/2017/04/22/trump-team-asked-carter-page-to-cease -calling-himself-a-campaign-advisor/

55. https://www.documentcloud.org/documents/3259984-Trump-Intelligence -Allegations.html, dossier at 35

56. Ibid.

57. Ibid. at 20

58. http://www.bbc.com/news/world-europe-26304842

59. http://www.telegraph.co.uk/news/2016/05/31/ukraines-fallen-leader
-viktor-yanukovych-paid-bribes-of-2-billio/
60. https://www.rferl.org/a/ukraine-russia-yanukovych-trial-absentia-treason
/28467538.html
61. https://www.documentcloud.org/documents/3259984-Trump-Intelligence
-Allegations.html, dossier at 20
62. http://www.latimes.com/world/europe/la-fg-trump-russia-spy-2017-story
.html
63. https://www.wsj.com/articles/russian-tech-entrepreneur-denies-link-to
-donald-trump-hacking-report-1487096190
64. http://www.vanityfair.com/news/2017/03/how-the-explosive-russian-dossier
-was-compiled-christopher-steele
65. http://www.nbcnews.com/news/us-news/clinton-ally-says-smoke-no-fire
-no-russia-trump-collusion-n734176
66. http://www.dailymail.co.uk/home/moslive/article-2011951/John-Le-Carre
-In-day-MI6—I-called-Circus-books—stank-wartime-nostalgia.html
67. http://www.nbcnews.com/news/us-news/clinton-ally-says-smoke-no-fire
-no-russia-trump-collusion-n734176
68. Ibid.
69. https://www.craigmurray.org.uk/archives/2017/01/hitler-diaries-mark-ii
-hope-changed-mattress/
70. http://www.independent.co.uk/news/world/americas/donald-trump-who-is
-christopher-steele-man-behind-the-trump-dossier-perverted-sexual-acts
-mi6-agent-a7524191.html
71. http://insider.foxnews.com/2017/01/16/garbage-document-woodward-says
-trump-owed-apology-over-unverified-russia-dossier
72. http://www.bbc.com/news/av/uk-politics-38607833/ex-mi6-officer-trump
-dossier-hard-to-believe
73. http://www.bbc.com/news/world-us-canada-39435786
74. http://dailycaller.com/2017/03/05/obamas-intelligence-director-strongly
-denies-any-secret-warrants-against-trump-or-campaign-video
75. https://www.documentcloud.org/documents/3259984-Trump-Intelligence
-Allegations.html, dossier at 1
76. https://www.documentcloud.org/documents/3259984-Trump-Intelligence
-Allegations.html, dossier at 1-2
77. https://www.documentcloud.org/documents/3259984-Trump-Intelligence
-Allegations.html, dossier at 2
78. https://www.documentcloud.org/documents/3259984-Trump-Intelligence
-Allegations.html, dossier at 32
79. https://www.documentcloud.org/documents/3259984-Trump-Intelligence
-Allegations.html, dossier at 25
80. www.newsweek.com/alfa-bank-buzzfeed-trump-dossier-616763
81. https://www.documentcloud.org/documents/3259984-Trump-Intelligence
-Allegations.html, dossier at 25
82. www.bbc.com/news/world-us-canada-39435786

FOUR

1. https://www.theguardian.com/uk-news/2017/apr/13/british-spies-first-to
-spot-trump-team-links-russia?CMP=share_btn_tw
2. Ibid.

3. Ibid.

4. https://www.nytimes.com/2016/07/22/us/politics/donald-trump-foreign-policy-interview.html?_r=0

5. http://thehill.com/homenews/administration/314432-trump-nato-is-obsolete

6. http://www.bbc.com/news/election-us-2016-35906493

7. http://www.independent.co.uk/news/world/americas/us-politics/donald-trump-latest-brexit-european-union-act-together-uk-angela-merkel-a7663641.html

8. http://thehill.com/blogs/ballot-box/presidential-races/291818-trump-they-will-soon-be-calling-me-mr-brexit

9. https://www.nytimes.com/2017/01/27/opinion/sunday/is-donald-trump-mr-brexit.html

10. https://www.theguardian.com/news/defence-and-security-blog/2016/jun/20/remain-in-eu-say-former-uk-security-and-intelligence-chiefs

11. https://www.thesun.co.uk/news/2360529/mi6s-chief-warns-theresa-may-her-brexit-deal-must-not-damage-britains-intelligence-network-across-europe/

12. https://www.theguardian.com/news/defence-and-security-blog/2016/jun/20/remain-in-eu-say-former-uk-security-and-intelligence-chiefs

13. http://www.telegraph.co.uk/news/2016/06/16/why-this-lifelong-patriot-is-voting-remain/

14. https://www.theguardian.com/world/2014/apr/06/among-the-russians-in-london

15. http://www.cityam.com/214488/sunday-times-rich-list-2015-london-has-more-billionaires-any-city-world

16. http://www.tmz.com/2017/01/16/mariah-carey-russian-billionaire-wedding

17. http://www.telegraph.co.uk/news/2016/12/17/russia-accused-waging-secret-war-against-britain-using-cyber/

18. Ibid.

19. https://www.theguardian.com/uk-news/2017/apr/13/british-spies-first-to-spot-trump-team-links-russia

20. Ibid.

21. http://www.dailymail.co.uk/news/article-4114008/MI6-officers-never-ex-Russian-embassy-issues-dark-tweet-Christopher-Steele-scandal-claiming-British-spies-briefing-ways-against-Moscow-US.html

22. http://www.motherjones.com/politics/2016/10/veteran-spy-gave-fbi-info-alleging-russian-operation-cultivate-donald-trump/

23. http://ijr.com/2017/04/857604-spy-behind-trump-dossier-admits-judge-raw-unverified-intel/

24. http://www.independent.co.uk/news/world/americas/donald-trump-dossier-mi6-christopher-steele-russia-documents-alex-younger-a7528681.html

25. https://www.theguardian.com/uk-news/2017/jan/23/gchq-chief-robert-hannigan-quits

26. http://www.dailymail.co.uk/news/article-4113576/Former-MI6-spy-hiding-Russians-Trump-dirty-dossier-1million-two-years-working-undercover-supplying-FBI-information-cracked-open-corruption-FIFA.html

27. http://www.dailymail.co.uk/news/article-4111608/Will-look-cat-Ex-MI6-spy-worked-murdered-Litvinenko-flees-1-5m-home-fearing-life-leaving-pet-neighbours-outed-man-dirty-dossier-Donald-Trump.html

28. http://www.dailymail.co.uk/news/article-4119148/Theresa-told-dirty-dossier-Donald-Trump-MONTH-ago-Boris-Johnson-amid-fears-sex-allegations-cause-diplomatic-crisis.html

29. https://www.theguardian.com/us-news/2017/jan/13/uk-british-former-mos cow-ambassador-andrew-wood-trump-dossier

30. http://www.npr.org/2016/12/12/505261053/13-times-russian-hacking -came-up-in-the-presidential-campaign

31. http://time.com/4528049/hillary-clinton-john-podesta-emails-hackers -russia/

32. http://www.npr.org/2016/10/09/497056227/fact-check-clinton-and-trump -debate-for-the-second-time

33. https://www.nytimes.com/2016/10/10/us/politics/transcript-second-debate .html

34. http://www.cnn.com/TRANSCRIPTS/1610/19/se.01.html

35. http://www.msnbc.com/msnbc-quick-cuts/watch/clinton-putin-would-rather -have-a-puppet-as-president-789608003695

36. http://www.history.com/this-day-in-history/churchill-delivers-iron-curtain -speech

37. http://thefederalist.com/2016/07/25/5-times-liberals-mocked-mitt-romney -for-warning-about-russia/

38. http://dailycaller.com/2016/12/30/the-cold-war-wants-its-foreign-policy -back-2012-obama-laughs-in-romneys-face-for-worrying-about-russia-video/

39. http://www.nationalreview.com/corner/424840/becoming-putins -poodle-arthur-l-herman

40. https://www.theguardian.com/world/2014/mar/25/barack-obama-russia -regional-power-ukraine-weakness

41. https://www.amazon.com/dp/B000N2HCM4/ref=dp-kindle-redirect?_en coding=UTF8&btkr=1

42. http://www.cnn.com/2017/01/20/politics/trump-churchill-oval-office/

43. https://www.theatlantic.com/international/archive/2017/01/the-week -in-global-affairs-writing/513632

44. https://millercenter.org/president/fdroosevelt/foreign-affairs

45. Nicholas John Cull, *Selling War* (New York: Oxford University Press, 1996).

FIVE

1. https://www.brainyquote.com/quotes/quotes/j/jamesresto147742.html

2. http://www.latimes.com/politics/washington/la-na-essential-washington -updates-contractor-is-charged-with-leaking-top-1496716102-htmlstory.html

3. http://www.nytimes.com/1995/12/10/magazine/the-cia-s-most-important -mission-itself.html?pagewanted=all.

4. http://www.nytimes.com/1997/06/19/us/house-panel-says-cia-lacks-exper tise-to-carry-out-its-duties.html

5. http://articles.latimes.com/2004/apr/15/nation/na-tenettext15

6. http://www.nytimes.com/1997/07/20/weekinreview/aging-shop-of-horrors -the-cia-limps-to-50.html

7. www.truth-out.org/article/john-yoo-architect-imperialism

8. http://www.nytimes.com/2007/07/06/books/06book.html

9. Ibid.

10. Ibid.

11. Ibid.

12. Ibid.

13. Ibid.

14. Warwick Funnell, Michele Chwastiak, *Accounting at War* (New York: Rout-ledge, 2015), p. 164.

15. http://www.nytimes.com/2001/10/07/weekinreview/the-nation-hide-and
    -seek-to-fight-in-the-shadows-get-better-eyes.html
16. https://georgewbush-whitehouse.archives.gov/news/releases/2002/08/2002
    0826.html
17. www.vox.com/2016/2/16/11022104/iraq-war-neoconservatives
18. https://books.google.com/books?isbn=1610392388
19. edition.cnn.com/2002/ALLPOLITICS/10/07/bush.transcript/
20. http://freebeacon.com/politics/46-times-president-obama-told-americans
    -thats-not-who-we-are/
21. http://www.nbcnews.com/id/31052241/ns/world_news-terrorism/t
    /cheney-gitmo-holds-worst-worst/
22. Author interview with Frank Gaffney, April 3, 2017.
23. http://foreignpolicy.com/2012/09/19/the-seven-deadly-sins-of-john
    -brennan/
24. http://freebeacon.com/politics/cia-director-once-voted-for-communist-presi
    dential-candidate/
25. https://spectator.org/leaky-john-brennan/
26. Ibid.
27. Author interview with source, April 7, 2017.
28. https://www.dailydot.com/layer8/cia-john-brennan-waterboarding-donald
    -trump-brookings-institution/
29. http://dailycaller.com/2017/01/17/outgoing-cia-director-known-for-wearing
    -rainbow-lanyard-at-office-to-show-lgbt-solidarity/
30. http://investigatingtrump.com/wsj-cia-director-calls-trumps-nazi-germany
    -comments-repugnant-denies-leaking-kompromat-dossier/
31. Author interview with source, April 7, 2017.
32. http://articles.latimes.com/2012/feb/23/world/la-fg-iran-intel-20120224
33. https://spectator.org/donald-trump-rants-and-raves-at-the-press/
34. Ibid.
35. https://spectator.org/leaky-john-brennan/
36. http://thehill.com/homenews/administration/314436-trump-on-outgoing
    -cia-director-was-this-the-leaker-of-fake-news
37. http://freebeacon.com/uncategorized/lt-col-tony-schaffer-reveals-who-was
    -directly-behind-mike-flynn-phone-call-leaks/
38. http://www.breitbart.com/video/2017/01/22/priebus-the-former-cia-director
    -has-a-lot-to-answer-for-in-regard-to-the-leaked-documents/
39. https://spectator.org/confirmed-john-brennan-colluded-with-foreign-spies-to
    -defeat-trump/
40. John Fund and Hans von Spakovsky, *Obama's Enforcer* (New York: Broadside
    Books, 2014). Kindle edition.
41. Ibid., p. 411.
42. Ibid., p. 1224.
43. Ibid., p. 1165.
44. http://www.nationalreview.com/bench-memos/331374/dojs-partisan-dis
    parate-impact-litigation-agenda-part-1-ammon-simon
45. Fund and Spakovsky, *Obama's Enforcer*, Kindle loc. 1238.
46. Ibid.
47. Ibid., 1248.
48. Ibid., 1257.
49. Ibid., 1271.
50. Ibid.
51. Ibid., 1271.

52. http://freebeacon.com/national-security/former-cia-analyst-believes-leftover
    -obama-staffers-withholding-intel-from-trump-admin/
53. Fund and Spakovsky, *Obama's Enforcer*, Kindle loc. 2595.
54. http://www.foxnews.com/politics/2009/09/18/raw-data-letter-cia-directors
    -president-obama.html
55. http://www.nationalreview.com/corner/186024/panetta-profanity-laced
    -screaming-match-nro-staff
56. Fund and Spakovsky, *Obama's Enforcer*, Kindle loc. 2605.
57. https://www.washingtonpost.com/opinions/the-cias-exoneration-and
    -holders-reckoning/2011/07/04/gHQASrfnxH_story.html?utm_term=.f4a
    52cc0c8f9
58. nypost.com/2009/07/17/a-bleeding-heart-to-fight-terror/
59. Ibid.
60. Ibid.
61. https://en.wikiquote.org/wiki/Otto_von_Bismarck

SIX

1. https://www.wired.com/2012/04/michael-flynn-dia/
2. Ibid.
3. https://www.washingtonpost.com/world/national-security/head-of-pentagon
   -intelligence-agency-forced-out-officials-say/2014/04/30/ec15a366-d09d
   -11e3-9e25-188ebe1fa93b_story.html?utm_term=.4710592ffb6b
4. Ibid.
5. Ibid.
6. https://www.defense.gov/News/Article/Article/603020
7. http://www.politico.com/magazine/story/2016/10/how-mike-flynn-became
   -americas-angriest-general-214362
8. Ibid.
9. Ibid.
10. http://www.latimes.com/nation/politics/trailguide/la-na-republican-conven
    tion-2016-live-passed-over-as-vice-presidential-pick-1468897531-htmlstory
    .html
11. Ibid.
12. http://www.politico.com/magazine/story/2016/10/how-mike-flynn-became
    -americas-angriest-general-214362
13. https://www.vox.com/policy-and-politics/2017/2/14/14609618/michael
    -flynn-trump-hillary-clinton
14. https://en.wikipedia.org/wiki/Ash_heap_of_history
15. https://www.washingtonpost.com/blogs/plum-line/wp/2016/12/06/donald
    -trumps-most-terrifying-appointment/?utm_term=.e6cbdeaf0c02
16. Ibid.
17. Ibid.
18. Ibid.
19. Ibid.
20. http://observer.com/2015/09/lieutenant-general-retired-michael-flynn-and
    -the-iranian-nuclear-agreement/
21. https://www.bloomberg.com/view/articles/2016-05-24/the-secret-history
    -of-the-iran-deal-echo-chamber
22. http://www.cnn.com/2017/02/01/politics/michael-flynn-condemns-iran
    -actions/

23. https://pjmedia.com/trending/2017/02/15/report-obama-loyalists-led
    -by-ben-rhodes-orchestrated-flynn-ouster/
24. Ibid.
25. Ibid.
26. Ibid.
27. http://content.time.com/time/specials/packages/article/0,28804,2036683
    _2036477_2036540,00.html
28. http://www.cbsnews.com/news/us-russia-sanctions-election-interference
    -2016/
29. https://www.theguardian.com/world/2017/mar/30/vladimir-putin-denies
    -us-election-interference-trump
30. http://www.foxnews.com/transcript/2017/01/15/mike-pence-on-rep-lewis
    -comments-us-russia-relation-brennan-on-russia-dossier.html
31. Ibid.
32. http://www.cbsnews.com/news/mike-pence-michael-flynn-russia-contact
    -strictly-coincidental/
33. http://www.nationalreview.com/article/445045/general-michael-flynn
    -national-security-adviser-fbi-investigation-phone-call-russian-ambassador

SEVEN

1. http://www.mediaite.com/online/trump-reportedly-told-mexican-president
   -you-have-a-bunch-of-bad-hombres-down-there/
2. http://www.foxnews.com/politics/2017/02/01/trump-tells-mexican-presi
   dent-to-stop-bad-hombres-down-there-in-phone-call.html
3. http://www.businessinsider.com/trump-australia-prime-minister-turnbull
   -phone-call-2017-2
4. https://www.bloomberg.com/view/articles/2017-04-03/top-obama-adviser
   -sought-names-of-trump-associates-in-intel
5. https://www.nytimes.com/2017/01/17/us/politics/donald-trump-obama
   -approval-rating.html
6. https://www.nytimes.com/2017/03/18/us/politics/trump-controversies
   -chaos.html
7. https://www.nytimes.com/2017/03/25/fashion/the-perverse-thrill-of-chaotic
   -times-world-war-ii-baby-boomers.html
8. https://www.nytimes.com/2017/02/02/business/donald-trump-management
   -style.html
9. https://www.nytimes.com/2017/02/02/business/donald-trump-management
   -style.html
10. https://www.nytimes.com/2017/03/30/us/politics/devin-nunes-intelligence
    -reports.html?action=click&contentCollection=Politics&module=Related
    Coverage&region=EndOfArticle&pgtype=article
11. http://www.politico.com/story/2017/04/bannon-ousted-from-national
    -security-council-236908; https://www.nytimes.com/2017/04/06/us/politics
    /stephen-bannon-white-house.htmh
12. https://www.nytimes.com/2017/04/06/us/politics/secret-service-trump
    -first-family-protection.html?action=click&contentCollection=us&module
    =NextInCollection&region=Footer&pgtype=article&version=newsevent&r
    ref=collection%2Fnews-event%2Fdonald-trump-white-house
13. https://www.nytimes.com/2017/04/05/us/politics/trump-interview-susan
    -rice.html?ref=todayspaper

14. https://www.washingtonpost.com/news/worldviews/wp/2017/01/12/this
-former-british-spy-was-identified-as-the-trump-dossier-source-now-he-is
-in-hiding/?utm_term=.f78511c9328b
15. https://www.washingtonpost.com/news/worldviews/wp/2017/01/12/this
-former-british-spy-was-identified-as-the-trump-dossier-source-now-he-is
-in-hiding/?utm_term=.281a6ad2537a
16. http://www.cnn.com/2017/01/10/politics/donald-trump-intelligence-report
-russia/index.html
17. http://www.cnsnews.com/blog/craig-bannister/trump-media-shouldnt-be
-allowed-use-sources-unless-they-use-somebodys-name
18. http://www.reuters.com/article/us-usa-trump-fbi-idUSKBN1631GC
19. http://bigstory.ap.org/article/03dd1b758ddc4693b5f2de2f23e169bb
/joke-president-trump-returns-conservative-confab
20. https://www.washingtonpost.com/world/national-security/candidates
-poised-for-classified-briefings-despite-spy-agency-worries-over-trump/2016
/07/28/865cd686-5500-11e6-bbf5-957ad17b4385_story.html?utm
_term=.56b1ec131875
21. http://www.reuters.com/article/us-usa-election-trump-intelligence-idUSK
CN0YO24T
22. https://www.nytimes.com/2017/02/18/public-editor/the-risk-of-unnamed
-sources-unconvinced-readers.html
23. https://www.nytimes.com/2017/06/02/public-editor/liz-spayd-final-public
-editor-column.html?rref=collection%2Fcolumn%2Fthe-public-editor&
action=click&contentCollection=opinion&region=stream&module=stream
_unit&version=latest&contentPlacement=1&pgtype=collection
24. http://www.factcheck.org/2017/05/trump-fire-comey/
25. Ibid.
26. http://www.andersen.sdu.dk/vaerk/hersholt/TheEmperorsNewClothes_e
.html
27. http://thehill.com/policy/national-security/333217-trumps-war-with-comey
-intensifies?rnd=1494669813
28. http://www.politico.com/story/2016/11/obama-hurt-by-trump-win-2016
-election-231103
29. http://nypost.com/2017/02/11/how-obama-is-scheming-to-sabotage-trumps
-presidency/
30. Ibid.
31. Ibid.
32. Ibid.
33. Ibid.
34. https://www.washingtonpost.com/politics/it-went-off-the-rails-almost
-immediately-how-trumps-messy-transition-led-to-a-chaotic-presidency
/2017/04/03/170ec2e8-0a96-11e7-b77c-0047d15a24e0_story.html?utm
_term=.ba273897d452
35. Ibid.
36. Ibid.
37. http://www.latimes.com/opinion/op-ed/la-oe-mcmanus-deep-state-2017
0219-story.html
38. https://www.washingtonpost.com/politics/slow-pace-of-trump-nominations
-leaves-cabinet-agencies-stuck-in-staffing-limbo/2017/04/25/0a150aba-252c
-11e7-b503-9d616bd5a305_story.html?utm_term=.1e02cea4df67
39. https://counterjihadreport.com/2017/03/18/obama-used-nsa-fbi-to-spy-on
-trump-veteran-cia-officer-gary-berntsen/

40. http://freebeacon.com/politics/obama-admin-loyalists-government-insiders-sabotage-trump-white-house/
41. http://www.frontpagemag.com/point/266212/obamas-people-tried-change-trumps-executive-order-daniel-greenfield
42. http://www.commondreams.org/news/2017/03/22/trump-presidency-has-had-most-failed-start-ever-says-historian
43. https://www.washingtonpost.com/blogs/right-turn/wp/2017/02/14/heres-how-to-save-the-failing-trump-presidency/?utm_term=.2fc4adc2ddc0

EIGHT

1. http://www.washingtontimes.com/news/2017/apr/7/hillary-clinton-blames-misogyny-lost-election/
2. http://www.cbsnews.com/news/hillary-clinton-says-she-would-have-won-the-election-if-it-were-held-oct-27/
3. http://www.foxnews.com/politics/2016/12/19/bill-clinton-bashes-trump-blames-angry-white-men-and-comey-for-wifes-loss.html
4. http://www.washingtonexaminer.com/hillary-clinton-blames-comey-and-wikileaks-as-determinative-factors-behind-her-2016-loss/article/2619597
5. http://www.cnn.com/2017/04/06/politics/hillary-clinton-russian-election-meddling/
6. http://thehill.com/policy/defense/253963-trump-i-would-get-along-with-putin
7. http://thehill.com/blogs/blog-briefing-room/news/263555-putin-praises-trump-hes-a-really-brilliant-and-talented-person
8. http://www.cnn.com/2017/02/04/politics/donald-trump-vladimir-putin/
9. http://www.patheos.com/blogs/dispatches/2015/12/20/trump-praises-putin-as-a-leader-even-after-being-told-he-kills-dissidents-and-journalists/
10. http://time.com/4153183/putin-trump-presidency/
11. https://www.theguardian.com/us-news/2017/jan/07/russia-us-election-hacking-uk-intelligence
12. https://www.nytimes.com/2016/12/13/us/politics/russia-hack-election-dnc.html
13. Ibid.
14. https://www.wired.com/2017/01/fbi-says-democratic-party-wouldnt-let-agents-see-hacked-email-servers/
15. http://thehill.com/policy/cybersecurity/310234-typo-may-have-caused-podesta-email-hack
16. Ibid.
17. https://www.washingtonpost.com/world/national-security/obama-orders-review-of-russian-hacking-during-presidential-campaign/2016/12/09/31d6b300-be2a-11e6-94ac-3d324840106c_story.html?utm_term=.657bbfcb574d
18. Ibid.
19. Ibid.
20. Ibid.
21. Ibid.
22. http://www.telegraph.co.uk/news/2017/03/30/vladimir-putin-says-read-lips-no-us-claims-used-propaganda/
23. https://www.theguardian.com/world/2017/mar/30/vladimir-putin-denies-us-election-interference-trump

24. http://www.cnsnews.com/news/article/melanie-hunter/clapper-russians
    -didnt-alter-vote-count-presidential-election
25. https://web.stanford.edu/~gentzkow/research/fakenews.pdf
26. Ibid.
27. Ibid.
28. Ibid.
29. http://www.kgw.com/news/politics/sen-merkley-vows-to-honor-the-peace
    ful-transfer-of-power/387358158
30. https://www.nytimes.com/2016/12/13/us/politics/russia-hack-election-dnc
    .html?_r=0
31. http://www.latimes.com/opinion/topoftheticket/la-na-tt-putin-trump-2016
    0912-snap-story.html
32. Ibid.
33. https://www.washingtonpost.com/news/the-fix/wp/2016/09/08/donald
    -trumps-answer-on-russia-and-vladimir-putin-at-the-commander-in-chief
    -forum-was-bananas/?utm_term=.93f99068ae31
34. Ibid.
35. https://www.usnews.com/news/articles/2016-08-15/ukraine-documents
    -detail-cash-payments-to-paul-manafort
36. http://www.politifact.com/truth-o-meter/article/2016/aug/04/did-trump
    -campaign-soften-platform-language-benefi/
37. http://www.politico.com/story/2016/07/trump-putin-no-relationship-226282
38. https://www.washingtonpost.com/world/national-security/intelligence-com
    munity-investigating-covert-russian-influence-operations-in-the-united-states
    /2016/09/04/aec27fa0-7156-11e6-8533-6b0b0ded0253_story.html?utm
    _term=.70e2c15bdf6a
39. http://www.nbcnews.com/news/us-news/could-russian-hackers-spoil-elec
    tion-day-n619321
40. http://www.politico.com/magazine/story/2016/08/2016-elections-russia
    -hack-how-to-hack-an-election-in-seven-minutes-214144
41. https://www.nytimes.com/2016/07/27/us/politics/spy-agency-consensus
    -grows-that-russia-hacked-dnc.html?_r=0
42. http://www.npr.org/2016/12/12/505261053/13-times-russian-hacking-came
    -up-in-the-presidential-campaign
43. Ibid.
44. https://www.washingtonpost.com/world/national-security/us-government-of
    ficially-accuses-russia-of-hacking-campaign-to-influence-elections/2016/10
    /07/4e0b9654-8cbf-11e6-875e-2c1bfe943b66_story.html?utm_term=.64ee
    3ef97373
45. http://www.nbcnews.com/news/us-news/what-obama-said-putin-red-phone
    -about-election-hack-n697116
46. http://www.cnbc.com/2017/04/06/us-military-has-launched-more-50-than
    -missiles-aimed-at-syria-nbc-news.html
47. http://myfox8.com/2017/04/07/putin-slams-trumped-up-us-strike-against
    -syria/
48. https://www.washingtonpost.com/politics/despite-early-denials-growing
    -list-of-trump-camp-contacts-with-russians-haunts-white-house/2017/03
    /03/a5b196d8-002d-11e7-8f41-ea6ed597e4ca_story.html?utm_term=.aa79d2
    4f8233
49. https://www.usatoday.com/story/news/2017/03/01/sessions-did-not-disclose
    -contact-russian-ambassador-justice-dept-says/98618758/
50. http://billmoyers.com/story/the-jared-kushner-timeline/

51. https://www.nytimes.com/2017/03/03/us/politics/trump-russia-links-wash ington.html
52. https://www.washingtonpost.com/world/moscow-had-contacts-with-trump -team-during-campaign-russian-diplomat-says/2016/11/10/28fb82fa-a73d -11e6-9bd6-184ab22d218e_story.html?utm_term=.527fe7a4a101
53. https://www.washingtonpost.com/politics/despite-early-denials-growing-list -of-trump-camp-contacts-with-russians-haunts-white-house/2017/03/03/a5 b196d8-002d-11e7-8f41-ea6ed597e4ca_story.html?utm_term=.03cad4c489c1
54. Ibid.
55. http://www.politico.com/story/2016/12/michael-morell-russia-us-elections -232495
56. http://www.express.co.uk/news/world/789961/Russia-Iran-respond-with -force-after-Donald-Trump-crossed-line-Syria-strike-Xi-Jinping

NINE

1. http://dailycaller.com/2016/11/28/attention-millenials-foreign-election-med dling-and-fake-news-are-nothing-new/
2. https://en.wikipedia.org/wiki/1996_United_States_campaign_finance_con trovers
3. http://articles.latimes.com/1999/may/12/news/mn-36489/2
4. http://www.washingtonpost.com/wp-srv/politics/special/campfin/stories/cf 021098.htm
5. https://www.washingtonpost.com/world/national-security/intelligence -chiefs-expected-in-new-york-to-brief-trump-on-russian-hacking/2017/01 /06/5f591416-d41a-11e6-9cb0-54ab630851e8_story.html?utm_term=.069 40ff38442
6. www.bookrags.com/research/who-lost-china-debate-aaw-04/
7. Telephone conversation between author Dick Morris and President Clinton, October 1995.
8. Ibid.
9. https://www.foreignaffairs.com/articles/russia-fsu/1996-09-01/why-yeltsin -won-russian-tammany-hall
10. Author conversation with Berger in spring 1996.
11. https://www.foreignaffairs.com/articles/russia-fsu/1996-09-01/why -yeltsin-won-russian-tammany-hall

TEN

1. erenow.com/common/legacy-of-ashes-the-history-of-the-cia/48.html
2. https://www.theatlantic.com/international/archive/2013/06/gentlemen -reading-each-others-mail-a-brief-history-of-diplomatic-spying/276940/
3. Curt Gentry, *J. Edgar Hoover: The Man and the Secrets* (New York: W. W. Norton & Company, 1991), Kindle edition, location 4119. Also available at https://books.google.com/books?isbn=0393343502
4. Ibid.
5. Read more at ibid., Kindle loc. 4324.
6. Ibid., Kindle loc. 4383.
7. Ibid., Kindle loc. 4383.
8. Ibid., Kindle loc. 4441.
9. Ibid., Kindle loc. 4376.

10. Ibid., Kindle loc. 4410.
11. Ibid., Kindle loc. 4410.
12. Ibid., Kindle loc. 4468.
13. Ibid., Kindle loc. 4479.
14. Ibid., Kindle loc. 4479.
15. https://en.wikipedia.org/wiki/Fruit_of_the_poisonous_tree
16. Gentry, *J. Edgar Hoover,* Kindle location 4490.
17. Ibid.
18. Ibid., p. 327.
19. Ibid., p. 357.
20. https://www.washingtonpost.com/archive/local/1981/05/22/maj-gen-harry
    -vaughan-aide-to-president-truman-dies-at-8/e96a79b4-811a-4ca7-b8c3
    -560c622ec9e5/?utm_term=.a8ec1cb59d63
21. https://history.state.gov/historicaldocuments/frus1945-50Intel/d3
22. http://www.history.com/this-day-in-history/churchill-delivers-iron-curtain
    -speech
23. https://www.trumanlibrary.org/publicpapers/index.php?pid=148&st=&st1=
24. https://global.oup.com/us/companion.websites/9780195385168/resources
    /chapter10/nsa/nsa.pdf
25. Ibid.
26. https://en.wikipedia.org/wiki/Deep_state_in_the_United_States
27. Richard H. Blum, ed., *Surveillance and Espionage in a Free Society* (New York:
    Praeger, 1972). Available at https://books.google.com/books?id=X1m-FL7ny
    o8C&pg=PA208&lpg=PA208&dq=I+had+the+gravest+forebodings+about
    +this+organization&source=bl&ots=x72378kEga&sig=5fejL0evqiThhW78
    ERmklAws3ak&hl=en&sa=X&ved=0ahUKEwizjPqQ7uXSAhVJzmMKH
    XmFAzkQ6AEIHDAA#v=onepage&q=I%20had%20the%20gravest%20
    forebodings%20about%20this%20organization&f=false
28. https://www.nationalchurchillmuseum.org/winston-churchill-and-the-cold
    -war.html
29. https://history.state.gov/historicaldocuments/frus1969-76v12/d149
30. https://williamblum.org/essays/read/overthrowing-other-peoples-govern
    ments-the-master-list
31. http://nsarchive.gwu.edu/news/20040925/index.htm; and https://en.wikipe
    dia.org/wiki/Salvador_Allende
32. Tim Weiner, *Legacy of Ashes: The History of the CIA* (New York: Anchor Books,
    2008), p. 355.
33. Ibid., p. 356.
34. Ibid. p. 365.
35. https://history.state.gov/historicaldocuments/frus1969-76v02/d218
36. research.omicsgroup.org/index.php/Richard_Helms241
37. Ibid., 5548.
38. Michael Holzman, *James Jesus Angleton, the CIA, and the Craft of Counterintel-
    ligence* (Amherst, MA: University of Massachusetts Press), p. 23. Available at
    https://books.google.com/books?isbn=1558496505
39. www.nytimes.com/2007/06/27/washington/27cia.html
40. Ibid.
41. www.amigospais-guaracabuya.org/oagmb002.php
42. Alexander Bloom, ed. *Long Time Gone* (New York: Oxford University Press,
    2001). Available at https://books.google.com/books?isbn=0198028946
43. Weiner, *Legacy of Ashes,* Kindle edition, loc. 6221

44. Ronald Kessler, *The Bureau: The Secret History of the FBI* (New York: St. Martin's Press, 2002), p. 127. Available at https://books.google.com/books?isbn=1250111269

45. Kessler, *The Bureau*, p. 209. Available at https://books.google.com/books?isbn=1250111269

46. Gentry, *J. Edgar Hoover*, p. 480.

47. Davin Cunningham, *There's Something Happening Here* (Berkeley: University of California Press, 2004), p. 114. Available at https://books.google.com/books?isbn=0520939247

48. http://www.openculture.com/2014/11/you-are-done-the-chilling-suicide-letter-sent-to-martin-luther-king-by-the-f-b-i.html

49. Kessler, *The Bureau*, p. 150.

50. https://www.washingtonpost.com/politics/how-mark-felt-became-deep-throat/2012/06/04/gJQAlpARIV_story.html?utm_term=.091e45147058

51. Kessler, *The Bureau*, Kindle loc. 5626.

52. https://www.washingtonpost.com/national/james-r-schlesinger-cia-chief-and-cabinet-member-dies/2014/03/27/e4a8f01c-b5bb-11e3-8020-b2d790b3c9e1_story.html?utm_term=.2825979572eb

53. Ronald Kessler, *Secrets of the FBI* (New York: Broadway Paperbacks, 2012), p. 54. Available at https://books.google.com/books?isbn=0307719707

54. http://www.nytimes.com/1975/01/20/archives/officials-of-fbi-will-be-summoned-on-congress-files.html

55. http://spartacus-educational.com/JFKschlesingerJ.htm

56. https://nacla.org/news/latin-america-and-cia%E2%80%99s-%E2%80%98family-jewels%E2%80%9D

57. https://www.usnews.com/opinion/blogs/peter-fenn/2014/12/10/cia-torture-report-shows-the-rogue-elephants-are-back

58. https://flashtrafficblog.wordpress.com/2013/11/04/inside-the-revolution-how-iran-seized-the-us-embassy-in-tehran-34-years-ago-today-we-were-just-plain-asleep-said-cia-director/

59. http://archive.millercenter.org/ridingthetiger/iran-in-oral-history

60. http://articles.baltimoresun.com/1991-09-20/news/1991263012_1_fiers-casey-central-america

61. Robert Gates, *From the Shadows: The Ultimate Insider's Story of Five Presidents and How They Won the Cold War* (New York: Simon and Schuster, 1996), p. 213. Available at https://books.google.com/books?isbn=1439127484

62. https://journals.lib.unb.ca/index.php/JCS/rt/printerFriendly/11711/12479

63. https://archive.org/stream/nsia-FBIKelleyClarenceMarion/nsia-FBIKelleyClarenceMarion/FBI%20Kelley%20Clarence%2047_djvu.txt

64. Ibid.

65. www.nleomf.org/assets/pdfs/nlem/oral-histories/FBI_Dyson_interview.pdf

66. www.nleomf.org/assets/pdfs/nlem/oral-histories/FBI_Webster_interview.pdf

67. https://www.fbi.gov/history/famous-cases/year-of-the-spy-1985

68. Ibid.

69. http://www.nytimes.com/1981/06/29/us/2-men-arrested-in-alleged-sale-of-us-secrets.html

70. https://www.washingtonpost.com/archive/opinions/1988/04/17/moscows-mole-in-the-cia/a976fac3-622a-475d-8c87-46b6170b1f4e/?utm_term=.535598d3c94c

71. https://www.army.mil/article/109525/Clyde_Conrad_arrested_for_espionage_August_23_1988

72. https://www.fbi.gov/history/famous-cases/robert-hanssen

73. Jane Corbin, *Al-Qaeda: In Search of the Terror Network That Threatens the World* (New York: Thunder's Mouth Press, 2002), p. 50.

74. Weiner, *Legacy of Ashes,* p. 438.

75. *InfoWarCon: International Conference on Information Warfare* (Darby, PA: DI-ANE Publishing, 1996), p. 6. Available at https://books.google.com/books?isbn=0788135414

76. James D. Boys, *Clinton's Grand Strategy: US Foreign Policy in a Post-Cold War World* (New York: Bloomsbury Academic, 2015), p. 94.

77. http://www.worldhistory.biz/sundries/33690-facts.html

78. www.chicagotribune.com/news/ . . . /ct-presidents-cia-intelligence-20170111 -story.html

79. http://www.today.com/news/louis-freeh-says-he-distrusted-bill-clinton -wbna9649832

80. https://books.google.com/books?isbn=1429904445

81. Quote from John Ehrlichman to John Dean during Watergate scandal, https://dictionaryblog.cambridge.org/2013/01/28/words-of-watergate-part-2/

82. http://www.nytimes.com/2002/10/01/us/threats-responses-terrorist -bombing-book-clinton-aides-says-saudi-diplomat.html

83. http://www.nytimes.com/1994/07/28/us/betrayer-s-tale-a-special-report-a -decade-as-a-turncoat-aldrich-ames-s-own-story.html?pagewanted=all

84. www.npr.org/templates/story/story.php?storyId=105090777

85. Ibid.

86. http://www.nytimes.com/1994/09/28/us/congress-decides-to-conduct-study -of-need-for-cia.html

CONCLUSION

1. http://www.slate.com/blogs/lexicon_valley/2014/11/25/sol_wachtler_the _judge_who_coined_indict_a_ham_sandwich_was_himself_indicted.html